Symbols of Nations and Nationalism

Symbols of Nations and Nationalism

Celebrating Nationhood

Gabriella Elgenius
University of Oxford, UK

© Gabriella Elgenius 2011

All rights reserved. No reproduction, copy or transmission of this publication may be made without written permission.

No portion of this publication may be reproduced, copied or transmitted save with written permission or in accordance with the provisions of the Copyright, Designs and Patents Act 1988, or under the terms of any licence permitting limited copying issued by the Copyright Licensing Agency, Saffron House, 6–10 Kirby Street, London EC1N 8TS.

Any person who does any unauthorized act in relation to this publication may be liable to criminal prosecution and civil claims for damages.

The author has asserted her right to be identified as the author of this work in accordance with the Copyright, Designs and Patents Act 1988.

First published 2011 by
PALGRAVE MACMILLAN

Palgrave Macmillan in the UK is an imprint of Macmillan Publishers Limited, registered in England, company number 785998, of Houndmills, Basingstoke, Hampshire RG21 6XS.

Palgrave Macmillan in the US is a division of St Martin's Press LLC, 175 Fifth Avenue, New York, NY 10010.

Palgrave Macmillan is the global academic imprint of the above companies and has companies and representatives throughout the world.

Palgrave® and Macmillan® are registered trademarks in the United States, the United Kingdom, Europe and other countries.

ISBN 978–1–349–59047–6

This book is printed on paper suitable for recycling and made from fully managed and sustained forest sources. Logging, pulping and manufacturing processes are expected to conform to the environmental regulations of the country of origin.

A catalogue record for this book is available from the British Library.

Library of Congress Cataloging-in-Publication Data
Elgenius, Gabriella, 1967–
  Symbols of nations and nationalism : celebrating nationhood / Gabriella Elgenius.
    p. cm.
  Includes index.
  ISBN 978–1–349–59047–6
  1. Nationalism—History. 2. National characteristics—History.
I. Title.
JC311.E475 2011
929.9—dc22
                                                  2011001478

10 9 8 7 6 5 4 3 2 1
20 19 18 17 16 15 14 13 12 11

For my parents

Contents

List of Figures	viii
List of Tables	ix
List of Illustrations	x
List of Maps	xi
Preface and Acknowledgements	xii
Introduction	1
1 National Symbols and Ceremonies: The Construction and Authentication of Boundaries	12
2 National Flag Origins: Religion, Revolution and Rivalry	27
3 National Flags, the Politicization and Sanctification of Nations	57
4 National Days in Nation Building: Similarities and Differences	94
5 National Day Design: Towards a Typology of Successful National Days	133
6 The Symbolic Regimes and Nation Building	186
Bibliography	201
Index	223

List of Figures

2.1	Crusader flags, 1188	32
2.2	Early war flags: white cross on red	35
2.3	The Dutch *Prinsenvlag*	35
2.4	The development of the Union Jack	39
2.5	The complexity of the French tricolour	42
2.6	Tricolour with Marianne	45
2.7	The Norwegian flag of independence	48
2.8	Flags with pre-modern origins	52
2.9	Modern national flags and the French Revolution	53
2.10	Post-imperial flags and the First World War	55
3.1	Flags of the USSR and the Soviet Socialist Republics	60
3.2	Flags of Belarus from 1991	65
3.3	Flags during the Spanish Civil War	68
3.4	Flagging loyalties in Spain	69
3.5	The flag situation in Bosnia-Herzegovina, 1992–98	72
3.6	The flag dispute in Macedonia, FYROM	76
3.7	Post-historical and counter-nationalist flags and Europeanization	76
3.8	The Dardanian flag	78
3.9	Flagging identity beyond traditional territories	92

List of Tables

3.1	Flags and political change	62
3.2	Symbolic regimes and flag categories in Europe	88
4.1	National days with pre-modern origins	97
4.2	National days and the age of nationalism	99
4.3	National days and the age of post-imperial nations	102
5.1	National personification and golden ages	135
5.2	Political events	135
5.3	National days and symbolic regimes	136
5.4	National day design and ceremonial variety	138
5.5	National anthems of Europe	142
5.6	Scandinavian rivalry and claims to nationhood	170
5.7	Successful national days: Norway, France and Britain	178
5.8	Is Britain a failed nation?	181
6.1	The symbolic regimes of Europe	196

List of Illustrations

4.1	Arc de Triomphe, flypast Champs-Élysées, Bastille Day, Paris	107
4.2	The military procession, Place de la Concorde, Bastille Day in Paris	107
4.3	Ceremonial focal point and the Constitution Day Parade in Oslo	119
4.4	Ceremonial focal point: the Cenotaph in London	126
4.5	Fields of Remembrance in London	130
5.1	Nationalism, Christianity and sacrifice, Remembrance Sunday	155
5.2	Women of the Second World War	159
5.3	The Golden Jubilee: pomp and circumstance	183
5.4	The multi-dimensional future of national day design	184

List of Maps

5.1 *Via Triumphalis* of Paris   147
5.2 The national and royal routes of London   148
5.3 Ceremonial route of Oslo   148

Preface and Acknowledgements

Colleagues, friends and family kept asking when the writing of this book would be completed. I can now say, with certainty, that it is not, or only as far as this particular version is concerned. Unexplored subjects such as these generate more questions than answers and there is still much to say about national symbolism and its intriguing and intricate relationship to nationalism and the building of nations. As this book is published, the research for another study exploring the patterns of national symbolism and symbolic regimes for the various continents should have commenced.

For invaluable feedback on the overall arguments made in this book, I am especially grateful to Professor Anthony Heath (University of Oxford), Professor Emeritus Anthony D. Smith (London School of Economics), Professor Göran Therborn (University of Cambridge), Professor David Miller (University of Oxford), Professor Margie Wetherell (Open University), Professor Emeritus David Martin (London School of Economics) and Dr Kevin Manton (School of Oriental and African Studies). A number of colleagues have also given constructive feedback on particular sections and I am especially indebted to Professor Thomas Hylland Eriksen (University of Oslo), Professor Peter Aronsson (University of Linköping), Professor Arne Bugge Amundsen (University of Oslo), Professor Stefan Berger (University of Manchester), Professor Stein Tønnesson (PRIO, Oslo), Professor John Breuilly and Professor John Hutchinson (London School of Economics), Professor Kaare Strom (University of California), Professor David McCrone (University of Edinburgh), Dr Gordana Uzleac (London Metropolitan University), Dr Michael Biggs, Dr Djordje Stefanovics and Jean Martin (University of Oxford), Dr Richard Mole (School of Eastern European Studies), José María Lanzarote Guiral (European University Institute), The Reverend Stephen Williams (Diocese of London), Dr John Nagel (University of East London), Dr Christel Kesler (Colombia University, NYC), Peter Del-Manso (UCL) and Richard Campanaro (LSE). Dr Kevin Manton (School of Oriental and African Studies) has generously read more than one version of this manuscript and Charles Laurie (University of Oxford) has kindly organized the many references and sources for the same. Thanks also to Carlos Gonzales Sancho (University of Oxford) for his help in arranging the index, and to Henrik Brandin for help with the maps.

I find myself in an inspiring environment at the Universities of Oxford and London and it is a privilege to be able to take part of the research conducted by colleagues at Nuffield College, the Department of Sociology at University of Oxford, the School of Oriental and African Studies and the London School of Economics at the University of London. I am especially grateful to the Department of Sociology at the University of Oxford for all the help I have received during my time here. As a Research Fellow of the British Academy I have worked on a few projects related to the politics of identity and notions of homeland also among Diaspora communities in Britain (funded by the BA), the decline of traditional identities in Britain (with Professor Heath, funded by the ESRC), and more recently on national museums in Europe (with Professor Aronsson, funded by the European Commission). During this time at the University of Oxford it has been a true privilege to work with Professor Anthony Heath who is a most inspiring mentor. Similarly, Professor Emeritus Anthony D. Smith (London School of Economics) and Professor Göran Therborn (University of Cambridge, Gothenburg University) provided much valued feedback in the early stages of this research and parts of the research for this book were completed while I held a position as a Marie Curie Fellow (European Commission) at the London School of Economics and Political Science. The Swedish Research Council of Social Sciences supported the early stages of this research as has the Swedish Institute, the Department of Social Sciences at Linnaeus University (Sweden) and the European Institute (LSE) for which I am truly grateful.

Finally, to my wonderful parents, sister and extended family I owe many thanks and love. My greatest debt is to my dear parents who have helped me in more ways than I can articulate here. This book is for them with all my love.

GABRIELLA ELGENIUS
NUFFIELD COLLEGE, UNIVERSITY OF OXFORD

Introduction

This book will explore the role of national symbols and ceremonies as markers of nation building, their role in the formation of nations and the mechanisms by which they operate. Scholars and the public alike often juxtapose symbolism to the real world, implying that symbols are decorative or of secondary importance to the world of politics and economics. This book will argue to the contrary: symbolism is, as far as nationhood is concerned, a significant element of the nation-building process as it authenticates boundaries. The complexity of nation building can even be traced alongside the establishment of symbols and ceremonies as these are introduced, adopted, altered, modified, contested, abolished and re-established during pivotal times of nation making. Moreover, when the information about symbolic measures, such as the adoption of flags, anthems and national days, is systematized distinct *symbolic regimes* emerge, in turn, forming pre-modern, modern and post-imperial narratives. Thus, whereas some nations are represented by pre-modern religious and monarchical imagery others reproduce the ideals of the modern and republican age. Post-imperial images point as a rule towards an 'ancient' past prior to more recent formations. In brief, in outlining the symbolic and ceremonial measures of nations it becomes clear that nations are layered and their formations ongoing and visible in the adoption of national symbols.

The main aims here are to demonstrate that symbols and ceremonies are markers of nation building and celebrate and commemorate nationhood and that they can play an important role in the formative processes of nations as they authenticate boundaries. The historical complexities are crucial in understanding how it is possible for a piece of cloth (national flag) to turn into such a powerful political symbol and how the celebrations of events often in a distant past (national day) continue to have such significance. In outlining the symbolic and ceremonial measures and the double-edged and contested nature of national symbolism, new conclusions within a neglected research area can be highlighted. Three crucial processes stand out here: self-reference – telling us who we are; differentiation – of us from others; and recognition – the struggle for affirmation against the negation of others.

Why are national symbols and ceremonies important?

Nations become visible through their symbols (flags, anthems and emblems), ceremonies (national days, regional festivities, national holidays and international sporting events), museums and monuments (collections, memorials and statues), the land itself (the landscape and the capital city as a historical centre for institutions and location for ceremonials) and defined borders (passports, membership, citizenship, nationality, insiders and outsiders). It has therefore been argued that the nation 'must be personified before it can be seen, symbolised before it can be loved, imagined before it can be conceived' (Walzer, 1967, p. 84). In order to be recognized internationally, nations have a certain number of characteristics besides their name, a capital city, defined borders, etc. – they all have a national flag, a national anthem and a national day that represents it. It is within this context that the existence of a national flag, for instance, has become a sign and a measure of success. The nations of Europe all follow this pattern and have signed up to the adoption of this congruous symbolic code distinguished by symbols (flag, anthem and national day) representing the nation and its presence among other nations. In this way, symbols and ceremonies mirror the pursuits of nations, the nation-ness becomes visible through these symbolic measures, and their acceptance provides a tangible measure of recognition – given from within and/or without.

National symbols and ceremonies are also used to express complex meanings related to nationhood and are for this reason challenged, contested, disputed, negotiated, mobilized and replaced during socio-political conflicts. Many examples in this book highlight changes and alterations to national symbolism as results of divisions and conflicts of various kinds. Many national flags and national days were (re)introduced and (re)modified after the French Revolution and the World Wars. It is precisely because historical events contribute to defining nations that the symbols representing these are contested at every level. The national flag is for this reason not only a piece of cloth fluttering in the wind; it makes claims to a historic territory, independence and nationhood. Flags have remained successful political symbols because they *authenticate boundaries* between those who belong and those who do not. This means that flags are not necessarily marked by their unifying qualities as their meanings are contested and challenged. Endless examples are to be found demonstrating how flags ignite passions and associations by their presence but also when defaced or burnt. National flags, much like national anthems, provide form to national self-celebrations, wave or sing the nation into action and move history into the present. As a rule national days celebrate, honour and validate official founding myths and identity. The choreography of *national day design* enhances these notions of sameness ceremonially. Belatedly, the politics of recognition (and patience) have entered ceremonial agendas to challenge such perceptions in order to highlight their potentially exclusive nature. For the reasons given above, national symbols and ceremonies can have an effect upon the community they represent as they *repeatedly* illuminate boundaries and raise awareness of membership. The appeal and reiteration of national ceremonies can therefore be understood as barriers against change or threats. The richness of keeping to traditional culture and ceremonies among diaspora groups further illuminate a sense of the security found in familiarity that regular ceremonies can generate.

National symbols and ceremonies also contribute to a civic or secular religion with a calendar of honouring founding myths, legends, national heroes and personifications, victories and sacrifices. The variety of celebrations and commemorations serve ultimately to glorify and sanctify nations. National flags are for this reason regulated by law and, in certain ritual contexts, protected as if they were sacred objects. In fact, it is the *relationship* between the nation and the flag, or the commemoration and dominant historical narrative, which is protected and justifies the cause of nations and states. Remembrance ceremonies, for instance, provide justifications for deaths that otherwise would go unexplained in an increasingly secular world and may provide comfort during times of war since these persist over time and conform – in form – to established patterns of mourning.

As indicated above, national symbols and ceremonies also have something to tell us about dominant and official versions of history that tend to promote established notions of nationality. However, because they are able to generate feelings they also generate anti-feelings and can be understood as exclusive objects or occasions for those who do not share the same history or remain excluded on other grounds. Ceremonial initiatives attempting to build bridges have in recent decades become part of the *politics of recognition, regret and apology* and are currently highly visible in multi-ethnic states where the contributions of previously marginalized communities are being recognized. Considerable ceremonial activity is also seen with reference to the re-invention of existing national ceremonies and the introduction of new inclusive ceremonies. Citizenship ceremonies (marking and celebrating the entry of new members) are introduced in a number of European countries, and nations thought lacking joyous national days attempt to rectify this by building on existing ceremonies or by introducing new ones. Notably, participation in ceremonies may raise awareness but do not necessarily create unity or cohesion for reasons that will be outlined. Little is known about individual meanings but, as will be demonstrated by a wealth of examples, national symbols and ceremonies constitute potentially divisive forces. However, there are ceremonial elements that contribute to successful national ceremonies in which participation is evident and these help us assess whether national days can be exportable to other nations. Recent national day initiatives in multi-ethnic and multinational nations are of particular interest here and also call for a discussion on the related issues with regard to ceremonial modernization, inclusion and reconciliation.

Symbols and ceremonies adopted alongside nation building vary in age. Flags appear early on and with time become attached to modern and national territories as the first national symbol. The role of the flag has generally been overlooked with reference to nation building but has continued to constitute a rallying point of reference. The national day constitutes a younger stratum of the nation and, as a rule, appears later in the nation-building process with the age of nationalism and mobilization. By dating and categorizing national flags, national anthems and national days, different regimes of symbolism emerge. Nation building can be understood in light of symbols and ceremonies appearing with reference to pre-modern (pre-1789), modern (*ca.* 1789–1914) and post-imperial (*ca.* 1914–) *symbolic regimes*. This terminology does not relate to a specific age of nations but relates to the nature and age of their symbolic expression and content. Pre-modern symbolism appears with religious or monarchial sanctioned communities. The Cross flags that survived to modern times were originally used in warfare whereas the national days with pre-modern origins, as a rule, were religious holidays later nationalized or transformed into national days. The national flags and national days that emerged during the modern symbolic regime honour revolutions, the signing of constitutions, the formation of unions and the declaration of independence as would be expected after 1789. The tricolour flags broke with earlier religious symbolism and appeared with secular ideals. Within the more recent post-imperial regime, established after 1914, nations display pre-modern heraldic devices or colours on their flags (heraldic flags) in order to justify the existence of the nation and the state in the present. Nationalists often wish to refer to an ancient past as a mechanism to sanction contemporary nations and/or states and it is *through such symbols that the past remains in the present* and tells us something about the importance of history in the making of nations. Having said this, an atypical form of flag symbolism has emerged recently and is characterized by its post-historical and counter-nationalist qualities. These flags avoid references to a specific national past altogether and point towards the future. Nations are, in other words, *work in progress* and nation building is ongoing and continuous, as demonstrated by ongoing activity within the symbolic and ceremonial spheres. The main theories of nationalism offer insights into different periods of the national building process, commencing at different times in different parts of Europe. Keeping in mind the debates on whether nations are pre-modern or modern, discovered or invented, we shall see that nation building is highly complicated and ongoing and cannot be reduced to neat conceptualizations in this regard. National symbols and ceremonies are challenged and contested through this process and thus replaced, (re)created, (re)constructed and (re)invented. For this reason they constitute powerful political instruments as symbols of unity but also of dissent, and by their capacity to express complex notions of nationality they are used in the pursuit of power.

Comparisons

Symbols and ceremonies of nations, as a whole, use references to the past in order to justify their existence and that of the states in the present. The past is, in other words, in the present. A comparative and historical approach allows for the study of origins and developments of national symbols and ceremonies, as well as for a comparison between different periods and places. The nation is made visible through a number of symbols and the national flag and the national day will be explored here. Little is known about the traditions of flags and of national days in Europe and about their relationships to nation building. Recent contributions include Eriksen and Jenkins (2007) on flag related symbolism and McCrone and McPherson (2009) on national days, but otherwise few comparisons have been made.

The symbolism of European nations must be explored with reference to their main 'symbolic and ceremonial statistics'. The origins of the national flags and national days have thus been dated and some exploration of national anthems is also to follow. Here we enter a contested and contestable area. The dates of origins are sometimes obscure and documentation is sparse, especially with reference to pre-modern (war and religious) flags or the development of early religious festivities transformed into national flags and days. The dates of origin and adoption of flags and national days as appropriated by nationalists are sometimes provided in order to highlight a considerably distant or glorious past. The dates referred to in this study with reference to the first introduction of the flag and the national day are also subject to interpretation and based on available material in a neglected field of research. The overall framework developed in order to highlight the layering of nations, the ongoing process of nation building and the appearance of distinct symbolic regimes do not suffer from the complexity of the data but rather confirms the significance and taken-for-granted nature of national symbolism.

Given that it is not possible to provide an in-depth account of the development of all the European national days and flags, a cross-case analysis of the development in Britain, France and Norway will be explored. These cases have been selected to illustrate different paths to nationhood and together highlight the complexity of nation building as expressed through symbolic and ceremonial activity and variety. A thematic approach to the case studies seeks to cover the main issues related to origins, developments and characteristics of national flags and days. Regional or ethnic diversity is not ignored but is beyond the scope of this study. Moreover, official national celebrations and symbols are appropriate to study as they uncover nation-making strategies in operation. Finally, this is not a book about national celebrations and commemorations as experienced by citizens, nor will it explore the effects ceremonies have on different national or ethnic groups as divided by sex, age, class, region and religion.

Definitions

Empirical curiosity is an important reason for this research: the symbolic and ceremonial manifestations of Europe are little known and no investigation into the symbolic patterns of nationhood has been undertaken from this perspective. In particular, knowledge about the systematic variety and pattern of symbolic expressions is missing. However, instead of asking why and when nations and nationalisms have arisen, the principal aim here is to identify the role of symbols and ceremonies in the layering and building of nations: to account for similarities and differences with regards to symbolism and ceremonials that have something important to tell us about the properties and components of nations. This raises questions of how concepts such as 'nation' and 'state', 'nationalism', 'nationhood', 'national identity', 'national symbolism' and related terms (national flag, national day, national day design) are to be understood. Attempts at defining nations have been singularly unsuccessful according to Seton-Watson (1977) and trying to establish a set of criteria to grasp the complexity, capricious nature and constantly changing conception of nations (Hobsbawm, 1992) is difficult. Instead of limiting attributes, definitions have therefore been designed to include general notions of the term (Anderson, 1991; Gellner, 1993; Hobsbawm, 1992) emphasizing the self-definitional dimension of nationhood and the imagination associated with this type of community (Anderson, 1991). The 'imagination of community' linked to and visualized through national symbolism is a useful concept here, although attention to that which is imagined must be given and is partly addressed through the embellishment of the past through symbols and ceremonies. (For an encompassing debate on the difficulty of defining these concepts, see Connor, 1992; Connor, 1994; Hutchinson and Smith, 1994; A.D. Smith, 1998, 2001).

A *working definition* of the nation will refer to the imagination of a community in terms of shared cultural, political and socio-economic elements (such as history, language, religion, ethnicity, territory, attainment of recognition). Many such variables can be employed to define nations but are cause for empirical confusion and difficult to date. However, all nations adhere to similar symbolic and ceremonial codes that raise boundaries against non-members and authenticate nations to the degree that they suggest that nations can be represented by *one* flag and its *raison d'etre* expressed through *one* national day. The national community is thus imagined as *one* and as characterized by *sameness*. The symbolic codes of nations are used in the process of attaining recognition, in political, social and cultural forums. With the French Revolution and the emergence of the modern nation characterized by mass-culture, mass-participation and citizenship, communal symbolism and ceremonies flourished. True, the term 'nation' was also in use pre-1789 but was then associated with different meanings (Greenfeld, 1992; Miller, 1995).

This brings us to the nexus of nation and state. The traditional idea of the homogeneous nation-state, the union of *one* people and *one* state (in terms of a sovereign political, judicial and military structure) has in today's increasingly multi-cultural world ceased to exist (if it ever did). However, the reality is less transparent as such aspirations have found expression in the promotions of one dominant culture (Elgenius, 2011; Guibernau, 1996). The nation is understood as the bearer of identity and culture within a framework usually provided by the state, which, in turn, is justified by the nation. (For related works on nation and state formation, see Breuilly, 1993; Hroch, 1995, 1996; Orridge, 1981; Plamenatz, 1976; Reynolds, 1997; Seton-Watson, 1977; Tilly, 1975; Tivey, 1981.) Thus, as a rule, national and state symbolisms are conflated and difficult to separate. Symbols of nations may also become symbols of state, unless the latter stand in opposition to the former. It is through these that people of the nation and the state are made ritually egalitarian and inequalities are in effect negated (Kapferer, 1988). The elites vary according to their involvement in the establishment and design of national flags and days. The role of governments also varies as does the involvement of the Church, the military, the intelligentsia and the financial elites. Clearly, nation-builders on the left played a significant role towards the end of the nineteenth century in Norway and in Germany and in the twentieth century counter celebrations were arranged by the left in France. In contrast, in Britain after the First World War, patriotism was encouraged in order to inhibit the growth of revolutionary sympathies. Intellectual and financial elites of the nineteenth and twentieth centuries played an important role with the forming of national institutions and industries. Adding to this, the branding of nations (Aronczyk, 2009, 2011) has become a central consideration. The only government that can 'afford to ignore the impact of its national reputation is one which has no interest in participating in the global community' (Anholt, 2007, p.13). The role of national imagery in the promotion of national products such as the flourishing business of producing regional folk costumes in Norway or the role of Guinness in the promotion of St Patrick's Day have emerged as noteworthy enterprises and with these notions associated with cultural copyright. With the transformation of this religious holiday into a national day in mind, it is interesting to note that pubs were regulated by law on St Patrick's Day up until the 1970s and the national campaigns commenced in 1995.

Nationalism is understood as operating on different levels: as an ideology of a world divided into nations; as a political movement for the attainment of autonomy or independence; and as a language of symbolism (see A.D. Smith, 1998, 2001). It is the symbolic dimension of nationalism – connecting these levels – that are explored in this book. Thus, nationality, nationhood and national identities are expressed with references to the socio-political elements of the nation and rest on various degrees of such imaginations of sameness. The concept of national identity thus refers to an active identity, the belief in a distinct and shared public culture, transmitted through symbols, expressed ceremonially in relation to historical complexities and geographical space. Nations are thus understood as 'communities that do things together, take decisions, achieve results' (Miller, 1995, p. 24). The idea of national identity as *one identity* is enforced by the dominant national narrative and hegemonic memory neglecting to acknowledge the competing strands of identit*ies* expressed through a dense web of symbolism. Continuity as claimed by nationalists, through flags and national day celebrations, in terms of continuous occupancy of a given territory, seldom survives critical reflection.

Historical narratives of nationhood justify social structures and hierarchies of power performed through a nexus of symbolism and ceremonials. These may have a series of meanings and associations attached to them. As the essence of symbolism and symbolic activity suggest, there is no likeness between the symbol and the ceremony to the entity it is supposedly representing. This relationship may seem arbitrary to the outsider as symbolic and ceremonial activity is defined by context and the means put into play seem inappropriate to their explicit or implicit ends (Sperber, 1974). Having said this, for the observer the ceremony may provide assurance and to the participant a form of renewing commitment.

National symbolism is set apart from other types of symbolism by its references to the nation, its claims to a specific history, sovereignty and distinctiveness. Here, will be explored the officially recognized national symbols (flag, anthem and national day) but also their informal equivalents, thought of as private in nature by references to sacrifice through membership (remembrance ceremonies for the fallen and associated symbols such as the poppy) that constitute *core symbolism* of nations. Both types are used to motivate patriotic action, enforce bonds, confer honour, justify or challenge authority (Cerulo, 1995). For the purpose of this book it is the *national* qualities of the flag and the national day that distinguish these from other flags or holidays. Some national flags have medieval origins whereas others have appeared recently as measures of success for the politicization of identities. Although pre-modern societies were rich in symbolism, it is too early in development to talk about *national* symbols in the Middle Ages. Similarly, the national day provides a platform for the performances and the on-the-streets aesthetics of official historical narratives, in turn, connected to the promotion and the appropriation of *one* dominant culture drawing on both traditional patterns and new designs. Here we focus on the Day recognized as the official 'national day' and, if no such day exists formally, with the day that operates as a community day. National days constitute a nexus of symbolism and symbolic activities that contribute to the visibility of nations and provide in their forms *seedbeds of virtue* (Etzioni, 2004) through ceremonial messages. National days, as a rule, are officially recognized public holidays claimed to celebrate founding moments of a community. *National day design* is intimately linked to nationalism and continues to occupy nation builders as connected not only to the transformations of ceremonial message and choreography but also to the desire to encourage inter-generational, multi-ethnic and multinational participation. The ultimate signs of successful national days are their ongoing celebrations or commemorations, despite being drained of original meaning and having been elevated to a sacred sphere in which they are difficult to criticize or beyond official criticism.

Outline

It is worth noting that the theoretical and empirical points of departure are briefly explored in Chapter 1 and reappear in their relevant contexts throughout subsequent chapters. Chapters 2 and 3 uncover the contexts in which flags became such important national and political symbols. The link between pre-modern and modern periods and the circumstances and the attachment of flags to national territories is investigated in Chapter 2. The nation-building process as seen from the perspective of the complex developments of the national flags in Britain, France and Norway are also analysed. Chapter 3 explores flags as instruments of elites and counter-instruments of peoples and as unifying and divisive symbols. Illuminating examples are also drawn from the former Soviet Socialist Republics; the Spanish Civil War; the flagging of national and regional loyalties in contemporary Spain; Belarus and independence; the flag conflict between Macedonia and Greece and the divisive nature of flag-symbolism employed in Bosnia-Herzegovina in the 1990s and the related developments with regard to the Europeanization of the symbolism of Bosnia-Herzegovina and Kosovo. The nature of successful flag symbolism is discussed and a typology presented in which national flags are linked to the symbolic regimes and corresponding pre-modern, modern and post-imperial narratives.

Chapters 4 and 5 explore the national days of Europe, the ceremonial statistics of what, when and how. The significance of national day design and constituent elements in nation building is explored in a number of cases. The differences and similarities with regards to ceremonial content and the origins of national days is identified in Chapter 4 with a comparative perspective of over 40 national days in Europe in mind. The complexity of ceremonial variety is explored with regards to Europe and through the different developments into Bastille Day in France, Constitution Day in Norway and Remembrance Sunday in Britain. The nature and variety of ceremonial choreography through parades and processions (military and/or civilian), ceremonial routes, nationalization of sacrifice through membership are also explored. The point of references for the national days (often foundation myths or personifications of a golden age) is contrasted to the actual dates of the first national events in order to highlight striking discrepancies. These dimensions in turn illuminate the emerging pattern of the making of successful national days and national day designs as presented in Chapter 5.

The concluding chapter brings together the study of national flags, national anthems and national days in order to identify the complex layering of nations – their expressions and counter-expressions – and the continuous nature of nation building. Many nations of Western Europe and northern Europe have been represented by the same flags for centuries whereas independence in the former Eastern Europe was interrupted and explains why many flags have been (re)introduced and (re)established relatively recently. Thus, continuity characterizes the symbolic expressions of Western and northern Europe and less so in Central and Eastern Europe. A consistent pattern is not found in southern Europe.

1
National Symbols and Ceremonies: The Construction and Authentication of Boundaries

Considerable activity is currently found in the sphere of national symbolism and ceremonials in multicultural states and connected to debates on nationality, citizenship and integration. Many governments seem to have adopted a Durkheimian approach hoping that celebrations of and participation in ceremonies of various kinds ultimately will contribute to cohesion. The British *Citizenship Review* of 2008 suggested that a British National Day (national citizenship day) be introduced as a permanent annual feature (Rimmer, 2008) in order to bring people together. This suggestion was part of a chain of initiatives as the Home Office had already introduced a Citizens' Day as a low key initiative in 2005 with the intention of breaking down barriers and providing an opportunity for people from all backgrounds to come together – in the first instance in ethnically mixed parts of Britain encouraging people to interact as British citizens and celebrate Britishness. The issue was perceived of in a comparative light which highlighted the lack of an all-inclusive and large-scale national celebration in Britain. As laid out below:

> Indeed, while Britain does commemorate the fallen on Remembrance Sunday, it is relatively unusual in not having any great public days of national celebration, such as Bastille Day in France, Independence Day in Greece, Constitution Day in Norway, Liberation Day in Bulgaria, or 4th July in the USA. (Heath et al., 2007, p. 28)

In line with the above, the former Prime Minister Gordon Brown suggested that Remembrance Sunday – the only existing day in Britain which commands a substantial amount of participation in one form or other – would be a suitable Britain Day. Remembrance Sunday commemorates Britain's fallen soldiers and, since 2000, has officially invited several faith communities and acknowledged their sacrifices. Drawing on existing ceremonial structures the government thus debated how to encourage the celebratory elements of Britishness. Closely related to such ceremonial initiatives are the recently introduced *citizenship ceremonies*, in Britain in place since 2004, marking the new status for new citizens. These ceremonies indirectly define British citizenship in terms of being earned, learned and celebrated (Andreouli and Stockdale, 2009; Elgenius, 2008). As acted out within the ceremonial sphere of nations, the celebration of citizenship is becoming more tied to the 'important underlying assumption of the earned citizenship discourse' which indicates that 'justice claims are grounded in a territorially bounded view of the world which supports the superiority of the entitlements of the native population' (Andreouli and Stockdale, 2009, p. 164). Citizenship ceremonies thus mark the approval for new graduating citizens and constitute in effect a nationalization of the citizenship debate.

Similar community-building projects are in operation world-wide and in a Durkheimian vein employed to celebrate, recognize, promote, (re)negotiate, (re)create and (re)enforce identities (Elgenius, 2008, 2011). Thus, participation in the same ceremonies is understood to (re)create a sense commonality and hereby strengthen communities, in which ceremonial imagery and performance is narrated in such ways that it justifies the current social order.

Something eternal in religion

It has long been recognized that social life is an important repository of symbols, whether in the form of totems, golden ages, flags, heroes, icons, capitals, statues, war memorials or football teams, which are – at the core – various forms of symbolic markers of social groups. Symbols provide short cuts to the group they represent and symbolism is by nature referential, subjective and boundary-creating. A Durkheimian departure is helpful but must be challenged on its functionalism and claim that symbols and ceremonies produce unity and cohesion. However, while national days may provide a unifying narrative, cohesion and solidarity do not necessarily follow their introduction. Whereas national day ceremonies are expressions of societal worship and affirmation of values, the effect of this worship continues to be assumed rather than proved. Having said this, in a much quoted passage Durkheim highlights the eternal forms of religious life as characteristic also of secularized ceremonies:

> there is something eternal in religion which is destined to survive all the particular symbols in which religious thought has successively enveloped itself. There can be no society which does not feel the need of upholding and reaffirming at regular intervals the collective sentiments and the collective ideas which make its unity and its personality. Now this moral remaking cannot be achieved except by the means of reunions, assemblies and meetings where the individuals, being closely united to one another, reaffirm in common their common sentiments; hence come ceremonies which do not differ from regular religious ceremonies, either in their object, the results which they produce, or the processes employed to attain these results. (1976, p. 427)

This 'eternal something' refers to the systems of practices, rites (cult) and ideas explaining the world (faith) and the eternal forms of religion in secular forms and guises can be revealed. Continuing in the forms of ritually active religious communities, national ceremonies are today understood as 'symbols of collective unity' used 'in more secular vein as the celebration of political ideals' (Giddens, 1991, p. 207). In line with this argument the nation has been perceived as 'a community of faith and as a sacred communion' (A.D. Smith, 2003, p. 24). National symbols have thus been described as modern totems as they merge the mythical sacredness of the nation into forms experienced by sight and sound by blending of subject and object beyond simple representations of nations: 'In a very real sense, national symbols become the nation' (Cerulo, 1995, p. 4). Along these lines, Durkheim had questioned the difference between an assembly of Jews commemorating the Exodus from Egypt, Christians celebrating Christmas, the honouring of a new political system or remembrance of significant historical events. Every society uses symbolic and ceremonial activity to attempt moral remaking. Many studies of political symbolism (Gusfield and Michalowicz, 1984) have built on these Durkheimian assumptions and have explored ceremonies as symbols of moral values (Shils and Young, 1953) whereas others have highlighted the impossibility of assessing the interpretations and feelings of the public (Lukes, 1975). The evidence highlights these dimensions and that ceremonies represent authoritative interpretations of society and contribute to the assertion of power. The participation in ceremonies may reinforce a feeling of social location as people come together on national days, carnivals, fairs, religious holidays, saints' days, joyful celebrations or solemn commemorations. The success of national days also provides evidence to the effect that they *can* constitute a shared experience and raise awareness of imagined communities and thus constitute building blocks in the making of nations. Therborn writes:

> A collective identity is not just an identity held in common in their souls by an aggregate of individuals. As a rule it is also a public thing, manifested in and sustained by public rituals. (1995, p. 223)

Perceptions of commonality, boundaries, us and others

Symbols are effective precisely because they are ambiguous, imprecise and their meanings are 'subjective' without undermining their collective nature. They 'exist as something for people to think with', to make and express meaning without imposing a static one. Nevertheless, they express social values in ways that allow for a common form to be retained and shared without compromising individual beliefs and associations linked to communities. So, 'rather than thinking of community as an integrating mechanism it should be regarded instead as an aggregating device' and commonality need not be uniformity (A. Cohen, 1995, pp. 19–20). Moreover, this does not mean that the interpretations of communal symbols are arbitrary or remain uncontested. On the contrary, they are formed in line with encouraged notions of traditions, ideology, power, beliefs, culture and social expressions that by nature can be highly divisive. It is true that individuals participate in ceremonies for all sorts of reasons, but whatever their motivations, the use of symbols are prominent in the repertoire of communal symbolism where boundaries are heightened and reinforced.

The transactional process of boundary creation has primarily become a matter of differentiation from others (Barth, 1969). Boundary-making ceremonies are multi-referential and multi-vocal by nature and revealed on a variety of levels to the members of a community (Turner, 1967, 1969) as they communicate the relationships of this group to other groups and to the world outside it. The construction of symbols and ceremonies help transform the reality of diversity into an appearance of commonality (of cultural forms and ways of behaving) contributing to the understandings of nationhood and membership. Thus, boundaries are simultaneously oppositional and relational and turn community itself into a boundary-expressing symbol (A. Cohen, 1995).

Ethno-political symbols related to language, culture, art, music, geography, ethnicity and religion contribute to mythic structures and to *mythomoteurs* that systematize and justify membership in relation to other groups (Armstrong, 1982). Religious symbols have been argued as particularly important for ethnic border guards as groups define themselves not (only) by reference to their own characteristics but by exclusion of strangers and in comparison to outsiders, which constitute part of the process of identifying with the in-group (Armstrong, 1982; Tajfel and Turner, 2004). When the variability of meanings become too encompassing and when geo-social boundaries are undermined, blurred or weakened (Alba, 2005; A. Cohen, 1995) notions of 'community' depend on the manipulation and embellishment of its symbols. Boundaries constitute in this manner and by nature 'sociologically complex fault lines' or systems of social distinctions that are 'imposed by the ethnic majority' (Alba, 2005, p. 20). Blurred boundaries are associated with ambiguity about membership whereas bright boundaries are not. It is the context of the former that national flags and national days help facilitate the brightening of these. Conflicts, struggles and wars have therefore been noted as significant in the process of raising boundaries and as characterized by considerable flag-waving (Colley, 1992; Eriksen and Jenkins, 2007; Marvin and Ingle, 1999; A.D. Smith, 2003). Sacrificial boundaries ultimately define boundaries by which nations become known, characterized by the commemorations of particular sacrifices and the lack of recognition of those of others.

Boundary creation is also related to perceived rights of cultural production, property rights and copyright protection and addresses notions of boundaries related to culture as owned by particular groups or traditions. This discussion is related to *the perceived rights* of defining culture and artifacts, protecting culture from infringement and benefiting from commercialization. 'Native essentialisms' have been highlighted as part of such political and commercial discourses. Cultural copyright is a phenomenon that has been held in connection with the production and use of national flags, the production of regional costumes (*bunad*) in Norway or the highland tradition in Scotland (T.H. Eriksen, 2005; Trevor-Roper, 1992) as has various forms of the musealization of cultural production (Knell et al. 2011).

Using national symbols and ceremonies

Since *blurred* boundaries are reinforced with the embellishment of symbolic content, symbols and ceremonies have come to constitute tools through which nationalist regimes attempt to mobilize populations in pursuit of power. It is beyond any doubt that a variety of elites are active in various stages and at various times in the nation-making context. However, it is also true that their attempts do not always work. Moreover, symbols (flags) and ceremonies (national days) also constitute powerful counter-instruments in the hands of people protesting against such authorities.

The *aesthetics of politics* and the work of Mosse (1975, 1993b) is an appropriate place to commence when exploring the nexus of myths, symbols and the new ceremonial styles linked to nationalism (Mosse, 1975, p. 20). In brief, during the eighteenth century allegiances to royal dynasties had begun to decline and populations emerged as a political force with the concept of popular sovereignty. The manifestation of a general will was transformed into a new form of politics and into conditions in which people worshipped themselves and hopes and fears were controlled within ceremonial and liturgical forms. A sense of permanence was hereby introduced or at least attempted and integrated into the daily life of people. National symbolism has a special reserve of *self-reference* distinguishing it from religious symbolism.

> Nationalist movements, like all mass movements, make use of symbols and ceremonies. These give nationalist ideas a definite shape and force, both by projecting certain images and by enabling people to come together in ways which seem directly to express the solidarity of the nation. Nationalist symbolism is able to do this in particularly effective ways because it has a quality of self-reference which is largely missing from socialist or religious ideology. Nationalists celebrate themselves rather than some transcendent reality, whether this be located in another world or in a future society, although the celebration also involves a concern with transformation of present reality. (Breuilly, 1993, p. 64)

It is through inventing traditions that elites attempt to establish continuity with a suitable past that, in turn, justifies the regimes of the present. The establishment of repeated practices, of a symbolic and ritual nature, help to enforce values and norms (Hobsbawm and Ranger, 1992). As new forms of national loyalties emerged, new traditions were invented and linked to new institutions that were required with rapid social transformations. Inventing traditions thus constitute tools by which the past can be controlled and the theatrical idiom of nationalism and related formation of ceremonial spaces contribute to maintaining social order. The mass production of public ceremonies and public monuments from 1870 to 1914 in the Third Republic of France and in the Second German Empire are examples of enforcing historical legitimacy. However, such perspectives do not explain all dimensions of national symbolism in nation building nor the appeal of symbols of nationhood or their importance for *nations-to-be*. National flags and national days are created for a number of reasons and not by elites only, but once established they are deliberately formalized and perceived as central to nation formation.

Symbols and ceremonies can be significant to nation building because they place the past – a foundation for nation-making – in the present where it can be directed towards the future. Thus the past constitutes a powerful resource in the making of boundaries raised against other nations. Celebrations and commemorations of historic events can also be emotionally charged reminding people of why they belong together. Scholars such as Smith, Stråth, Hutchinson, Hastings and Armstrong emphasize the importance of foundation myths – visible through symbols chosen to represent nations. Smith highlights the significance of historic landscapes with reference to 'golden ages' in the formation and in the maintenance of national identities as symbols, memories, myths and traditions constitute the core of nations (A.D. Smith, 1986, 1988, 1998). He states:

> Symbols such as flags, emblems, anthems, costume, special foods, and sacred objects, give expression of our sense of difference and distinctiveness of the community [...] myths of origins, liberation, the golden age, and chosenness link the sacred past to a sense of collective destiny. Each of these elements articulated a vital dimension of the culture-community. (A.D. Smith, 1995)

The notion of a national destiny is linked to the founding myths of communities (Stråth, 2000). Historical images root communities in territories and sites for mythologies and references to golden ages link nations with respective myths of heroism. Notions of national birth, growth, maturity, decline and rebirth may also be central as they provide communities with a sense of direction and references to the past, present and the future (Hutchinson, 1994; A.D. Smith, 2003). However, as demonstrated further on, founding myths are crucial in the formative years of national ceremonies but as a sign of true success for those that survive over time we may even say, on the contrary, that the opposite is true. Successful national days that have survived over time have, as a rule, been drained of their original meanings but nevertheless achieve a sacred status. Many national day celebrations and commemorations were in their origins exclusive and pitted against others and the transformation of boundary-related matters are crucial for survival over time. Moreover, the nostalgia for the past has often been explained by the waning of religious beliefs and the need for new measures of immortality through posterity. However, the significance of history in the building of nations must also be considered with reference to the potentially divisive nature of its interpretations within nationally or ethnically-divided territories. Whereas national symbolism in Europe – as a rule – makes references to a distant, glorious or suitable past justifying the existence of the states in the present – a post-historical and counter-nationalist narrative has emerged, forced to avoid historical references altogether.

Moral direction

The glorification of nations in the present provides fuel in nation making as the (re)constructed relationship between the past, present and future contributes to (an illusion of) unity in the present. The glorifying of nations also contributes to the formation of moral communities as moral remaking takes place through ceremonies and symbols referring to significant events, heroes, wars and sacrifices. A moral stance naturally follows when related norms and values are uncovered and involved by the honouring of certain historical events, birthdays, enterprises, personifications and sacrifices but not others, as in the remembering *our* fallen and by definition *not* the fallen killed by these. Remembering, we understand in the imagined sense of the word. National symbols constitute in this fashion master or dominant symbols (Wright in Dillistone, 1986; Turner, 1967, 1969) or moral symbols that by nature provide moral codes of justification. Nationalism, death and sacrifice are intimately linked with their equivalent religious constellations enforced by sacrifices given willingly for a worthy cause and that involves saving the group by leaving it. The nation thus achieves its morality directly created from 'the flesh of its citizens' (Marvin and Ingle, 1999, p. 75) and sacrifical boundaries are established on the basis of these. It is in such contradictory contexts that ceremonies are employed to justify and exhort people to war and violence and that conflicts are perpetuated (Kertzer, 1989, p. 129). It is not only in context that the notion of 'imagined communities' (Anderson, 1991) is useful. The commemorations of fallen soldiers are highly significant in the creation of moral communities and have strong affinity with religious imaginings as aptly linked below:

> No more arresting emblems of the modern culture of nationalism exist than cenotaphs and tombs of Unknown Soldiers. The public ceremonial reverence accorded these monuments precisely *because* they are either deliberately empty or no one knows who lies inside them, has no true precedents in earlier times. To feel the force of this modernity one has to imagine the general reaction to the busy-body who 'discovered' the Unknown Soldier's name or insisted on filling the cenotaph with some real bones. Sacrilege of a strange, contemporary kind! Yet void as these tombs are of identifiable mortal remains or immortal souls, they are nonetheless saturated with ghostly *national* imaginings. (Anderson, 1991, p. 9)

Nations become distinctive through their particular style of imagination and their persuasive power is manifested in the citizens' willingness to die for their communities (Anderson, 1991) and act against their self-interest. Remembrance ceremonies also help shed light on the nature of commemorations related to sacrifice (Moriarty, 1991) and on the justification of existing social structures.

The politics of (non)recognition and protest: victory and defeat

In the process of challenging the direction of nations, existing symbols and ceremonies are replaced, discovered, re-discovered, constructed, re-constructed, invented and re-invented. Since national flags and national days express meanings about nationhood they are therefore also contested. The altering of city names has throughout history been a legacy of new political regimes. St Petersburg (called Petrograd in 1917) was given the name Leningrad in 1924 to mark the victory of the Bolsheviks over the Provisional Government. The city retrieved its name – St Petersburg – in 1991 with the shift away from Communism. The city Tsaritsyn, founded in 1589, became Stalingrad for the period 1925–61 and has been known as Volgograd since 1961 (Arvidsson and Blomqvist, 1987; Overy, 1997). The revival of national symbolism in Eastern Europe following the collapse of the Soviet Union after 1989 produced new sets of national symbols, flags, anthems and national days to celebrate the new nations and states – a course, at times, long and complicated as symbolic battles ensued. Innumerable changes were made to the designs of national flags and days as a result of such sociopolitical conflicts. The reverence for national days and flags and their continued associations to nationhood are illuminating with reference to the politics of recognition and protest; whereas national elites attempt to protect national symbols and their relationship to the nation by laws and regulations, national flags and days remain double-edged or counter instruments. As such they express dissent as flags are defaced and burned in protests against political systems, ideologies and regimes, both within and outside nations.

Part of the politics of recognition, regret and apology is the re-invention of existing ceremonies and the introduction of new ones that acknowledge previously marginalized groups. The federal government in Canada has introduced a National Aboriginal Day (21 July) as has Australia with Aboriginal Day. However, Australia Day (26 January), in contrast, commemorates the landing of the first fleet in Sydney Cove in 1788 and has as such been challenged by the association of the Australian Aboriginal Sovereign Nations as a day of British colonialism. In Britain a monument to Women of World War II was unveiled in Whitehall (in 2005) on the ceremonial route of remembrance at the Cenotaph (dedicated to fallen soldiers) in London. This monument was dedicated to the seven million women who contributed to the war effort, their work recognized in this form *60 years* after the end of the Second World War (BBC, 9 July 2005).

Community-bridging strategies visible in these examples above stand in sharp contrast to strategies of *non-recognition* and exclusion employed during and after the Second World War. In Nazi Germany 1933–45, Jews were forbidden to fly the Swastika flag from 1935 but by 1945 the flag had become an (im)moral symbol tainted as it was with the results of Nazism. Finding an anthem and a national day in the aftermath of the Second World War was therefore a challenge. The ramifications of the nation's moral boundaries being undermined resulted in an absence of symbolic expression in Germany after the Second World War. The symbolism of the victorious nations was equally exclusive as one may expect. In the Moscow Victory Parade on 24 June 1945, 12 000 soldiers participated in honour of the millions who never returned. The regiments that had most distinguished themselves paraded with the 36 banners of their units. At a poignant point the music accompanying the military parade stopped and was replaced by a drum roll increasing in volume as a column of soldiers carrying 200 captured Nazi banners appeared. As the column drew up to Lenin's Mausoleum in Red Square each rank made a sharp right turn and a soldier flung his Nazi banner to the ground at the steps of the Mausoleum. The Victory Parade was carefully documented and photographs subsequently appeared in countless Soviet textbooks and journals. The most publicized scene was that of the contemptuous throwing down of the Nazi banners and standards, their eagles and swastikas crashing to the ground (Clayton, 1995). The imagery represented a new era of iconography – the people's triumph over fascism and the glorification of the Soviet Union, its leaders and military power. By defiling the Nazi banners – the enemy was crushed at the foot of the founder of the nation – and the gloves of the soldiers holding the banners were ceremonially burned (RussiaToday, 2010a).

As a result of colonialism and related wars, similar symbolic battles fought over names of streets, districts, towns, cities and provinces are found, for example, in Vietnam during the latter half of the twentieth century. Many places have been known by three or more names in the wake of colonialization, divisive political struggles and the renegotiation of nationhood and ideology. Round one attempted to erase the French colonial past by replacing all French names except those of Albert Calmette, Marie Curie, Louis Pasteur and Alexandre Yersin. New names were also allocated to South Vietnam in an attempt to erase references to the Viet Minh's anti-French exploits from 1956 onwards. As we may expect, names associated with the United States established during the Vietnam War were also replaced after the formal reunification of North and South Vietnam in 1976. The victorious North Vietnamese communists changed the name of the capital from Saigon to Ho Chi Minh City (HCMC) in 1975, significantly on the first day of their victory (Florence and Jealous, 2003). In 2000 a People's Committee originally set out to rename 25 new streets in order to redefine parts of Ho Chi Minh City; however, this generated considerable debate so the committee decided to rename another 152 streets. In the midst of the battle in Iraq, with the claiming of victory the new political regime was quick to erase all previous national days and establish new ones. With the fall of Saddam's regime in Iraq, the first decision made by the interim council (July 2003) was to abolish all previous holidays (Podeh, 2010). A new Iraqi national day (9 April) was adopted as a celebration of Saddam's ousting, a decision significantly taken on the 45th anniversary of the revolution that annihilated the Hashemite monarchy – a date celebrated by all Iraqi regimes.

Successful national days and national day design

A sense of commonality in modern nations can thus be produced through the use of the same symbols and participation in the same ceremonies. The diverse reality is, at least temporarily, transformed by participation into an appearance of similarity, something which alone does not necessarily produce cohesion. Simmel (1964) drew attention to the role of threats, external war and conflict as a form of *sociation* that makes boundaries more distinct. Cohesion, in this context, does not refer to an absence of conflict or to national idyll. In nineteenth-century Norway the national day became part of the struggle for democratization in times of internal disunity. In Britain during the First World War expressions of unity were found in the war effort and conflict with the external world created a national bond. At the same time, domestic disunity was channelled through strikes and demonstrations for peace. According to Nairn (1977) the First World War virtually saved England from civil war.

While national symbols and ceremonies can serve as convenient means of analysing nation building and raise awareness of membership some remain contested and others go unnoticed. Comprehensive studies of the French Revolution and its festivals highlight the fact that the attempt by the revolutionaries to restructure French society by re-ordering the celebratory year was ultimately unsuccessful (Ozouf, 1988). However, the annual celebrations of Bastille Day turned into a popular national day celebration at the centenary in 1880, in the age of nationalism and at a time when Bastille Day could be drained of the violent associations of the revolution. As a sharp contrast, the lack of celebrations on Unification Day in Germany demonstrates that national days must be seen within their historical context. German national days have throughout history constituted a source of conflict and, today, Unification Day has attempted but not yet succeeded in drawing people into the celebrations of unification, except for those in 1990 and 2009. Some ceremonies do not even create consensus as to what is commemorated. In Russia, the former national day, the Day of the Great October Socialist Revolution, after the collapse of the Soviet Union became known as the Day of Accord and Reconciliation, but was exchanged for Russia Day in 2004 (12 June) on the grounds of being ideologically outdated.

The findings of ceremonial success with reference to Norway's Constitution Day are in particular illuminating in its context of encompassing participation over time. This is attributed to a number of factors that include the existence of unifying narrative: the historical genesis and the Day's status as a symbol of independence before statehood had been achieved. Successful national days are as a rule public holidays and official and private celebrations are integrated or follow each other. Whereas historical complexities are understood as particularly important in the formative years, the design of national days is crucial for continued success and appeal. Many successful national days have emerged against 'others' and transform over time with regards to the ceremonial message and corresponding national day design. One sign of truly successful national days is that they have been drained of their original meaning so that nationhood is celebrated with changing associations. Moreover, many national days have acquired a sacred status and are not easily criticized in the public sphere.

Symbolic regimes and narratives

Symbolic regimes are built on the formation of successful symbolic codes. This study distinguishes between pre-modern, modern and post-imperial symbolic regimes. The pre-modern regime refers to symbolism introduced before the French Revolution, the modern regime from 1789 to the First World War when the post-imperial regime appears, three periods used as pivots for categorization of symbolic expression. This framework is not exhaustive, but different narratives become visible when comparing these periods to the designs of flags and to the celebrations of national days. Something can also be said about the context of nations that in the modern period required tricolours and celebrated days of revolution and independence. The context in which the many pre-national cross flags survived is also significant as is the context of the heraldic flags, designs adorned by historical devices and colours, introduced in a post-imperial age after the First World War with many new state formations. It is interesting that the retained pre-modern cross flags actually demonstrated dissent from papacy at the time. Whereas the modern tricolours became symbols of revolution and change, the many post-imperial heraldic flags staked out claims for nationhood against empires and foreign rulers with displays of colours and devices from the middle ages. Nation making relies on the standardization of cultural expressions associated with the status of independent states, something which is also seen with the relative standardization of national flags and days, flag types and ceremonial styles.

The call to display a Christian cross on the Italian tricolour flag in 2009 following the decision to ban the construction of minarets in

Switzerland is thus significant when we consider that the early cross flags were once chosen to justify conflict during the crusades. Swiss voters had approved a proposal to ban the construction of minarets after a campaign that labelled mosque towers symbols of militant Islam. The latter used posters displaying the Swiss flag pierced by minarets (*Guardian*, 29 November 2009). Following the Swiss vote, the conservative deputy minister of infrastructure and transport in Italy – Roberto Castelli of the Northern League – argued that 'Europe has the right to safeguard its own identity... it is necessary to return to our roots' (Adnkronos International, 30 November 2009).

What do national symbols and ceremonies mean to people?

It is difficult to appropriately assess individual sentiments associated with national days, anthems and flags in the absence of adequate or comparative qualitative or quantitative data. It is arguable that national ceremonies may create a feeling of community but that this sense of community is dissolved as soon as the crowd or audience is dissolved (Uzelac, 2010). However, we cannot assume that national ceremonies mean the same to everyone. Nationals marching through the streets may have a sense of 'being in this together' but their experiences will be multi-faceted. The degree to which ceremonies have a spill-over effect in everyday life is also hard to assess as is when and how national fervour is dissolved. It is, however, possible to determine that national symbols and ceremonies have been adopted alongside the process of nation building and re-adopted in new socio-political conditions. In observing the procedures associated with national days and flags, we may also say something about their appeal and success in providing a unifying focus. The respect they demand, as regulated by law, helps illuminate the ways in which national symbols help sanctify the purpose of nations and constitute components of national worship. Protests involving the burning of the Tricolour on Bastille Day or shouting during the two minutes silence on Remembrance Sunday are defined as acts of desecration. Symbols are thus able to ignite conflicts of various kinds and we find them contested and divisive.

In consulting the World Value Survey (WVS, 2005) and International Social Survey Project (ISSP, 2003) we find that people continue to be considerably proud of their nationalities despite their suggested decrease (Beck and Beck-Gernsheim, 2002). The high numbers indicate percentage of being very proud or quite proud of nationality as follows: Poland

96 per cent, Finland 94 per cent, Norway 90 per cent, Italy 90 per cent, Slovenia 90 per cent, Sweden 88 per cent, Switzerland 87 per cent, Serbia 86 per cent, Romania 84 per cent, Bulgaria 81 per cent, Ukraine 73 per cent (European Values Study Group and World Values Survey Association, 2006). Similar figures (of being very proud or somewhat proud) account to the following numbers in: Ireland 98 per cent, Portugal 95 per cent, Hungary 94 per cent, Austria 92 per cent, Denmark 90 per cent, France 89 per cent, Slovak Republic 86 per cent, Russia 85 per cent, Czech Republic 81 per cent, Netherlands 78 per cent and Latvia 76 per cent (ISSP, 2003). These figures appear to confirm that nationality matters with increased fragmentation and heterogeneity. Interestingly, high figures are also noted in multi-national states such as Spain 95 per cent (WVS, 2005) and Britain 87 per cent (ISSP, 2003), which suggest that survey material of this nature is more complex than first meets the eye. It is unlikely that a representative sample of nationals within these states would have been collected. However, if we instead consider the relative importance of nationality in comparative terms (see e.g. Heath et al., 2007) the ranking of identities (ISSP, 2003; Spreckelsen, 2010) continue to demonstrate that nationality matters. The significance of social identities across Europe has been ranked in the following order: family, occupation, gender, nationality, age, region, class, ethnicity, religion and political party. The figures above point towards the continued appeal of nations and nationhood and also contribute to an explanation as to why symbols associated with nationality continue to matter.

Exploring patterns with regard to the history of flags and national days will help assess their significance in expressing, representing, recognizing and building nations. Moreover, these patterns help demonstrate the ways in which nations are uniquely honoured, glorified, celebrated and commemorated. Thus a representative of the British conservative press described Herman van Rompuy after his election to the EU Presidency in 2009 as a 'fanatical federalist' who was even backing the replacing of national symbols such as national flags and anthems with their EU equivalents (*Daily Mail*, 20 November 2009).

2
National Flag Origins: Religion, Revolution and Rivalry

The introduction of national flags constitutes markers of nation building in the modern period and reflects political change. The *national* flag appears as a symbol for mass-participating nations that emerged with new notions of citizenship and 'oneness' after the course of 1789. Some flags survived from pre-modern times and were transformed into national flags as they were adopted by nations without states and states without nations. Elites in pursuit of power have played an essential role in the selection process throughout history. In this chapter we explore the reasons why flags became attached to nations and explain why some flag designs survived over time and others did not. Flag-related symbolism will be explored with reference to the latter part of the Middle Ages (1100–1500) to the early modern period (1500–1800) up to the modern period from 1800 onwards. The flags of Britain, France and Norway are discussed in detail as they represent different nation-building processes reflected in the adoption of their *national* flags. The conclusions drawn from the role of national flags in the building of nations will be discussed in this chapter and the next. The first building block is laid in this chapter by exploring the current national flags of Europe and by identifying different flag types aligning these with three main symbolic regimes and corresponding narratives developing in the ages of pre-modern, modern and post-imperial nations.

What we mean by national flags?

Symbols such as flags constitute a ubiquitous feature of social life not exclusive to nations. In the modern world, flags came to constitute powerful political symbols early on and continued to glorify nations by nature of their usage. They constitute 'routinely familiar habits of language' (Billig, 1995, p. 93) and visually display to people the ideology of nationalism in a world divided into nations. Flags may therefore, in Durkheimian sense, be described as modern objects of worship and as the extension of a secular form of divinity. While the early flags illuminate the cause of differentiation along pre-modern lines and that territorial loyalties existed early on – in one form or other – it is anachronistic to talk about national flags of the Middle Ages, a matter neglected by the authors of vexillological literature (see Crampton, 1989; Crampton, 1992; Hulme, 1915; Preble, 1980; W. Smith, 1969, 1975a). However, with reference to the modern period a 'certain definition of a nation is adherence of its people to common symbols – and first and foremost a national flag' (W. Smith, 1975a, p. 54). The adherence to national flags is impossible to assess but flags adopted prior to 1789 were not 'national' in the modern sense of the concept representing a more democratic vision of community. Whatever variables facilitate the formation of nations – language, religion, perceptions of a shared history, a political agenda, economic integration or a combination of these elements – national flags reflect the supremacy of nations. While little can be said about individual feelings towards these we can decipher the patterns of their usage and identify their links to territorial loyalties and, later on in the modern period, say something about the ongoing process of nation building. Flags became significant political symbols because of their simple and abstract representation of complex notions of nations and nationhood and have continued through their usage as visual declarations of independence and claims to historically distinct and designated territories (Elgenius, 2007c).

The use of flags throughout history

The term *vexillology* – the study of the history and symbolism of flags – became a separate study in the 1960s and was coined by Whitney Smith whose work on the history of flags is central in this context (Elgenius, 2007c; W. Smith, 1969, 1975a). Vexillology refers to the vexillum (from velum) referring to flag-like 'sails' (FOTW, 1999) and to the Roman cavalry flags or standards used by a 'vexillation' or detachment from the legion. Standards, in turn, refer to flags based on heraldic shields that represented military units in battle or to those personal flags of a monarch or other high official (Hulme, 1915). The related term 'vexilloid' refers, in turn, to objects (such as animal figures and signs of the zodiac) on poles. These were employed to identify an assembly or a military unit and also to identify and mark the presence of a notable person or to communicate the attributes of a person or a god. The Roman empire was the first to systematize the use of standards in order to mark units of the army. Several vexilloids were used as emblems of identification as well as weapons. The two most famous vexilloids reproduced the images of the emperor or the eagle. The eagle could appear together with the symbol of Jupiter, the patron of Rome, with a thunderbolt – symbolism thought to add strength to Rome. The empire used different kinds of animals on standards until 104 BC, after which the eagle became the sole standard of the Roman legions. Each legion had an eagle and the different detached units carried also a vexillum (among the first vexilloids in fabric). The grand parades in ancient Rome provided the context for these. Lavish parades with standards and soldiers in battle dress intended to compensate for the weak distribution of military resources. The parading of flags and regalia captured from vanquished peoples further associated the vexilloids with conquest. The eagle standards were honoured as if they were sacred objects and their divinity transferred to the empire. As an example, the standards and vexilloids of foreign troops, serving in the Roman army, had to be given official recognition within the sanctuary of the Roman Pantheon. Roman vexilloids were also introduced into the Temple of Jerusalem, by order of Pilate in AD 26, as a mark of authority. These early vexilloids were linked in their function to modern flags, as in their capacity as totems that provided a foci for the given cult. 'Flags' in this form were distinguished by their plasticity, omnipresence and usefulness as they could be seen by great numbers of people simultaneously.

There are a number of suggestions as to the exact origin of the cloth flag (see W. Smith, 1975a). Flag symbolism has ancient roots and some depictions of flags are claimed to date to 4000 BC (Crampton, 1992). The Chinese used flags, as lateral cloth attachments to staffs, following the invention of silk farming as the development of sericulture around 3000 BC brought new possibilities of producing light, enduring and colourful flags used outdoors. One of the earliest cloth flags has also been dated to the Egyptian Middle Kingdom around 2000 BC. The Roman empire, as far as we know, used two kinds of fabric flags, one with the image of the goddess of victory and the other (known as the *flammula*) with red streamers attached to the spear marking the presence of a general. This usage is derived from the Greek *phoinikis* (a red cloak), which marked the commander of a ship, a practice later copied by the Roman empire. Another fabric standard used by the Christian Roman emperors was the *labarum*, employed as early as AD 400 by the Roman Emperor Constantine (Hulme, 1915), constituted a Christian version of the earlier Roman vexillum. The *labarum* was a jewelled square purple cloth and has been dated to Constantine's victory over Licinus in 324. It marked an evolution of flag-related symbolism as it displayed a portrait of the emperor and his family (or government officials) and atop the staff, the monogram of Christ (the *Chi-Rho*). The fourth century historian Eusebius writes in *Life of Constantine* that the emperor saw a sign of the cross in the sky before the victory over Maxentius in 312 with the words *In hoc signo vinces* [In this sign thou shalt conquer]. A myth that was to be recycled a century later. These portable deities described above were not flown from flagpoles but represented and identified various units.

Flags and banners in the Middle Ages

The Koran's injunction against representational art encouraged the development of flags in the Muslim world early on. These flags relied on abstract patterns and calligraphic inscriptions – often religious texts – in embroidery, appliqué or painting. Before the rise of Islam, flags of black and white were used in the early part of the seventh century. Mohammed (570–632) used one black and one white flag and the *liwa* (black with a white border) is also associated with him. The Arab world developed the tradition of using contrasting colours and inscriptions for different dynasties and leaders and contributed to the modern flag tradition by inventing cloth flags with greater adaptability with their colours (and inscriptions) affirming a 'dominant ethos'. So the banner (a flag carried by a military unit) of the Moorish State of Granada from the eighth century displayed the inscription 'There is no conqueror but God' on red background. The association of specific colours with dynasties and individual leaders reinforced political identities and became the basis for all modern flags. The colours of the early Arab flags were chosen on the basis of the association with Mohammed, and selected on the basis of an affiliation to values and leaders (W. Smith, 1975a).

The flags of Western Europe were inspired by these Arab military banners and introduced during the Crusades as a direct result of the wars and conflicts between Christians and Muslims. The first cross flags indicated that the military operations of the crusaders were sanctioned by the Pope. Many of the national flags, their colours and designs, were influenced by preceding coats of arms which originally used to identify soldiers on the battlefield (Tenora, Unknown). In the Christian world, the practice of bestowing banners previously blessed by the Pope also became of high significance during the Middle Ages and followed the ceremonial forms set by pre-Christian Rome as part of the politics of legitimizing power. These banners, or *pallia*, were flags that originally had been garments as is also the case with the cloak of and later the flag of Mohammed. *Pallia* were bestowed on St Augustine (354–430), Charlemagne (742–814) and William the Conqueror (1028–87). The cloak of St Martin was another garment turned flag and later became part of the cult objects of Frankish kings. The banner bestowed on William the Conqueror by the Pope before his invasion of England was an exchange of worldly power and moral authority, the cross as a symbol of the Roman Catholic Church. From the eleventh century onwards the cross started to identify Christians in the Crusades but, in the usage described above, took on a more secular meaning as a symbol of the worldly power of the emperor.

The influence of heraldry, as in the 'systematic hereditary use of an arrangement of charges and devices on a shield' (Woodcock and Robinson, 1990, p. 1), on modern flags has been substantial. Heraldic devices and colours emerged in the mid-twelfth century over wide areas of Europe and, with the use of arms on the seals of ecclesiastics, an early collective principle was deduced. Namely, that seals from the twelfth century onwards symbolized the body of the ecclesiastics represented, cities or educational establishments. These coats of arms, livery colours (main colours of the field of the principal motive of a coat of arms) and badges (distinctive emblems) would be displayed during tournaments in the Middle Ages and were associated with strength and distinction. Thus, the first badge used during the Crusades was the cross and was worn as a garment on the chest or back of the warrior. The Crusader flag – a white cross on red – was originally used by Christians against the European 'pagans' and became the flag employed by the Holy Roman Empire (from 800 onwards), thus symbolizing the holy cause of (FOTW, 2004b; W. Smith, 1975a).

Different colours were in use for crusaders from different areas by 1188 (see Figure 2.1). In 1188, King Philip Augustus of France got his colours on his cross flag (red cross on white), as did King Henry II of England (white cross on red) and Count Philip of Flanders (green cross on white). These colours were later reversed and, while the reason for this remains unclear, England embarked on what today is considered a continuous tradition of displaying a red cross on white from 1277, whereas France displayed a white cross, first on red, then on blue. Thus emerged St George's Cross (red cross on white), the Cross of St Denis (a white cross on red) and the cross flag of the Teutonic Knights (black cross on white).

32 *Symbols of Nations and Nationalism*

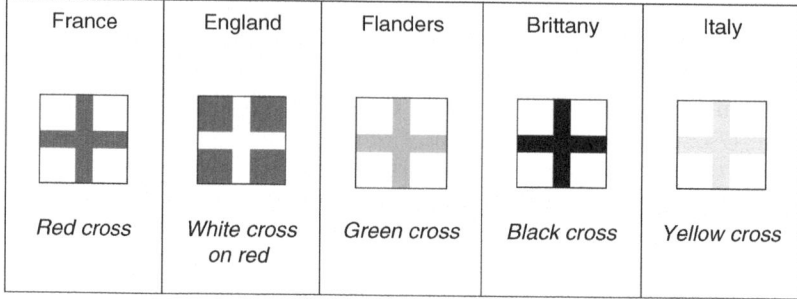

Figure 2.1 Crusader flags, 1188
Sources: (Crampton, 1989, 1992; FOTW, 2007; Preble, 1980; W. Smith, 1975a). Flag images courtesy of: (FOTW, 2010b).

Early modern flags

The first known cloth flag in the Christian tradition, the Cross Flag, constitutes a significant link between the representations of the early religiously sanctioned communities and nations. The Crusader Cross (red couped cross on white) influenced the development of three main streams of cross flags. First, the *coloured cross on white* as in the cross flags adopted by England, Genoa, Milan, Padua, Sardinia (all displaying a red cross on white), by Finland (blue cross on white) and by Nantes (black cross on white). The second version of the Crusader Cross was *the white cross on a coloured* background as in the flags of Denmark, Savoy, Malta and Vienna (white cross on red) and the flags of France and Greece (white cross on blue) and Sweden (yellow cross on blue). Thirdly, the *Saltire cross* (diagonal cross) used by Ireland (red diagonal cross on white also known as St Patrick's Cross) and by Spain (red diagonal cross on white) and served as inspiration for the white diagonal cross on blue used by Scotland (St Andrew's Cross) and the blue diagonal cross on white adopted by Russia (also known as St Andrew's Cross) (W. Smith, 1975a, pp. 46–52). As standardized measures were taken towards a uniform mode of representation, the use of these arms of dominion would gradually be restricted and flown only by monarchs and their appointed agents. This process started after the Crusades, when the nobility transformed their coats of arms into a formal system and hereby restricting their usage. The systematization of heraldic coats of arms and the heraldic tradition became a matter for professional heralds and tied the ruling elites (nobility or other magnates) to a specific territory via specified arms of dominion or town flags associated with 'local rights'. As the system was elaborated, it continued with specifications such as confirming the size of flags to rank. With the loss of relevance on the battlefield and with the growth of new social classes, novel means of representation were created. The Cross of St George, originally seen as a less important flag, became as a result the flag to represent England used by the English trading companies as a basis for their own flags at sea. Many current national flags are derived from the arms of dominion (originally used by rulers of empires, kingdoms, principalities and states), or the armorial flags (depicting the shield of the coat of arms) or the livery colours of these arms such as the flags of Spain, Sweden, Austria, Poland, Hungary and Belgium.

The sharp ideological divisions (religious divisions, dynastic affairs, and pre-national claims) and the military encounters based on these in the fifteenth and sixteenth centuries were reflected in the flags and banners carried by the troops. As a result, new groupings were identified with specific colours adopted during the revolutions preceding the modern nations. Emerging in times of warfare and the crusades, the livery colours of individual monarchs and noblemen, gained symbolic value and their attributed associations slowly became national in character. As part of smaller communities or corporations certain sections of society had also been represented through church banners and guild flags. As a general rule, a contrast is found between two kinds of flags that emerged after the sixteenth century: on the one hand, the elaborate and complex designs of flags connected to armorial bearings, and, on the other, simpler flag designs. The latter inspired the new system of elementary flag designs and served as a basis for modern ones. The complex honorific flags preserved for magnates and the simplistic flags figured side by side on land as two distinctive symbols of identification. A main reason for the standardization of flag designs, corresponding to the signal system at sea, was the growth of standing armies and the need for 'ordering infantry by company and battalion' (Hulme, 1915; W. Smith, 1975a). Subsequently the Cross of St Denis started to figure on France's infantry colours, whereas the English made use of the red cross of St George, which provided an indication of growing notions of differentiation. The symbolism in this early modern period operated on the basis of the separation between the elites – the nobility and the sovereigns – and the people. They acted, nevertheless, as predecessors to the modern flags when this separation formally would decrease in usage.

Religious and monarchical representation

Several flags survived from the Middle Ages into modern times. The early flags appeared as political symbols and transformed from religious (together with or via monarchical) representation to flags of nations. Their exact dates of appearance are usually unknown. Some are claimed to date to as early as the twelfth century but later dates usually indicate a formal decree or a first depiction of the flag. The flags that survived from the Middle Ages to modern times retained in almost all cases their pre-modern designs for the reasons outlined below.

The Danish, English, Scottish, Swiss and Swedish Cross flags (examples below) appeared endorsed by legendary claims of divine sanction. A legend of chosenness endorses the origin of the Danish Flag, which bears a striking resemblance to the legend of the cross, and the monogram of Christ claimed to have appeared in the sky before the Emperor Constantine's victory over Maxentius in 312. The Danish flag, one of the oldest national flags in Europe, is linked to King Valdemar II (1170–1241) who allegedly had a vision of a white crucifix in the darkening sky on the eve of the Battle of Lyndanisse on 15 June 1219, a vision taken as a sign of Christ's protection in the battle against the pagan Estonians. The flag is also described as having fallen from heaven, thereby accounting for the turning of defeat into victory. The Danish flag was later formally attested to the arms of King Valdemar IV Atterdag (reigning 1340–75) (Crampton, 1992; Devereux, 1992). Similar cross flags were used by small states in the Holy Roman Empire (Switzerland and Savoy) and also the design of the war flag of the Holy Roman Empire and its provinces (white cross on red). The latter is likely to have inspired the Danish Cross flag (Notholt, 1995). Similarly, the Swiss flag (current form of white couped cross on red, square in shape) is also archetypical European and inspired by the Imperial War Flag. It evolved over centuries with the formation of the Confederation. One early flag (red without cross) is said to date from 1240 Schwyz, one of the three cantons forming the original league in 1291, when a red flag with a narrow white cross in the canton was used (W. Smith, 2004c). The Confederation had received recognition to represent the crucifixion of Christ in the upper right field on their flag a few years earlier (1289) (History of Switzerland, 2004). As the Confederation fought the Holy Roman Empire at the Battle of Laupen in 1339, it used a white cross on a red shield and one early Confederate Flag is dated to 1422 (Battle of Arbedo) and takes a four-folded shape during the fourteenth century and with the formation of the Confederation of Schwyz, Lucerne, Nidwalden and Uri in 1480. The use of the current Swiss flag was restricted until the nineteenth century and formally adopted in 1848 as the official standard of the army and with the new constitution established in 1889 (Crampton, 1989, p. 57; Pedersen, 1992; Znamierowski, 2004).

National Flag Origins 35

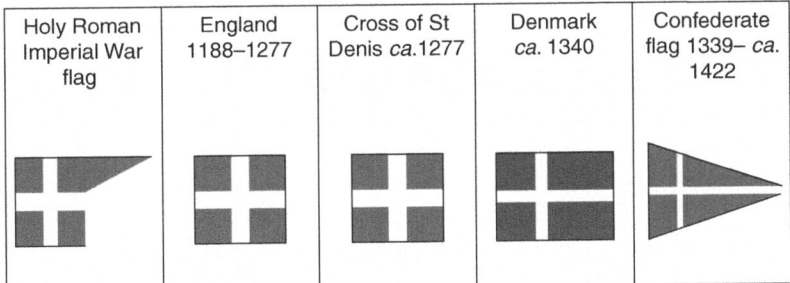

Figure 2.2 Early war flags: white cross on red
Note: Dates are subject to availability and interpretation.
Sources include: (FOTW, 2010g; W. Smith, 1975a). Flag image courtesy of: (FOTW, 2010b).

The early war flags, many on which appeared the white cross on red, and as such used, for example, in the conflicts between the Confederation and the Holy Roman Empire, with minor differentiating elements of design only (see Figure 2.2).

Break with tradition: tricolorization and designs of liberty

The development of the Dutch tricolour signifies a first step towards a new era of representing and inciting communities by means of flags. Whereas flags with pre-modern origins, as a rule, are cross flags, the Dutch tricolour is the first exception. The Dutch *Prinsenvlag* emerged as a flag of resistance and as a symbol for liberty during the 80 years' war that led to the formation of the United Provinces of the Netherlands (FOTW, 2003a; W. Smith, 1975d) (see Figure 2.3).

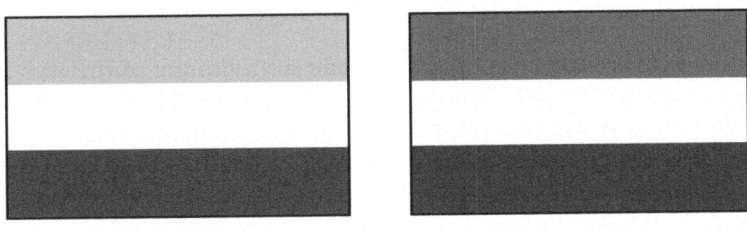

Orange-white-blue   *Red-white-blue*

Figure 2.3 The Dutch *Prinsenvlag*
Note: The Dutch Prinsenvlag, a first version of which displayed the colours orange-white-blue (1597). Red replaced orange in 1648 (1630–60).
Source: Flag image courtesy of: (FOTW, 2010b).

The first Dutch tricolour displayed the colours orange, white and blue, originated from the livery colours of the House of Orange, adopted by supporters of William of Orange (reigning 1572–84). From 1597 onwards it was used as the flag, although during the first decades of the Republic (created in 1581, recognized as independent in 1648 with the Peace of Westphalia), 'red' replaced 'orange' over the period 1630–60 as a sign of political change and the growing dissociation with the House of Orange. The red, white and blue tricolour was abolished when the Netherlands was annexed by the French in 1810, but was reintroduced in 1815 after the overthrow of Napoleon. The Dutch tricolour inspired Peter the Great of Russia and the Russian design for a merchant tricolour (white, blue and red) adopted in 1705. The French tricolour was also inspired by the Dutch (Devereux, 1992).

The French and Russian flags would later come to influence the other European tricolours and symbolized the struggle against oppression with its colours (red, white and blue) known as the three 'colours of liberty'. The tricolour flag emerged as a concept associated with new political programmes and political transformation during the American Revolution (1775–83). The 'Stars and Stripes' made a significant contribution to the modern flag tradition in Europe as it officially claimed to represent a 'whole population' and its government, reflecting the egalitarian ideas of the time. This process had started with the Declaration of Independence in 1776 and the flag was officially adopted on the 14 July 1777 and used during the remainder of the War of Independence (Crampton, 1992; W. Smith, 1975a). Interestingly, the United States and the colonial states (with separate flags) did not have one flag representing it prior to the conflicts with England.

Modern national flags: contested and challenged

The end of the eighteenth century marks the official beginning of the national flag as it developed in the aftermath of the American (1775–83) and the French (1789) Revolutions and the adoption of many national flags in Europe became part of the struggle for independence. In France, the context is provided by the break with the *Ancien Régime* and demand for participation in the political process. Before the outbreak of the Revolution, the flags of the Bourbon dynasty were mainly white as in the case of the Naval Ensign and the Royal Standard, the latter displaying the golden fleur-de-lis and the royal arms. Besides, individual flags of red, white and blue had been in use long before the Revolution (see the case study below) and combinations of these three colours had a past as royal livery colours. The process of renegotiating the official representation of France began with the introduction of cockades (a rosette or bow of livery or a badge in the national colours). From 1789 onwards, the troops of the Paris Militia – later the National Guard – were required to wear the livery colours of Paris: blue and red (white was added shortly afterwards); and an official naval flag of red-white-blue was adopted in October 1790 (Crampton, 1992).

The many uprisings in nineteenth-century Europe, inspired by the French Revolution, had fundamental effects for the development of national symbolism. The tricolour as a symbol appeared, for example, in Germany (black, red and gold) during the War of Liberation (1813–14), in the fight against France when it marked resistance against French administration. The hundreds of German-speaking states, belonging to the Holy Roman Empire of the German Nation until it ceased to exist in 1806, fought for unification under the tricolour as a symbol of liberty during the Napoleonic Wars. The German colours originated from the uniforms of the Lützowian Free Corps (black with gold and red details) who started the German resistance. The influence of these colours was later reinforced when they were displayed in the patriotic rallies at Warburg Castle (1817) and Hambach (1832). The German tricolour was adopted by the new German parliament in 1848; in 1867 Bismarck's tricolour of black-white-red superseded it, but the original tricolour was restored with the Weimar Republic in 1919–33. During the period 1933–45 the flags became again black, white and red, so after the Second World War the Federal Republic reverted back to the black-red-yellow colour combination of the first republic in order to dissociate itself from the previous Nazi regime.

The revolutions of 1848–49 adopted similar symbolism to that of 1789. The tricolour flag became the mark of revolutions and several new tricolour flags appeared in 1848 combining the successful tricolour formula of 1789 with their respective national colours and traditions. Tricolours were adopted in Romania, Hungary and Schleswig-Holstein in 1848. The tricolour flag also appeared in Slovakia (using the Russian colours) and in Ireland the same year. In Ireland, the colours were adopted with unification in mind and as a blueprint of what political bonds ought to look like: 'white' to express peace and unity between the traditional 'green' of Ireland and 'orange' for the supporters of the late King William of Orange (1650–1702). The tricolour also appeared in Italy and produced flag-related changes in Parma, Venice, and Naples. Savoy-Sardinia established a tricolour as early as March 1848 (adding the shield of Savoy with a blue border) hoisted again in

1859 with the movement to free 'Italy' from Austrian rule. With some modifications the tricolour flag was adopted by the unified Kingdom of Italy in 1861. However, several of the tricolours flown during the revolutionary year 1848 were lowered in 1849, although some were later restored.

National flags and nation building: case studies

In order to explore the paths towards the establishment of national flags and demonstrate their relationship to the nation-building process, three examples are explored in the order they appeared: the Union Jack, the French Tricolour and the Norwegian Cross flag.

The Union Jack: combining traditions and crosses

The 'Union Jack' officially represents the United Kingdom (England, Wales, Scotland, Northern Ireland, the Channel Islands and the Isle of Man) (see Figure 2.4). The Union Jack is a union-flag and as such a composite of the cross flags of St George of England (red on white), of St Andrew of Scotland (white diagonal cross on blue) and of St Patrick of Northern Ireland (red diagonal cross on white). The Welsh flag is not included in this cross design.

The soldiers in the Middle Ages would paint images of saints on their armour in hope of divine intercession – a hope not seemingly affected by the fact identical practices were employed by the rival armies. Several saints were depicted in this fashion until St George became popular with soldiers after his legend was discovered in the Near East in the crusades. So popular indeed was he that soldiers would display this cross on an armband if they were not allowed to wear the livery colours or badges of a noble lord. The first reference to a flag of St George is found in 1277 but the prominence of St George's cross flag is dated a whole century later (1348) when Edward III formally made St George the patron saint of the Order of the Garter. After the Battle of Agincourt in 1415, Henry V ordered all soldiers siding with the English to wear a band with the colours of St George (W. Smith, 1975a).

The second cross of the Union Jack is the Saltire (diagonal) Cross of St Andrew. There are early records of St Andrew's cross dating from 1165 AD and by 1180 is said to be incorporated into the seal of St Andrew's. The cross was shown as the emblem of Scotland on the seal of the guardians of Scotland. A later decree stated that all soldiers of the combined Scottish and French army had to wear the white saltire as their distinguishing mark in 1385 (W. Smith, 1975f). Gradually, the colour

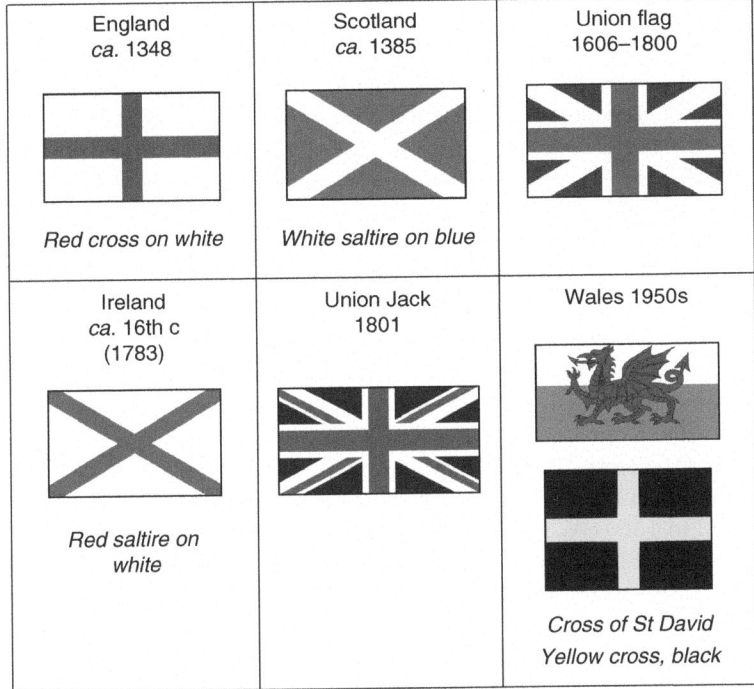

Figure 2.4 The development of the Union Jack
Note: Dates are subject to availability and interpretation.
Sources include: (FOTW, 2004c, 2007, 2009i; 2004; Government Publications, 1989; S. Notholt, 1996; W. Smith, 1975f, 2004d; Stilling, 1995). Flag images courtesy of: (FOTW, 2010b).

combination of the blue background for the white saltire became associated with the flag. The cross of St Patrick (red saltire on white), in turn, has been argued to originate from the arms of influential Anglo-Irish families (Devereux, 1992) sent to Ireland to represent Henry II of England and did not necessarily have any historical associations to St Patrick considering that the chief emblem for Ireland had long been the harp and the national colour green. This cross flag first appeared in the sixteenth century and was adopted as the emblem of the Order of St Patrick established in 1783 (Znamierowski, 2004). St Patrick's cross was incorporated into the Union Jack in 1801.

The Union Jack initiated a new era of British national flags, after the succession of the Stuart dynasty to the throne and during the growth of British naval power. The first reference to the Union flag dates from a proclamation of 12 April 1606 declaring the personal union of the crowns of Scotland and England, when King James VI of Scotland (1567–1625) ascended the English throne, thereby becoming James I of England (1603–25). The design of the first union flag was formed by superimposing the red cross of England on top of the white saltire of Scotland. However, the flags of England and Scotland continued to be flown separately on land. The use of the first Union Jack (uniting the crosses of England and Scotland) remained restricted, being allowed only at sea from 1634 on ships of the Royal Navy (S. Notholt, 1996). This first version influenced the jacks in several countries that hoisted similar designs in different colours such as Russia, Bulgaria, Latvia and Estonia. For a period of 200 years, a great variety of ensigns[1], jacks and pennants[2] were devised and all were essentially variations of the Union Jack displaying the recognized British colours. In the period known as the Protectorate (1649–60) the golden Irish harp was displayed in one variation of the union flag. It was, however, removed with the restoration of Charles II in 1660 (W. Smith, 2004d). In the Act of Union (1707), England and Scotland joined together as the United Kingdom and the two combined crosses were officially recognized (S. Notholt, 1996) and lasted until 1801 (Znamierowski, 2004).

In the final design of the Union Jack the cross of St Patrick was counter-charged (counterbalanced) with the Scottish saltire and as such adopted on 1 January 1801 when the United Kingdom of Great Britain and Ireland was formed. In order to manage the incorporation of St Patrick's cross (red diagonal cross on white) in accordance with the heraldic principles, the heraldic advisers to the king suggested St Andrew's cross be divided diagonally and red appear below and above the white (on the hoist half of the fly and above on its fly half) since red may not border the blue background, so a white narrow border (fimbriation) was added in between. This also held for the centre where a white border separated the crosses of St Patrick and St George (W. Smith, 1975f). Devising the colours in this fashion guaranteed the incorporated flags equal status.

The Union Jack has remained unchanged since 1801 and was confirmed by an Order in Council on 9 July 1864. The name Union Jack became the official name for the flag later in the nineteenth century. We note in this context that neither of the Welsh flags (the red dragon on white-over-green nor the cross of its patron St David, yellow cross on black) were ever included in the official representation, which has been cause for debate. The colours of the Welsh national flag have been influenced by the livery colours of the Tudor dynasty (fifteenth century) and the dragon is also claimed to date from the fifteenth century and has been the official badge for Wales since 1801; whereas the flag was not formally recognized until the 1950s and, in contrast to the cross of St David, has been used as a national flag in Wales.

No other flags in British flag history have rivalled the Union Jack (Crampton, 1992; W. Smith, 1975a, 2004d). The flag began as a distinguishing flag of a ship, as an auxiliary of the principal flag and evolved into the main flag of Britain and its empire. Today the Union Jack is flown for government and military purposes. Traditionally the Union Jack was incorporated into other flags, as authorized in civil, governmental, military, naval or royal contexts and is, for example, displayed in the canton of the British Blue Ensign and the British Red Ensign. It also constitutes part of the flags of the Commonwealth nations such as Australia (and its states of New South Wales, Queensland, South Australia, Tasmania, Victoria, and Western Australia), New Zealand and Tuvalu; and, in addition, of the US state of Hawaii and the three Canadian states of British Columbia, Manitoba, and Ontario.

The French Tricolour and revolutionary symbolism

The French Tricolour (vertical of blue, white and red) had a turbulent past before being finally established as a national flag during the Third Republic (1870–1940). Despite being perceived as a revolutionary symbol, the colours of the French Tricolour are understood to be inspired by pre-revolutionary flags of France: the blue of the cloak of St Martin (*cappa Sancti Martini*) and the Banner of France, the white of Joan of Arc and the Bourbons, and the red of Charlemagne and St Denis (W. Smith, 1975b, pp. 130–9) (see Figure 2.5).

The earliest standard claimed by the French was the blue cloak of the fourth-century bishop and patron saint of France, St Martin. The cloak of St Martin became legendary with military success following the battle of Vouillé in 507 and replicas were thereafter used but this tradition ended with the defeat suffered by the French at the Battle of Poitiers in 1356. St Martin's cloak stood in sharp competition with the imperial golden red oriflamme (originally the standard of the King) with six gold discs (possibly roses) bordered in dark blue and red and a flame-like tail at its end (Montjoie of Charlemagne) and used by Charlemagne as a symbol of his empire. It has been suggested that a symbolic continuity exists between the modern Tricolour and the red, white and blue colours of a tassel below the spearhead of the flag of Charlemagne. Another oriflamme became associated with St Denis, the first bishop of

42 *Symbols of Nations and Nationalism*

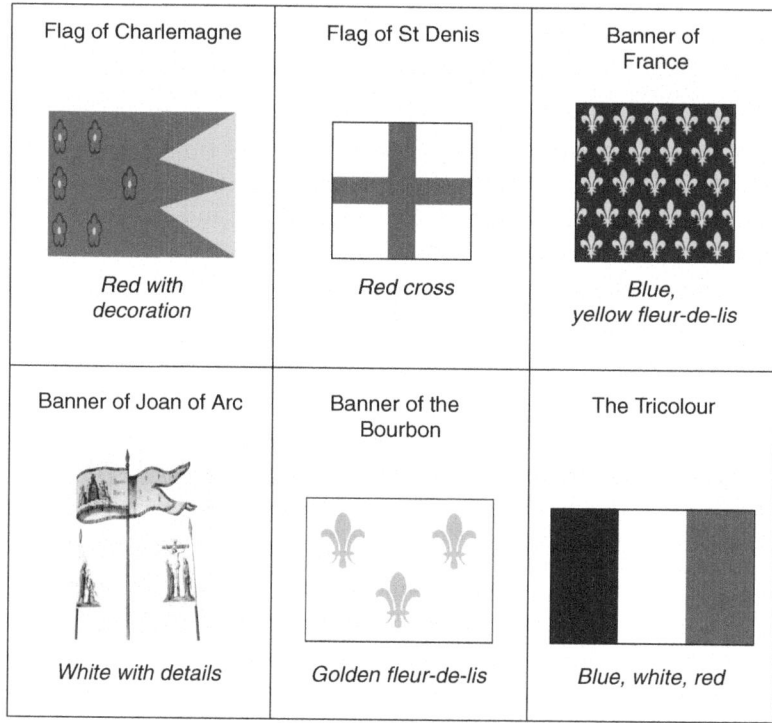

Figure 2.5 The complexity of the French tricolour
Note: Dates are subject to availability and interpretation.
Sources include: (Colrat, 2010; FOTW, 2005a; French Embassy Official Website, 2000; Girardet, 1998; Joan of Arc Museum, Unknown; W. Smith, 1975a, 2004a). Flag images courtesy of: (FOTW, 2010b).

Paris. This red oriflamme, first chosen as a war flag by King Louis VI in 1124, was carried during four Crusades and seventeen other wars. Its service ended with the dramatic French defeat by the English at the Battle of Agincourt in 1415. The flag of St Denis was matched by the Banner of France, the royal flag that displayed the golden fleurs-de-lis on a square blue field. This banner was used under King Louis VI (reigning 1108–37). Later, under Charles VI (reigning 1380–1422), the fleurs-de-lis were reduced to three in honour of the Holy Trinity. Although considered as the personal emblem of the king, it figured in battles from the Crusades onwards. The Banner of France ranks, alongside the war flag of the Holy Roman Empire (black eagle on gold) and the armorial banner (shield of arms made into a flag) of England (three gold lions on red), as the most famous heraldic banners of the Middle Ages (W. Smith, 1975b).

White emerged as a colour on French flags during the fifteenth century with the influence of Joan of Arc and the House of Orléans. When Joan of Arc was standing trial for heresy and sorcery in 1431, she described her banner as a field sprinkled with lilies. According to legend it was protected by an angel on each side carrying the inscription *Jhesus Maria* above three fleurs-de-lis. The flag, on the reverse, displayed the arms of France. The standard of Joan of Arc is important in the vexillological history of France. It was to a great extent through its influence, after Joan's death in 1431 until the French Revolution of 1789, that white came to serve as the principal French national colour. In 1590, white had gained added strength at the Battle of Ivry, during the French Wars of Religion, where Henry IV is said to have employed his white scarf as a flag in the struggle against the Holy League and before he eventually converted to Catholicism in 1593. White was also used in various forms and shapes in the personal livery of the kings of France and the plain white flag was known as the Bourbon Banner. Furthermore, during the sixteenth century, white, having spread from a few royal flags, in the form of a cross or as a background colour, became the predominant flag colour of French military flags both on land and at sea. This predominance lasted until 1794, and was briefly revived between 1815 and 1830. Several flags were used to demonstrate loyalty to a pre-modern France, which is noticeable from a print of the warship *La Couronne* in 1636 which carried no fewer than five flags. This suggests that standardized designs were not yet in place. Besides, individual flags of red, white, and blue had been established in France a long time before the Revolution, and combinations of these three colours had also been used in the royal livery in the past.

Against such a complex background, the coat of arms of the city of Paris (blue and red), combined with white as a national colour, has been identified as the principal source of inspiration for the first Tricolour. The traditional colours of Paris, blue and red, were popular in revolutionary circles and the royal white of the Bourbon (also a colour used in memory of Joan of Arc) was often added to the flags. In July 1789, the troops of the Paris Militia (later the National Guard) were required to wear cockades of the municipal blue and red. The combination of blue, red and white as recommended by Marquis de La Fayette was officially adopted in October 1789 as the colours of the cockade, then a most important political symbol. Red and blue had been used as early as 1358 when Parisian commoners revolted against royal authority. Ironically, flags of plain white also associated with the Bourbons were displayed in 1790 at the Festival of the Federation (see Chapter 4) celebrating the first anniversary of the overthrow of the Bastille. The initiative for replacing white, recognized also as a royal colour of France, with red-white-blue came from the French navy which protested against having to fight for France under the old white flag, and demanded that the National Assembly should establish an official naval flag incorporating the three national colours. A law granting its wish was adopted in October 1790. Three-quarters of the new war ensign remained white, but its canton (the upper hoist quarter of the flag) displayed three vertical stripes of red-white-blue within a frame of the same colours, thus the reverse of the modern order. The design of this canton also served separately as the French Jack, flown at the bows of ships. A new system of army colours was also devised in 1791 based on what had become the new national colours.

The final form of the Tricolour design (during the first revolutionary period), the first version of which was introduced in 1789, dates from 1794 when the modern Tricolour was substituted for the two previous flags, the Jack and the Ensign, flown at sea and exhibiting vertical stripes of blue, white and red. This design was made by Jacques-Louis David on behalf of the National Convention, when the French navy once again demanded alterations to the flag. The design exhibiting vertical stripes took shape as a direct result of the navy's protest to the National Assembly. The pattern was meant to correspond to the morals, ideas and principles of the Republic. The predominance of the Tricolour at sea was not immediately matched on land. Instead, the Tricolour was abolished three times: during the short restoration of the French monarchy in 1814, Louis XVIII insisted on the supremacy of the white cockade and the white flag, but during his Hundred Days, Napoleon re-established the blue-white-red in 1815. After his defeat at Waterloo the white cockade and flag were instituted once again. The July Revolution of 1830, brought constitutionalism to the French monarchy and the re-introduction of the colours of the Tricolour through a decree signed by King Louis Philippe. As a consequence of the revolution of 1848, which overthrew the monarchy, a plain red flag was originally suggested as the main flag but a red rosette was added to the top of the Tricolour for a period of two weeks. This sparked a bitter debate and the French minster of Foreign Affairs, Alphonse de Lamartine, argued with passion:

> The Tricolour has made a tour of the world with the name, the glory, and the liberty of the fatherland! If you take away from me the tricolour flag, you take away from half the force of France, both here and abroad! (W. Smith, 1975a, p. 137)

Figure 2.6 Tricolour with Marianne
Note: Blue, white (Marianne) and red. Flag images courtesy of: (FOTW, 2010b).

Since 1848 no official modifications have been made to the Tricolour of France. During the Commune in 1871, however, the plain red flag reappeared, and, afterwards, for a while, it seemed as if the white flag was to be re-established. But, even though minor modifications of the colours blue, white, red and the relative widths of the stripes (varied from 1853 and formalized as equal in 1946) have been made over the years, the French Tricolour survived. It broke with its pre-revolutionary symbolism but does, after all, constitute a combination of the same.

In contemporary France the Tricolour flies outside all public buildings and provides the backdrop for presidential addresses to the public. The blue, white and red, with their associated values of Liberty, Fraternity and Equality and the symbol of Marianne were appropriated for a state emblem in 1999 intending to make the 'state more accessible' and symbolically unify all official correspondence (French Embassy Official Website, 2000) (Figure 2.6). The new federating 'identifier' – combining the main symbols of France – was thus a 'new' creation by the French Government Departments and appears on all material, brochures, publications, letter headings, business cards, publicity campaigns and so forth at centralized and regional levels of government.

The Norwegian flag – a symbol of independence

The adoption of a distinct Norwegian flag resulted in a 77-year long struggle between the Norwegian and Swedish parliaments as Norway attempted to achieve formal recognition for its flag while part of the enforced union with Sweden (1814–1905). The adoption of a national flag in 1821 occurred at a significant time in the nation-building process and is extraordinary for two main reasons. First, the flag became a highly-charged political instrument in the fight for independence and a mass symbol by the end of the nineteenth century through celebrations of the Norwegian national day. Secondly, it came to constitute *the* token symbol of Norwegian independence as the parliament struggled for its recognition. The story of the use and adoption of a distinct flag for Norway is illuminating in terms of politics of recognition, nationalism and nationhood.

The colours of the Norwegian flag (white cross on a red background, with a blue cross superimposed on the white cross) (see Figure 2.7) were inspired by the French Tricolour but its design expressed Scandinavian loyalties and became known as the Scandinavian Cross. The story of the Norwegian flag spans a relatively short period compared with Britain and France but has, in turn, inspired two other more recent flags – Iceland and the Faroe Islands.

Norway's history is closely linked to its neighbouring kingdoms. Norway was joined to Sweden in 1319. From 1380 onwards Norway and Denmark were a single unified state. Modern nation building in Norway commenced with the Treaty of Kiel (14 January 1814) signed towards the end of the Napoleonic Wars. Denmark had sided with France against the victorious alliance opposing Napoleon including Sweden, and as a result lost Norway to Sweden. This radically altered the power structure between the two rival kingdoms and the imperial approach of transferring Norway from one neighbour to another caused outrage in Norway. Nationalism arose as an attempt to prevent this new political reality. A popularly elected National Assembly was thus convened at Eidsvold (*ca.* 60 kms north of Christiania or Oslo) in April 1814 to provide Norway with a constitution of its own, successfully brought to a conclusion on 17 May 1814. On the same day the Assembly elected Prince Christian Fredrik of Denmark, governor of Norway since 1813, as King of Norway (Mykland, 1996). Provoked by these events, Sweden embarked on a military campaign in July and forced Christian Fredrik to abdicate as a condition of the cease-fire (and de facto peace) agreement of the Convention of Moss in August. A few months later (November 1814) the Swedish king, Karl XIII, was declared King of Sweden and Norway, and Norway was forced into a union that lasted until 1905 (Østergård, 1997).

Interestingly, Norway attempted to achieve independence (in 1814) under a Danish flag (white cross on red) displaying the Norwegian arms (a crowned lion and axe) in the canton (left corner of the flag) claimed to date from the thirteenth century (1230) (Nelson, 2007b). Not surprisingly, this flag was introduced by the Danish Prince Christian Frederik shortly after the Treaty of Kiel in 1814 and expressed opposition to the prospect of Swedish rule (Engene, 1997a; Nevéus, 1993). However, this Danish-inspired flag was used also by groups wanting freedom from Denmark. After the union was established with Sweden in 1814 Norway was first restricted to using the Swedish flag (yellow cross on blue) with a saltire or diagonal version of the Danish flag in the canton until 1844.

The protests over flying the Swedish flag with the Danish cross grew and the prompted a competition for a *Norwegian* flag, which resulted in a series of flag proposals in 1814, 1815, 1821 and 1836 (Nelson, 2007a). Despite the restrictions imposed by Sweden, a flag was chosen from a proposal in 1821 when the Danish white cross on red was overlaid by a blue cross (design by Frederik Meltzer) and adopted by the Norwegian parliament. The new design may be understood as a diplomatic necessity by displaying both the Danish and the Swedish colours. However, the combination of red, white and blue provided a code in echoing the colours of the French Tricolour and the ideals of *liberté* and *fraternité* (Grimnes, 2007). Thus the adoption and the battle for formal recognition of the distinct Norwegian flag commenced. In 1838, the use of the Norwegian flag was allowed at sea; the sanction, however, had come with a warning that Norwegian ships could not expect to receive protection if they did not fly the official union flag of Sweden–Norway.

Significant changes in the union symbolism began after 1844 when the king attempted to meet the demands of nationalists on both sides (Nilsson, 2004) by introducing what was to become the despised 'union emblem' by combining the crosses of Norway and Sweden in the canton of the Norwegian and Swedish flags. This meant that both countries could fly their own flags with the 'union symbol' in the canton. This gave some recognition to the Norwegian flag although it was never officially acknowledged (Engene, 1997b). The negative associations of the flag gave rise to the derogatory nickname of the 'herring salad' (*sildesalaten* or *sillsalaten*) in view of the mix and complexity of its design (seen in Figure 2.7), which through the number and designs of colours constituted a violation of the heraldic principles by which flags are usually designed. In short, the Norwegian and Swedish flags with their 'union badges' attempted to mix that which cannot be mixed – whether colours, nations or herrings.

The struggle for independence and nationhood displayed a new form of purpose with the claims for a 'pure' flag, first formulated by the radical and anti-unionist wing in the parliament in 1879 (A-L. Seip, 1995). These claims were followed by the formation of the Kristiania Flag Association (Kristiania Flagsamlag) in 1882, which also started to

48 *Symbols of Nations and Nationalism*

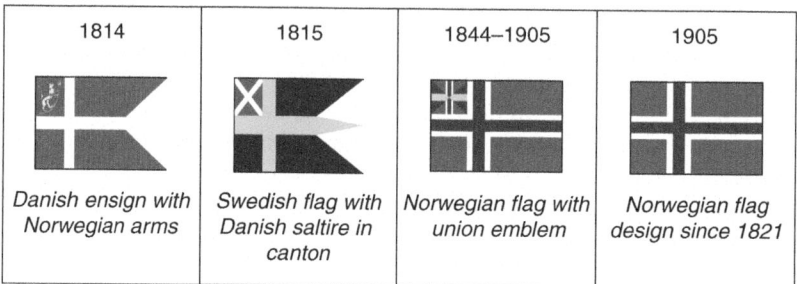

Figure 2.7 The Norwegian flag of independence
Sources: (Elgenius, 2011; Engene, 1997a, 1997b, 2000a, 2000b; A. Eriksen, 2007; Grimnes, 2007; Nelson, 2007a, 2007b; Nevéus, 1998; W. Smith, 1975c). Flag images courtesy of (FOTW, 2010b).

work for the recognition of the 'unmarked' flag. Its influence increased with the importance of flag-related symbolism during the 1890s when the 'cleansing' of the flag became a sensitive political issue (Grimnes, 2007). This was exemplified by extensive debates over whether the 'pure flag' or the 'union-flag' should be used in processions on national day. Through these processions, the unmarked Norwegian flag was transformed into a powerful political instrument. The parades organized by Venstre (the Liberal party founded in 1884) used the unmarked flag as did those organized by the socialists (the Labour Party founded in 1887) as they protested against the traditional ruling classes. The current flag became, in other words, first associated with the politics of the liberals and the socialists articulated against their more union-friendly opponents. With time, however, the unmarked flag started to appear alongside the union flag in the so-called 'ordinary' (conservative) processions (Grimnes, 2007). The unmarked flag became a highly politicized symbol in the national day parades as the struggle for independence intensified towards the end of the nineteenth century by which time it had become a powerful political symbol for a Norway unified in opposition to the Union.

The process of achieving recognition for a distinct Norwegian flag lasted no less than 77 years during which the Swedish parliament repeatedly refused to recognize it. The Norwegian parliament, in turn, continued to pass laws that intended the removal of the union emblem in 1893, in 1896 and in 1898. In the end the Swedish monarch was left no choice but to accept the law by adding a provision to the constitution and the Norwegian flag was signed into effect on 15 December 1899. In the process of active mobilization against the union, the flag and its use on the national day celebrations became closely interconnected (Grimnes, 2007) especially as the union came to an end. When Norway gained full independence in 1905, the flag design of 1821 was officially recognized as the national flag. The lion and axe (used in the first design) was adopted as the royal standard and national arms the same year.

The controversies surrounding the Norwegian flag did not end with the breakup of the union in 1905 and continued true to its politicized beginnings in the decades to come. In the 1920s the left-wing sympathizers in Norway came to perceive the celebrations and flag-parades as bourgeoisie symbols. They organized rival events to the national day on International Labour Day on 1 May and in the weeks before the national day (17 May) (Kolstø, 2006). A period of reconciliation between the left and right is described as taking place during the occupation of Norway in 1940–45, a period of considerable significance for nation building. With referenda in 1972 and 1994 and a majority of Norwegians voting against the EEC/EU, the national flag was once again politicized and the national colours used in the campaigns *for* as well as *against* membership in the European Union. Thus, protests were noted after the inclusion of some European flags in celebrations in the 1970s (Mykland, 1996).

In recent protests against globalization and unemployment smaller communities hoisted white flags at half-mast, initiatives receiving national coverage (NRK 1, 2002). An interesting debate also flared up before with the annual 17 May celebrations in 2005 when members of the Sami community wanted to use Sami flags in the parades (Eriksen and Jenkins, 2007). In 2008 there was a similar debate about whether the use of flags representing Norway's immigrant communities ought to be allowed in the parades (Barstad and Buan, 2008; Ryste, 2008). This despite the evidence that 10.6 per cent of the population are either immigrants or children of immigrants (Statistics Norway, 2009). Symbols may invariably enhance divisions in societies (Schöpflin, 2000) but the emphasis on similar symbols supports the notion of sameness and demonstrates also that the flag remains a powerful component in the process whereby the nation is sanctified.

As a final note with reference to the 77-year long struggle for the Norwegian flag and the context of rival nationalisms in Scandinavia, it is interesting that the concept of the Scandinavian cross flag developed at all. As a cross flag it was first in place in Denmark, as seen previously, and variations of this flag were later adopted by Sweden, Norway, Finland, Iceland, the Faroe Islands and the Åland Islands, communicating to the world their independence but loyalty to each other in the relative standardization of their designs. The adoption of the national flags in Finland (1863) and Iceland (1915) also reveal outstanding claims of recognition. Sweden lost Finland in 1809 as a result of a war that established Finland as an autonomous Grand Duchy within Imperial Russia. The notion of 'Sweden proper' hereby vanished (Østergård, 1997) although the Scandinavianists in Sweden wished to believe that the Finns longed for reunification (Barton, 2005). Iceland, in turn, attempted to break away from Denmark in two phases in 1918 and 1944 (Østergård, 1997) and the Icelandic government was forced to seek approval from the Danish king when introducing a distinct Icelandic flag in 1915. Approval was given with several reservations and the flag was not fully recognized until Iceland became a republic in 1944. The newly established Sami flag has completely broken with the tradition of displaying a Scandinavian Cross (Grimnes, 2007) (see Chapter 3).

Pre-modern, modern and post-imperial narratives

Thus, national flags have something to tell us about the properties and development of nations. The novelty of the national flag, compared with the earlier flags of identification, was its reflection of egalitarian ideas and availability to all citizens rather than a small privileged group, or to special occasions or situations. The prescribed arrangements of flags are especially important at their time of origin as with time they are drained of original meaning. Two European national prototypes were identified in the Danish cross flag and the Dutch tricolour. These survived into modern times representing modern nations. St George's cross of England was also an influential flag but its importance was rivalled by the Union Jack. The Danish cross flag inspired the so-called Scandinavian crosses and the Dutch tricolour influenced the French and the Russian tricolours that, in turn, inspired the many tricolours established in the nineteenth and the twentieth centuries. The routes to nation formation, as seen through their flags, vary greatly as with the combination of the cross flags of England, Scotland and Northern Ireland in reflecting the stages of development with the political union. France was rich in pre-revolutionary symbolism, but owing to its severance with the past the Tricolour appears with the formation of the Republic as a symbolic code and the means by which the moral values of modern France were asserted. In turn, the Norwegian flag was formally accepted after a 77-year long struggle with Sweden and ultimately with the dissolution of the Union by which time it had come to symbolize independence and resistance.

Symbolic forms and modes of expression let us distinguish between pre-modern, modern and post-imperial symbolic regimes. The Middle Ages, the French Revolution and the First World War are natural pivots for these narratives. The symbolic regimes can, in turn, be aligned to four types of flags (cross flags, tricolours, heraldic flags and post-historical flags).

Type 1: Cross flags and the age of pre-modern nations

The Danish, English and Swiss cross flags date to the fourteenth century. The Danish and Swiss crosses are based on the imperial war flag of the Holy Roman Empire (white cross on red). The myths associated with the early cross flags give us valuable information about these first European cross-flag prototypes and that which was required to become powerful symbols. Naturally, these flags display a notion of chosenness with the sign of the Cross but appear as flags of war and conflict. Many territories used variations of the crusader cross flags, but as national flag the cross only remained in a handful of countries. The original use of the medieval cross flags were, for example, adopted by England, Denmark, Savoy, Spain, Milan, Padua, Genoa and Russia and justified the cause of holy missions against non-Christians. Only some of these survived into modern times and came to represent England, Denmark, Scotland, Switzerland and Sweden (see Figure 2.8).

The process of establishing a date of origin for medieval cross flags and their colours is highly complex and contestable as records of early usage are obscure, hard to come by or non-existing. Some can be dated as depicted on the arms of ruling monarchs or as tied to founding of an order as with the flags of Denmark, England, Scotland and Sweden. Two pre-modern flags break with this pattern above – the Dutch and the Russian tricolour flags – as they originally came to provide a symbolic code for revolution and protest.

Type 2: Tricolour flags and the age of modern nations

As the Dutch tricolour breaks with earlier and required religious symbolism, it became associated with independence, liberty, religious and political freedom and a republican form of government. This is later reinforced by the French tricolour adopting the same colours in a

52 *Symbols of Nations and Nationalism*

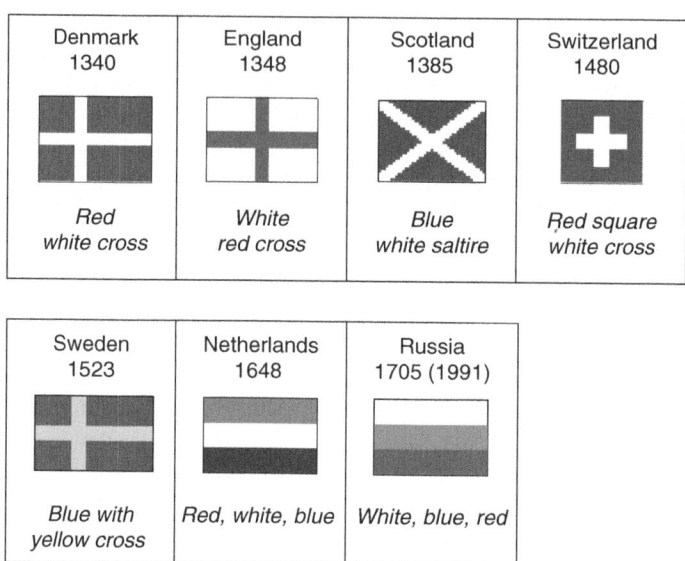

Figure 2.8 Flags with pre-modern origins
Note: Dates are subject to availability and interpretation.
Sources: (Elgenius, 2005a). Flag images courtesy of FOTW.

vertical version. This design and colour combination expressed adherence to the ideals of liberty, equality and fraternity, a visual promise of a new 'democratic' era and, at times, a justification for actions that turned out to be far from these ideals. In this context, the Greek flag is interesting as it has combined the cross with 'revolutionary' stripes representing the motto 'Liberty or Death'. Hereby, the flag acknowledges the role of Christianity in the formation of the Hellenic Nation raising boundaries during the war of independence (1821) against the Ottoman Empire (when a similar Greek flag was in use). In Spain a number of dynastic flags existed long before the design of the current Spanish flag appeared in 1783–85 and an armorial banner was in use in Portugal before the present flag was proclaimed with the Republic in 1910. Interestingly, the flags of Norway and Finland illuminate outstanding claims of nationhood and independence, and adopt pre-modern symbolism. In these two cases, this is a question of foremost positioning in relation to Denmark and Sweden. The colours of the Norwegian flag, as described in Figures 2.7 and 2.9, have been justified both in terms of being a diplomatic necessity but also as inspired by the colours of the French tricolor.

National Flag Origins 53

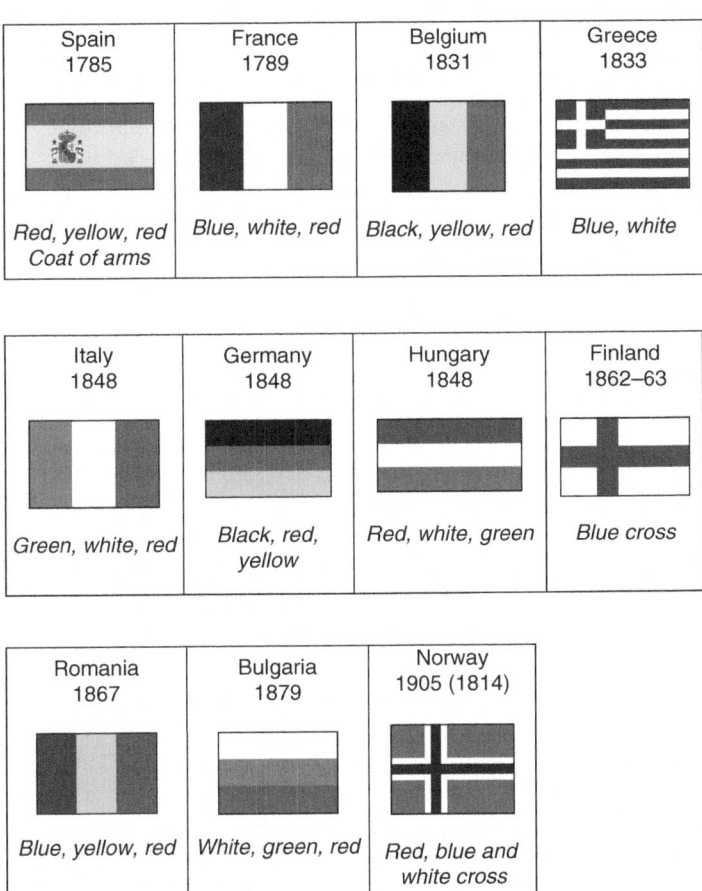

Figure 2.9 Modern national flags and the French Revolution
Note: Dates are subject to availability and interpretation.
Source: (Elgenius, 2005a). Flag images courtesy of FOTW.

Type 3: Heraldic flags and the age of post-imperial nations

The introduction of heraldry and the adoption of coats of arms by European royalty in the twelfth and thirteenth centuries have influenced many national flags of Europe, in many cases, centuries later. Some heraldic flags are bi-coloured with specific reference to livery colours of the coat of arms (Austria and Poland) or display heraldic devices on the flags (Portugal, Croatia, Slovakia, Slovenia, Ukraine and Albania). The Croatian, Slovak, Slovenian and Serbian flags – tricolours with coat of arms – symbolize in colours and composition the affiliation with Russia. It is, however, the heraldic devices that make these flags distinctly national. Other politically charged symbols are also used such as: a triangle (used to signify a union) – the Czech Republic; a national ornament – Belarus; a sun – Former Yugoslav Republic of Macedonia. Whether a heraldic device or a political symbol is displayed, these flags have one thing in common: device and colours carry territorial justifications chosen to further distinguish the nation from others (see Figure 2.10).

The sheer number of flags that appear in the age of post-imperial nations is striking and tells us a great deal about nation formation in Europe. Many of the flags in Figure 2.10 were adopted early but could not be maintained as the nations they represented became part of empires or unions as in the cases of Poland, Romania, Bulgaria and Lithuania. In Austria the flag was instituted in 1918, with the formation of modern Austria after the dissolution of the Austro-Hungarian Empire. The claims to a historic territory long before the existence of Austria re-emerged with the legend dating the red-white-red stripes from the flag to the Third Crusade of 1189–92 when Duke Leopold V fought in the Battle of Acre (Ptolemais) in 1191. The white stripe in the middle symbolized the only part of his uniform that had remained white after his belt was removed and an otherwise red uniform was drenched in blood. Red and white are also the colours of the arms of Duke Frederick II (1230) depicting the spread black eagle of the Holy Roman Empire with the shield of red and white at its centre. The past is thus crucial for post-imperial flags as golden ages and myths of heroism are reclaimed through heraldic colours and devices. When Poland, finally independent in 1918, adopted a new flag, it was based on the old coat of arms dating from the Polish-Lithuanian union (fourteenth century). When independence was declared in 1918, Lithuania too revived a heraldic banner claimed to date from this period before it changed to the tricolour. Pre-modern elements and colours are also displayed in the flags of the Czech Republic, Croatia and Slovakia. The flag of Slovakia (tricolour with coat of arms) displays the double-barred cross on the Carpathians claimed to originate in the ninth century. The tricolour itself appeared in 1848 (when Slovakia was part of Hungary) but the coat of arms was not given official recognition until 1918 with the formation of Czechoslovakia. Slovakia has claimed that the flag of Czechoslovakia, adopted in 1920, was already in use in Slovakia in 1848. The Ukrainian flag (yellow and blue), adopted in 1992, is claimed to reproduce the colours of the coat of arms of medieval 'Ukrainian' cities,

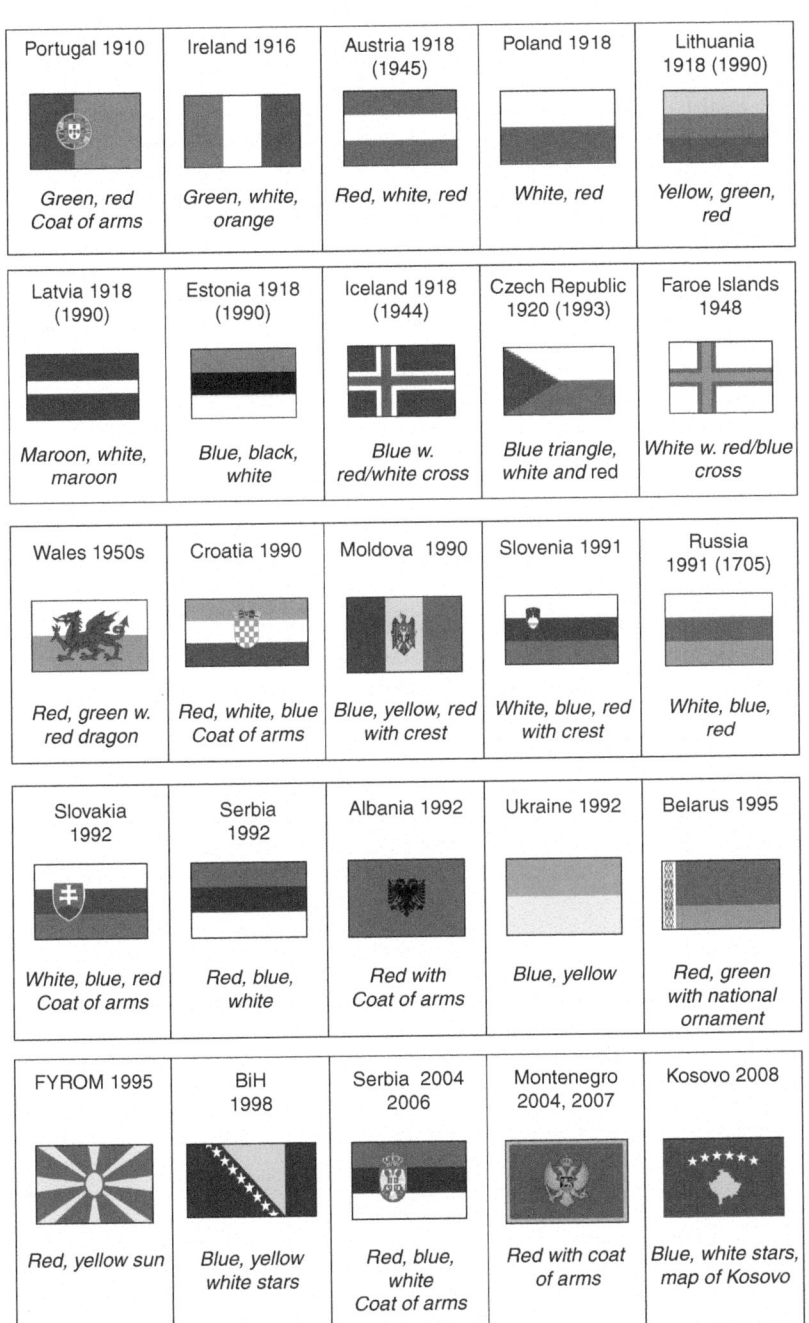

Figure 2.10 Post-imperial flags and the First World War
Note: Dates are subject to availability and interpretation.
Source: (Elgenius, 2005a). Flag images courtesy of FOTW.

as does Albania's flag (the black double-headed eagle on red field), again adopted in 1992 but the eagle was chosen to represent Skanderbeg who led the fight against the Ottomans in the 1440s. Other post-imperial flags have modern roots (Estonia and Latvia) whereas others are related to the short-lived period of independence starting after the First World War (Lithuania and Slovenia). The Baltic States restored their national flags from 1918 in 1989–90.

Type 4: Post-historical, counter-nationalist flags of post-imperial nations

The embellishment of design as described above with reference to the post-imperial flags has also continued with the flags of Bosnia-Herzegovina (stars and triangle) and Kosovo (stars and map). However, with these flags we see a new flag type emerging that breaks the previously established patterns formed along non-hereditary principles and claimed as *flags of the future*. These flags are *a*typical because historical references have been avoided completely for reasons that will be explored in the next chapter.

In brief, national aspirations are closely interlinked with symbolic manifestations in Europe and, as demonstrated, flag-related politics did not end with the nineteenth century. The disintegration of the Soviet Union towards the end of the twentieth century and the resurgence of nationalism in Eastern Europe produced vast changes in flag-related symbolism. Most countries in Central and Eastern Europe redefined themselves by selecting new national symbols (flags, anthems and national days) from 1989 onwards, a process that has continued in the 2000s.

Notes

1. An ensign is a flag flown at the stern of a ship, while jacks are flown at its bows.
2. A pennant is a tapering flag – that may be swallow-tailed – and is used to signify rank or similar.

3
National Flags, the Politicization and Sanctification of Nations

We move now to consider the context in which flags have become significant political symbols. The sacred nature of their treatment, induced and attained through the ritualization of nationhood, explains why burning a piece of cloth is considered an act of desecration and lays bare the flag's intricate relationship to the nation. The contradictory and contextualized nature of national flags is now investigated as flags continue to constitute meaningful yet empty vessels, treated as both sacred or mundane objects depending on context. Flags can be uniting yet divisive symbols, and used as instruments or counter-instruments; some are used to honour, others to dishonour. National flags have remained successful political symbols over centuries because they authenticate boundaries by symbolizing commonality. Physically, flag poles displayed on either side of territorial border crossings highlight such claims as the flags here eliminate ambiguity. The signalling of territorial claims and commonality also turn flags into highly divisive agents as they are used to threaten and warn strangers of membership boundaries. Flags are used to bestow honour on allies but their usage also extends to dishonour or condemn enemies. In this chapter we build on the flag-typology and the symbolic regimes identified previously and explore the contexts and developments of these and the nations that they represent.

Meaningful yet empty

National aspirations are projected and advertised through the flags having attained pre-eminence over other national symbols in this regard. The sociological literature in general and the literature on nationalism in particular have become increasingly conscious of this (see e.g. Eriksen and Jenkins, 2007) whereas a typical definition in a

58 *Symbols of Nations and Nationalism*

dictionary may read: 'a piece of cloth, bunting, or similar material displaying the insignia of a community' (*Encyclopaedia Britannica*, 2004). It is here the puzzle lies: national flags have become much more than a 'piece of cloth' for nations, states and people. The answer is partly explained by their condensed nature (Turner, 1967) and their narration as key symbols (Ortner, 1967). As an illustration, the extract from a government publication below explains this link between the association to the nation and its key symbolism: The national flag, the national anthem and the national emblem are the three symbols through which an independent country proclaims its identity and sovereignty, and as such they command instantaneous respect and loyalty. In themselves they reflect the entire background, thought and culture of a nation (Firth, 1973, p. 34; Hobsbawm and Ranger, 1992). Durkheim addressed the extraordinary relationship between the piece of cloth and the poignant meanings attached to it by highlighting the transference of emotions to objects and from nations to flags:

> The soldier who dies for his flag, dies for his country; but as a matter of fact, in his own consciousness, it is the flag that has the first place. Whether one isolated standard remains in the hands of the enemy or not does not determine the fate of the country, yet the soldier allows himself to be killed to regain it. He loses sight of the fact that the flag is only a sign, and that it has no value in itself, but only brings to mind the reality that it represents; it is treated as if it were the reality itself. (Durkheim, 1976, p. 221)

In order for the flag to be treated as if reality itself it must constitute an *empty vessel* (Eriksen and Jenkins, 2007) so that it can be filled with meanings but also allow for change over time. Flags are in this way compact yet simple. Their compactness is illustrated by the combination of simplicity in terms of design and the complex associations of nationhood attached to flags that can evoke powerful emotions and constitute rallying points for group action (Firth, 1973, p. 77). Scholars in the Durkheimian tradition (Carlyle, Sapir, Nehru, Honigman, Boas, Linton and Levi-Strauss) argued that symbols fundamentally reinforce solidarity. Firth (1973) also contends that flags constitute prime vehicles for conveying attitudes or expressing sentiments, because simple actions, such as waving them, imply complex themes of loyalty. As seen in the material below, flags convey a number of sentiments many of which are also associated with exclusion and aggression. With the origins of the European national flags as identified by warfare, revolutions, independence and state-constitution in mind, there is more to say about their multi-faceted repertoire. Whereas flags continue to be used as political symbols, as tools of propaganda and control, as devices for inclusion and division, they also reserve an uncontroversial space in everyday life.

Flags as political symbols: contested, challenged, divisive

The national flag became an effective medium early on because political messages could be passed on to people without having to rely on a certain level of literacy, first on the traditional battlefield or at sea and later outdoors in national ceremonies, public spaces, streets and squares. The intensification and the *tricolorization* of the modern flag tradition followed with the vision of a more democratic community and with the emergence of mass-politics. Flags managed to attain prominence over other forms of political symbolism because of their flexibility and their combination of active and graphic forms (see W. Smith, 1969). Thus, flags are waved in national day parades, celebrations, royal weddings and elections or used with increased honour in commemorations with the saluting of the flag or standing up when singing the national anthem in celebration of the nation. Graphic symbolism conveys meanings through colours and designs regardless of where represented, such as the cross, the hammer and sickle, the swastika and the star. As a qualifier, verbal symbols were found in conjunction with graphic symbols reinforcing the former, as with the Red flags of the Baltic States during 1945–53 when the initials of their Republics were displayed together with the hammer and sickle emblem identifying them as part of the Union of Soviet Socialist Republics, poignant symbolism revised and modified on a number of occasions.

The Red Flag became a highly contested political symbol in the age of mass-politics associated with symbolism of protest and resistance but also oppression. In modern times, the Red Flag was first hoisted during the French Revolution but its first reference as flag of defiance was with the siege of Ostend when the city held out against the Spaniards in 1601–4. The Red Flag was brought out again in the revolutions of 1830 and 1848 in France and during the (Paris) Commune of 1870, and, in this way, became associated with Communism. In Russia, the Red flag was used in the revolutions of 1905 and 1917 with coloured inscriptions, one version of which was chosen to represent the Republic from July 1918 onwards. The Red flag with the golden hammer and sickle emblem, as it became known, was adopted in 1923 as the flag of the USSR. The adoptions of variations of this Red flag in the Soviet republics took place in two main phases. First, the Red flags displayed stylized inscriptions or abbreviations and, with time, also the hammer and sickle emblem.

60 *Symbols of Nations and Nationalism*

Ukraine, for instance, flew a number of Red flag versions, the first of which was adopted in 1919 and then revised in 1923, 1927, 1930s, 1937 and the 1940s. The second phase included elaborations of the original designs in which national elements or deviations were allowed. In the Soviet Socialist Republic of Ukraine the longest serving flag was adopted in 1949 and in the Baltic States after the death of Stalin in March 1953. Figure 3.1 shows a sample of designs associated with the Union of Soviet Socialist Republics (USSR).

With reference to the many flag-related changes in Eastern Europe, the Baltic States were forced to introduce communist symbols upon their incorporation into the Soviet Union – that is, the Red Flag with the

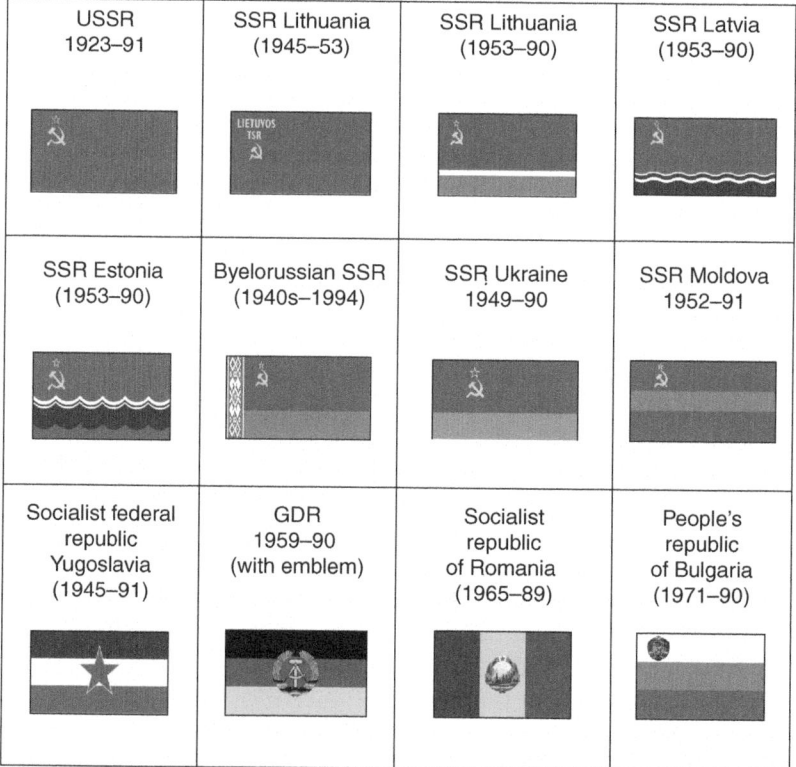

Figure 3.1 Flags of the USSR and the Soviet Socialist Republics
Note: Dates above indicate the use of the flags and not necessarily dates of regimes. Dates are subject to availability and interpretation.
Sources include: (Arvidsson and Blomqvist, 1987; Crampton, 1992, pp. 127–8; Z. Heimer, 1996a, 1996b; Znamierowski, 2004). Flag images courtesy of: (FOTW, 2002, 2010b, 2010f).

hammer and sickle emblem. After the end of Nazi occupation, the first version of the Red Flag displayed in the upper hoist yellow Latin initials of the country and the hammer and sickle emblem and new flags of the Socialist Republics were adopted in 1953 in Lithuania, Latvia and Estonia (see Figure 3.1). The current national flags of the Baltic States (Figure 2.10) were readopted as symbols of protests before the Baltic States officially proclaimed their independence 1990–91 and the Soviet emblems, associated with the deportation or execution of thousands of Estonians, Lithuanians and Latvians by Stalin, were immediately removed. The 1989 revolution in the GDR (1949–90) used as a symbol the GDR flag but the communist emblem had been cut out (the hammer represented heavy industry, dividers for scientific progress and wheat-ears for agriculture and had been adopted 1959). Crowds in Bulgaria and Romania employed the same kind of symbolism. Romania flew, at the time, its third Soviet-inspired flag as two older flags had been replaced in 1948 and in 1952. Ignatieff concluded: 'A state that has a flag with a hole in it is a state that no longer knows what it is' (Ignatieff, 1993, p. 45). This may be the case, but the opposite may also be true. A hole in the flag is definitely also an indication of change of direction and national re-definition in terms of what *not* to be.

Changes of ideological regimes thus lead to modifications of flags and/or adoption of new ones. Classical examples are the flags created after the French and the Russian Revolutions, during and after the Spanish Civil War, by the former Soviet Union for the Socialist Republics, and in the Balkans where newly established national flags were adopted in the 2000s. Table 3.1 identifies the main modifications and alterations with the current national flags in Europe in a few representative cases identifying the ruptures in continuity. Major changes are linked to revolutions, occupations, independence, formation of unions; transformations from monarchies to republics (Netherlands, France, Italy, Russia) and vice versa (France 1814, Italy 1861); communist domination (the Baltic States, Central and Eastern Europe) and anti-communist transformations (with removal of communist emblems); and fascist (Italy and Germany and their satellite states during the Second World War) and anti-fascist transformations (with national flags re-adopted).

Continuous changes, modifications and (re)adoption tell us that flags have been established as political symbols par excellence and are intimately connected to nation building. The reasons are not only related to the efforts by elites but also to the role they can play in the expression of nationhood. Thus, a 'new national flag is a potent symbol, a highly

Table 3.1 Flags and political change

Flag	Flag-related changes, modifications*
Denmark	1340 (arms of King Valdemar IV Atterdag), *1696* (1941–45, occupation)
Switzerland	(Cross variations: 1289, 1339 and 1422) 1480, restricted until 1848, *1889*
Sweden	1523, *1663* (1844–1905 with union emblem) *1906*
United Kingdom	*1606, 1707, 1801* (reflecting building of union) (see case study)
Netherlands	(1597 version of *orange*-white-blue) 1630 (red-white-blue) *1648* (1810–15 annexed by France) (1940–45, occupied)
Russia	1693 (naval ensign), *1705* (merchant flag), (1914, tricolour with imperial arms) (1917–91, Red Flags), *1991*
Spain	1783 (naval ensign), *1785* (royal decree) (1873–74, 1931–39 republics) (1936, 1938–45, 1945–77 Franco inspired designs) 1978, *1981*
France	1789, (1794) (1814–15) (1830) *1848 (see case study)*
Italy	1796, 1848 (1861, with arms of Savoy), 1946 (Republic), *1948*
Greece	1821–22 (colours), *1833* (colours), *1970 (design)*
Norway	(1814) (1815) 1821, 1938 (allowed at sea with sanctions), (1844–1905, with union emblem) (see case study) *1893, 1896, 1898 (Norwegian parliament) 1905*
Germany	1848–50 (1867–1918, Bismarck's tricolour) 1919 (1933–45) *1949, 1990*
Hungary	1848, (1867–1918 ensign of Austria-Hungary) 1918–45, (1949–56, 1958–89 with communist emblems) *1957*
Finland	1862, *1863* (1917–18) 1918 (republic) *1995* (alteration of shade of blue)
Serbia	1882–1918 (1918–45, Kingdom of Serbs, Croats and Slovenes) (1945–92 with star), *1992, 2004, 2006* (with coat of arms)
Portugal	(1830–1910 monarchial flag), *1910* (republic)
Austria	(1786 naval ensign with colours) (–1806, 1867–1918 imperial flags) 1918 (1938–45) *1945*
Lithuania	(1918 Heraldic design) 1918 (1940–41, 1941–44 occupations), (1945–53, 1953–1990, Red flags) 1988, 1989, *1990*
Ukraine	(1918 with trident in canton) (1919, 1923, 1927, 1930s, 1937, 1940s, 1949–1990 Red flags) 1991, *1992*

Note: *Dates are not exhaustive but in following order and in reference to the current national flags: year first claimed to appear, established by law in italics; periods not in use (in parentheses) that indicate that another flag was used. Other dates indicate modifications and changes with reference to colours and designs, and most recent date of adoption. Dates are subject to availability and interpretation.

condensed focus of sentiment which emphasizes the independence of the newly created unit' (Firth, 1973, p. 347). From this follows that the entries of new states admitted to the United Nations are accompanied by the display of their new flags. This does also suggest that flags invariably have become part of the politics of recognition and nation making in cases *before* the attainment of statehood. We see this with the flags of Norway (1821), Ireland (1848), Slovakia (1848), Finland (1863), Iceland (1915) and the Baltic States (1918, 1988–89). In these cases, flags have contributed to the justification of the state and have also been described as costly possessions, the loss of which would have pointed to more than the loss of a piece of cloth.

Symbols of control and dissent: honour and dishonour

Controlling national symbols is a means of managing the past and has become a consideration for elites as one way of maintaining social order. Firth maintains that flags are instruments of negotiating power, also described as 'master symbols' (Wright-Mills, 1963) or 'dominant symbols' (Turner in Dillistone, 1986), that in effect become moral symbols of justification. State control and legitimation of authority is exercised through flag laws and notions of 'desecration', which shed light on the political as well as the sacred nature of the national flag (and the nation). Naturally, flag legislation is less about the desecration of the flag and more about preventing ideological deviation from official patriotism and about restricting control from below (Baumgarten, 1984). The outrage following an attack on a national flag has been compared to an attack on the imagined national body (Cerulo, 1995) as the notion of the flag being 'defaced' or 'desecrated' also suggests. There are naturally variations in judicial interpretation of the laws of the state as regards the protection of national flags and this indicates that the flag is not handled by law as an object, but rather, as a relationship – the relationship between the object of the flag and the nation.

First, states control and restrict all elements relating to flag composition. Their designs, shapes, sizes and material are controlled by its institutions. States control the usage of national flags as they appear on state buildings, embassies, airlines, national museums, national monuments, capital city squares and stationery. Specific protocols are used with reference to the national flags at the headquarters of the United Nations and the European Union. The state, too, specifies the days when the flag is to be flown and the official flag days.

Secondly, the symbolism of contempt is significant as states may control the usage of national flags as a matter of exclusion. Thus, the legal framework that restricted the use of the Swastika flag in Nazi Germany from 1933 onwards was exercised by the withholding of access to the flag as a measure to exclude certain groups. Within a ritualized national and political calendar this flag was used as a condensed symbol of party propaganda and a political tool to intimidate opponents. The recognizable design of the Swastika flag and its standards were reproduced on a grand scale and used in large-scale party parades and rallies. The Nazi authorities issued nearly 2000 decrees against the Jewish population and among these the Nuremberg Flag Law (Reich Flag Law) written with the intention of making the Law for the Protection of the National Symbols from May 1933 more specific (Sensen, 1997). Paragraph 4:1 dictated that: 'Jews are forbidden to fly the Swastika national flag' (*Reich Law Gazette*, 15 September, 1935). The penalty for breaking the laws was officially penal servitude, imprisonment and/or imposition of a fine (paragraph 5). In such contexts, the Nuremberg Laws also stipulated that 'Citizenship in the Reich is limited to those of German and related blood' (Citizenship Laws, paragraph 2:1) (*Reich Law Gazette*, 15 September, 1935) and 'Marriages between Jews and citizens of German or kindred blood are forbidden' (Law for the Protection of German Blood and German Honor, paragraph 1:1) (*Reich Law Gazette*, 15 September, 1935).

Thirdly, whereas states and nations legally protect their own flags against defiling and desecration, the maltreatment of enemy flags and standards is used to dishonour enemies. The treatment of captured standards and flags in wars and conflicts is illuminating. An early example related to nation formation was the defiling of captured rebel standards after the Battle of Culloden (1746) during the Jacobite struggle against the English Hanoverian kings who crushed the Highland resistance. Rich in the symbolism of contempt, standards were handled by executioners and thrown in the dust before being destroyed by fire and turned to ash:

> They [the rebel standards] were carried by the chief hangman of Edinburgh and by chimneysweeps, with an escort, and laid in the dust, while a proclamation was read explaining why they were to be burnt by the public hangman. Each standard was then laid over the flames, while the senior herald named the Scottish clan that had marched behind it to battle. (Firth, 1973, p. 356)

In the 1945 Victory Parade in Moscow, the captured Nazi standards received similar treatment when at a poignant point the music accompanied by a drum roll increasing in volume, as when condemning a person to death or as in this case a nation, 200 captured Nazi banners where thrown at the ground on the steps of Lenin's Mausoleum. Invading forces throughout history have used their flags to signal invasion and take-over, one of many examples being the draping of buildings in Soviet flags in Berlin in 1945.

Fourthly, the symbolisms of dissent and protest have a double-edged character. Because of the meanings associated with flags, they are easily used as counter-instruments and as symbols in reverse. While nations exercise control and attempt to master the use of the flags, nationals and citizens also exercise control over the state in their display of these. Thus flags can be used to demonstrate discontent with governmental institutions and decisions, protests against authority or against single actions or general ideological condemnation against nations. National flags may, in other words, operate in reverse, against the interests the flag officially represents. The reactions to the flag are constituted in two parts: the action of the protesters and, in turn, the reaction of other people to their protest. We see here that the flag is treated as a surrogate and the 'national symbol is manipulated in order to assert moral value over existing power value' (Firth, 1973, p. 365). The significance of flags becomes transparent when flags are maltreated and defiled. The winner of a photo competition in Nice in 2010 submitted a photo of someone wiping their bottom with the French Tricolour, which led the Minister of State for Justice to react and to a revised flag law stipulating that culprits be fined 1500 euro for such offences (Lindblad, 2010).

Flag-related symbolism in Belarus after independence is an interesting example of protest against authority (see Figure 3.2). Belarus employed a white, red and white tricolour after independence (1991–95) but restored unexpectedly a modified version of the red and green flag used during the Soviet era in 1995 (without the hammer and sickle emblem and with the national ornament in inverted colours) (FOTW,

Figure 3.2 Flags of Belarus from 1991
Note: The white-red-white tricolour of Belarus 1991–95. The red and green flag with a national ornament established in 1995.
Sources: (FOTW, 1991a, 1991b). Flag images courtesy of: (FOTW, 2010b).

1991b). When the tricolour of independence (1991) was outlawed by the authorities it became an instant symbol in the protests that followed. On the day of the anniversary of the new constitution, which had given President Lukashenko and his government extensive powers, Belarussians demonstrated by waving a vast number of tricolours of independence in 1991 and the reports stated that: 'Some flags were so large that the authorities had to use heavy-duty equipment to remove them' (Newsline Radio Free Europe, 1997). Similar tactics were used in the dispute over the Ukrainian presidential election in Ukraine – the Orange Revolution – November 2004 to January 2005, which claimed to be marred by corruption and fraud in favour of sitting President Viktor Yanukovych. Nationwide protests succeeded and a re-run was ordered by the Supreme Court, which showed a victory for Viktor Yushchenko (52 per cent). Civil disobedience and strikes were organized by the opposition movement during this period as it expressed its dissatisfaction by flagging orange items, waving orange flags, wearing orange scarfs and hats and other orange items of clothing, giving name to the Orange Revolution. Orange was associated with Yushchenko's party and non-violent means of protest. Independence Square in Kiev turned orange on the anniversary in 2005 (BBC, 22 November 2005).

The burning of national flags highlights their potentially divisive agency as an immediate way of demonstrating dissatisfaction against nations, states, causes, wars and ideologies. Classical protests include the controversial burning of American flags by Vietnam veterans in the United States in the 1970s. This remains a poignant debate in the United States as a recent 'flag desecration debate' demonstrates: in the case of *Texas* v. *Johnson* (1989) the Supreme Court ruled that flag burning was warranted under the constitutional right of freedom of speech (Goldstein, 2000). This ruling was followed by protests and protest groups calling for flag burning to be outlawed (Madriaga, 2007). Europe has witnessed the burning of a number of flags in recent years. In London, Union Jacks were burnt in 2004 by protesters against the Iraq war, something which gained considerable attention in the media. Following the aftermath of the cartoon controversy in 2005 when satirical drawings linking Islam with terrorism were published by the Danish newspaper *Jyllands-Posten*, Danish flags were burned around the world. The cartoons were published in late September 2005 and drew nearly 3500 people to demonstrate in Copenhagen. Following the demonstrations other European newspapers re-published the cartoons which triggered, in turn, more demonstrations and a number of reactions such as boycott of Danish goods. In Damascus the Danish embassy was set on fire as was the Danish General Consulate in Beirut (Hansen and Hundevadt, 11 March 2008; MacAskill et al., 4 February 2006).

Flags and division

An exploration of flags as political symbols inevitably leads to their use as devices that invariably enhance division in politically and ethnically divided societies (Schöpflin, 1997, 2000) unless uniting narratives and symbols are found. The use of competitive flags in Spain during the Civil War but also in contemporary Spain, the establishment of a flag for Bosnia-Herzegovina (1992–98), and in Serbia and Montenegro (2004–7) are a few examples – among many – that highlight the potentially divisive nature of flag usage.

The number of flags in use during the Spanish Civil War (1936–39) demonstrates how loyalties were effectively negotiated and symbolized in conflict but also how flag-related competition in Spain remains unsolved and linked to the Spanish Civil War. A few years before the civil war, in 1931, with the formation of the Second Spanish Republic, Spain adopted a republican tricolour (red, yellow and purple with coat of arms, see Figure 3.3). Different versions of the older *royal* bicolour flag (along the lines of the current flag, see below) were also in use simultaneously (FOTW, 2003e; W. Smith, 1975e). The republican tricolour provided, at the time, a contrasting ideological commitment as 'purple' was specifically chosen as a republican colour pledging protection against the pressures of feudal institutions, church privileges and foreign monarchs. (The first republic, 1873–74, made a similar commitment by removing the crown from the top of the shield on the flag.)

Adding to this further complexity, the many political forces on both sides in the civil war – Falange, Requeté, the communists, the anarchists, the Basque units – also had their own colours and flags. Thus, Franco decided to introduce a new flag in 1936 modelled on the earlier royal and pre-republican bicolour flag in order to rally the forces under one banner. This differentiated Franco's forces from the republicans and identified him as *the Leader* protecting traditions and in charge of their future. Franco's flag (bicolour, crowned and modified coat of arms seen below) intended to recall the golden ages, the era of Spanish Greatness and the days of Isabella and Ferdinand, which he claimed should not be forgotten. To its coat of arms, Franco also added the black eagle of St John, the yoke and arrows – the symbol of his Falange supporters – under the slogan *Una, grande, libre* (One, great, free) (FOTW,

68 *Symbols of Nations and Nationalism*

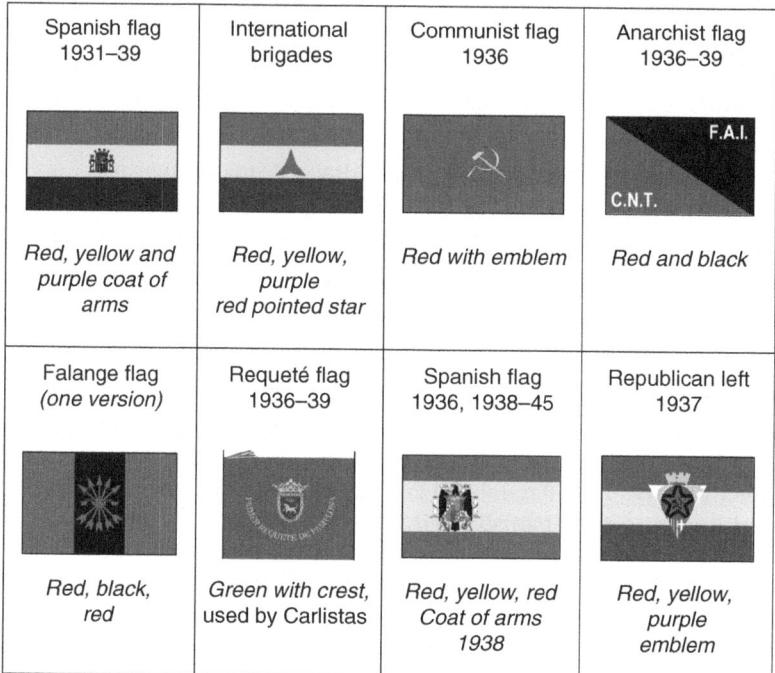

Figure 3.3 Flags during the Spanish Civil War
Note: Dates are subject to availability and interpretation.
Sources include: (FOTW, 2003b, 2003c, 2003d, 2003e, 2003f, 2010e; Gutiérrez, November 2004; Ministerio de Asuntos Exteriores, 1987; W. Smith, 1975e, 2004b). Flag images courtesy of: (FOTW, 2010b, 2010e).

2003b, 2003c, 2003f; W. Smith, 1975e, pp. 124–9). The yoke and arrows had originally been created for the Catholic kings (the arrows, *flechas*, for Fernando, and the Yoke, *Yugo*, for Ysabel) as a symbol of the dual monarchy, prosperity and warfare. The Falange adopted this in 1933. After the Second World War, Franco modified the coat of arms on the flag to incorporate a larger design onto the bicolour flag. This was in use until 1977, two years after Franco's death.

It is against such complex background that the development of the current Spanish flag (with national coat of arms, see Figure 3.4) and the competition between this and other flags in Spain must be understood. A first version of this was found in the naval design (1783) and adopted by royal decree in 1785. The colour scheme of red and gold appear in the arms of Aragon, Castile and Navarre, the shield displayed on the flag combine the arms of Castile, Aragon, Leon, Navarra and

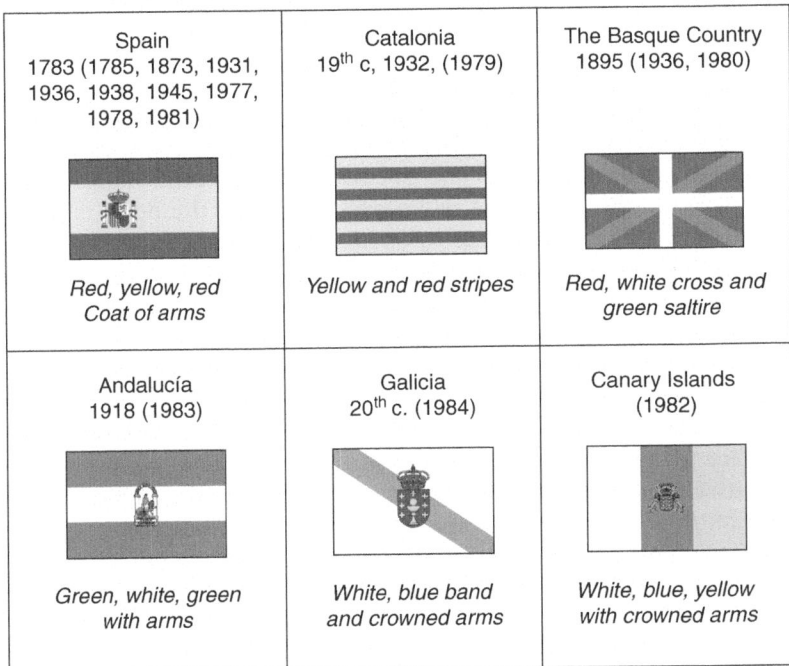

Figure 3.4 Flagging loyalties in Spain
Note: Dates are subject to availability and interpretation. Date of formal adoption in parentheses.
Sources include: (Basque Country, 2010; Catalonia, 2010; España, Kingdom of Spain, Reino de España, 2010). Flag images courtesy of FOTW.

Granada. Previously, the Bourbon dynasty (seventeenth–eighteenth centuries) had used a white flag with various combinations of the arms, including the Pillars of Hercules with the motto *'Plus ultra'* ('More Beyond') reflecting Spanish discoveries that had also inspired Franco. The path towards the establishment of the current Spain flag is complex and has evolved through a number of modifications and changes. The flag was significantly modified during and after the republican periods in 1931 and 1936, as mentioned, but also in 1938 and in 1945. The modification of the flag was one of the elements of the consensus reached during the process of Transition to Democracy. One condition for the legalization of the Communist party in 1977 was also its promise to refrain from pledging in favour of a republic and flagging the previous (red-yellow-purple) tricolour. Modifications to the design also took place in 1977 and was formalized in the Spanish Democratic constitution in 1978 and stripped off the symbolic elements added by Franco. The current design formally dates from December 18, 1981. However, the contested nature of the Spanish flag was not over with the civil war as it remains associated with conservative forces despite the removal of the Franco-inspired symbolism. Today, it continues to be seen with scepticism from the left but also generally speaking in the central state (Shachar, 2010) and contributes to a wider explanation of the development of national and regional flags in Spain. When the Historical Memory Law of 2007 intended for the recognition of victims on both sides of the Civil War and asked for the removal of statues and plaques in Franco's honour, pro-France demonstrators were quoted as shouting at the Valley of the Fallen and Franco's burial place: 'Viva Franco! One Spain, one flag!' (Kingstone, 2007).

A number of national and regional flags displays competing loyalties in contemporary Spain and had emerged as instruments of nationalism by the twentieth century and as counter-symbols of Spanish hegemony. A pervasive feature of contemporary Spain is its dialectic relationship between the centre and periphery, the Spanish state and the nations of Catalonia and the Basque Country. Spanish nation-building has been described as triggering the emergence of these peripheral nationalisms (Muro and Quiroga, 2004), which has also been expressed with use of distinct national symbols. The *comunidades autonomas* were formally created with the 1978 Constitution with the aim of curbing the aspiration of self-government among the nationalist movements of Catalonia and the Basque Country. Catalonia, the Basque Country, Galicia and Andalucía were already at the time in possession of their own flags. Other regions also looked back for suitable pre-modern flag-material (Aragon, Navarra, Valencia and Castille) whereas the Canary Islands and the Autonomous Region of Madrid created new flags. Thus, in Figure 3.4 it is noted that Catalonia-Aragon, Andalucía, Galicia and the Basque Country have produced flags calling on pre-modern symbolism whereas many these flags were in fact created by nationalist and regional movements in modern times in the nineteenth or the beginning of the twentieth centuries. These flags would thus fall within the category of 'heraldic flags' adopted during a post-imperial symbolic regime. The Andalusian flag is from 1918 and used colours that connected the region to its Arabic heritage; whereas the Galician flag, based on the maritime province of La Coruña, was adopted by the Galician emigrants to the Americas in the late nineteenth and first half of the twentieth century. The coat of arms, however, is of medieval origin. For the Canary Islands a new image was found combining the colours of blue and white from Tenerife and yellow and blue from Las Palmas. All of these are official flags of the Spanish state, and by law public buildings flag them together: the European flag, the Spanish and/or regional, the latter depending on perspective.

Competing loyalties are particularly flagged in Catalonia (*Senyera*), the Basque Country (*Ikurriña*) but also in Galicia, Andalucía and the Canary Islands. The flag of the Autonomous Community of Catalonia (four red stripes on gold) has been claimed to be the oldest national flag in Europe, linked to the colours of Aragon originating in the ninth century. Catalan historians such as Marti de Riquer have discounted this theory as an illustration of an invented tradition (Massot, 2000; Riquer, 2001). However, documentary evidence is dated to the seal of Count Ramon Berenguer IV in 1150 and the flag of the Aragonese and Catalan conquerors (when conquering Valencia in 1238) is preserved in the City Hall of Valencia. The Catalonian flag is politicized as a historical flag in relation to the other sources of the Spanish flag such as the colours and arms of the united kingdoms of Castile (yellow tower on red) and León (a red lion on white) that date to the thirteenth century (1230). The Catalan flag clearly has medieval origins (the Crown of Aragon) and came to represent the kingdoms of Aragon and Valenica, the Balearic Islands and the principality of Catalonia. However, it has not been in continuous use since these early times. On the contrary, it is likely that a cross design (St George) was also used in this area previously (W. Smith, 2004b). The movement for cultural revival in Catalonia – *Renaixença* – started to use the four-striped pre-modern flag in the second half of the nineteenth century but it is said to emerge as a political symbol in the 1930s (CatalanAssociationVexillologia, 1995, 2010; Catalonia, 2010; Origins of the Aragonese-Catalan Flag (Spain) Senyera, 2010). The Catalan flag was formally adopted when Catalonia became an autonomous region 1979, whereas the other autonomous regions once represented by same flag adopted versions of this: Aragon with coat of arms, Valencia with a royal crown and the Balearic Islands with a small castle (once the flag of Mallorca). The flag of the Basque Country (white cross, green saltire on red), in turn, was created in 1895 by Sabino Arana (1865–1903), the founder of Basque nationalism. It was re-adopted in 1936 as the separatist movement culminated in a statute of autonomy in October and formed a government and an alliance against Franco. The flag was re-adopted in 1980 (Basque Country, 2010) with the created autonomous community.

In their symbolic communication these two flags constitute typical forms of heraldic flags of a post-imperial age by which nationhood is claimed in the present on the grounds of the past – in these cases flagged

72 Symbols of Nations and Nationalism

against the symbolism of Spanish hegemony. Similarly, the Catalan and Basque national days have emerged as contra days and both were banned during the Franco years but re-emerged in the 1970s (McCrone, 2009). Significantly, Catalonia commemorates the loss of government with the War of the Spanish Succession (their defeat of 11 September in 1714) whereas the Basque Country celebrates the day of the homeland *Aberri Eguna* (celebrated in conjunction with Easter Sunday, the theme of resurrection serving a symbolic purpose).

National flags authenticate boundaries that are often contested in newly reconfigured states and, far from unifying, they enforce divisions. One of the more highlighted cases refers to the complicated debate that emerged in Bosnia Herzegovina in 1992 (see Figure 3.5).

After the flag of the former Socialist Federal Republic of Yugoslavia (blue, white and red tricolour with red star, 1945–92) was abolished, a new flag of Bosnia-Herzegovina (white a shield of fleurs-de-lis) was adopted in 1992 upon independence. The shield on this flag originated from the coat of arms of the Kotromanic family who ruled Bosnia in the fourteenth to fifteenth centuries (FOTW, 2009e). Meanwhile Croatia revived the Sahovnica flag in 1990 (the red-white-blue with the chequered shield) before proclaiming itself independent in 1991. This horizontal tricolour (red, white and blue) with the chequered shield of

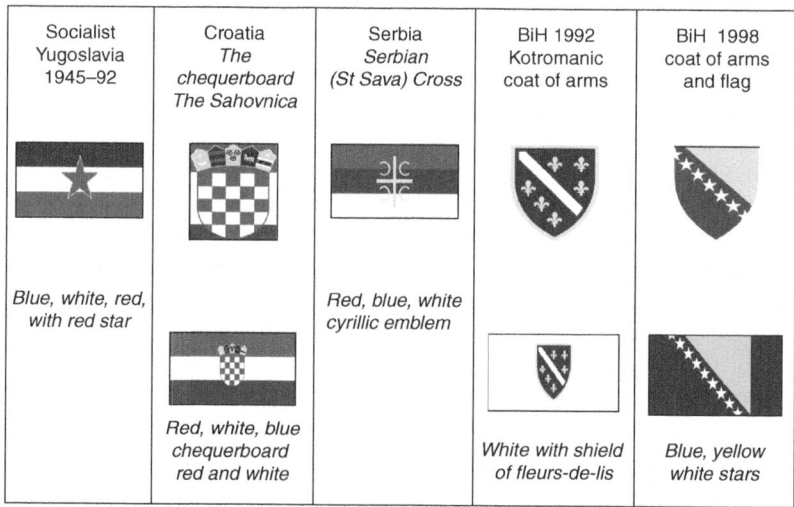

Figure 3.5 The flag situation in Bosnia-Herzegovina, 1992–98

Sources: (FOTW, 2004a, 2009e, 2010d; Kolstø, 2006; Office of the High Representative in Bosnia and Herzegovina (OHR), 1999; Office of the High Representatives, 1998; Poels, 1998; Velde, 1995; Westendorp Commission, 1998). Flag images courtesy of: (FOTW, 2010b).

red and white was the traditional Croat emblem and similar to the one used by the fascist regime of the Second World War (now with the order of the colours on the chequered shield in reverse), which led the Serbs to claim that the Ustaša had returned (Ignatieff, 1993). In the war of 1992–1995 the Croat and Serbs fought under their own flags: the Croats used the chequerboard and the Serbs often a tricolour adorned with four letters 'c' in Cyrillic, one interpretation said to be an acronym for *Samo Sloga Srbina Spasava* 'Only Unity Will Save the Serbs' or alternatively 'Only the Serbs Will Save Serbia'. As a symbol the latter was inspired by one of the flags of the Byzantine Empire.

In this context, the white flag with the fleur-de-lis became ethnicized and associated with the Bosnian Muslims (Kolstø, 2006). The use of the various ethno-national flags thus highlighted existing discord, which now was also visibly reinforcing existing divisions. Thus a complicated situation emerged when the parliament in Bosnia-Herzegovina was to choose a flag. By 1995 and the Drayton Agreement it was clear that a new flag was needed in this war-torn state so the parliament began to work on the 'flag-issue' in 1997. Various flags were proposed, one notably modelled on the Irish tricolour by displaying green (Muslims) red (Croats) and blue (Serbs) but this was rejected. With 44 per cent Bosniaks, 31 per cent Serbs and 17 per cent Croats, no comfortable majority decision could be reached. Kolstø (2006) writes that the Serbian deputies had a tendency to vote against all suggestions in order to deny the state legitimacy. Eventually, after long negotiations, the United Nations intervened and the High Representative in Bosnia (Westendorp) imposed the design that had received the most votes in the Bosnian parliament in 1998 (FOTW, 2004a, 2009a; Poels, 1998; Westendorp Commission, 1998). It has been claimed that the flag was imposed at the particular time because Bosnia-Herzegovina needed a flag at the Olympics in Japan: it 'would be a bad signal to send to the world if the Bosnian troop were to enter the stadium with no flag' (Kolstø, 2006, pp. 682–3). This flag was declared as a flag of the future but was met with considerable protests. A group of Bosniack intellectuals signed a petition against the imposed flag as 'the final way to kill the nation' (Kolstø, 2006, p. 683). The News Agency *Republika Srpska* reported that the Mayor of Zvornik had refused to accept the new flag 'In the name of the thousand mothers of killed Serbian veterans and the thousand war disabled persons' (FOTW, 1998a; Kolstø, 2006).

Recent developments regarding flag-related symbolism in the Balkans came to the fore in Serbia 2004–6 together with the process of Montenegro moving towards independence (2006). The national flag in Serbia since 1992 (see Figure 2.10) had been the tricolour with the pan-Slavic colours but this found itself in competition with the Serbian state flag (the same tricolour with the lesser coat of arms, see Figure 2.10). Thus the debate in 2004 came to focus on whether the national flag of Serbia ought also to display this coat of arms of Serbia (BBC, 2004b). With the establishment of the new constitution on 8 November 2006, the state and national flags were 'equalized' and their usage constitutionally sanctioned. However, when the parliament of Montenegro declared independence, formally confirming the result of the referendum, with a red flag displaying the Montenegrin coat of arms (Figure 2.10), the Serbian state flag with the coat of arms was hoisted in front of the UN building. Serbian restaurants, petrol stations and sport supporters also started to fly the flag with the coat of arms (FOTW, 2009h). Seen from this perspective, it was the national flags of Serbia and Montenegro that were 'equalized' by both displaying heraldic devices of the past. In Montenegro, with the formal adoption of the flag, anthem and national day, the parliamentary speaker Ranko Krivokapic stated: 'For the first time in history we have all three symbols of a nation' (BBC, 2004a, 2004b).

Flags and golden ages

It could easily be argued that national flags are among those symbols that posses a quality of special reserve in simultaneously representing the past together with aspirations of the future. Although references to the past are intricately connected to national imagery, the past can be highly problematic as seen with recent developments explored below. However, as a rule, national flags are vehicles that justify the present through the identification of a collective origin. The central message conveyed in many of the current flags in Europe is that of embattled peoples that despite the hardships have survived. For Smith, it is these myths of golden ages (heroism, victories, defeats) that provide groups with a sense of chosenness (A.D. Smith, 1986, 1998, 2003): 'Symbols such as flags, emblems, anthems, costume, special foods, and sacred objects, give expression of our sense of difference and distinctiveness of the community [...] myths of origins, liberation, the golden age, and chosenness link the sacred past to a sense of collective destiny' (A.D. Smith, 1995, p. 132). Clearly, national symbolism is appropriated along the lines of uniqueness and with the construction of 'border guards' and the embellishment of the past, one of many strategies used by nationalist regimes seeking to mobilize populations and nations-to-be (Armstrong, 1982). Franco's flag intervention in 1936 (see Figures 3.3 and 3.4) is a very good example of recalling the golden age of Spanish Greatness as the rebellious forces were also conveniently unified under one banner and under Franco. However, ancient material has also been useful in the choice and construction of signs displayed on the post-imperial flags introduced after the First World War that claim continuity with an often distant past by the use of medieval coats of arms and/or colours, for instance, with the flags of Portugal (1910), Austria (1918), Poland (1918), Latvia (1923), Czech Republic (1920), Wales (1950s), Croatia (1990), Slovenia (1991), Slovakia (1992), Moldova (1990) Albania (1992), Ukraine (1992), Macedonia (1995), Serbia (2006) and Montenegro (2007).

One illuminating example of the significance of the relationship between 'historical copyright' and perceived cultural authenticity is found in the debate that followed the adoption of the Macedonian flag (see Figure 3.6). More correctly, the Former Yugoslav Republic of Macedonia (FYROM), was forced to alter its flag (red with a sixteen pointed sun) in 1992 after a dispute with Greece that insisted that 'the sun of Vergina' was a Greek symbol as found on the sarcophagus believed to belong to Philip II (father of Alexander the Great). As expressed in unambiguous terms from a Greek point of view:

> The Vergina Sun, the emblem of Philip's dynasty, symbolizes the birth of our nation. It was the first time (4th century BC) that the Greek mainland (city-states and kingdoms) with the same language, culture, and religion were united against the enemies of Asia in one league. At the same time the fractured Greek world grew conscious of its unity. And, in this sense, we have never been apart since then. The 'Sun' was excavated in Greece in 1978, and it is sacred to us. (FOTW, 2009b).

We might mention that the name 'Macedonia' was in itself disputed by Greece which objected on the grounds of the name of the adjacent Greek region of Macedonia and with reference to related historical concerns. The claims above were disputed by the FYROM, which had to redesign its flag and adopt the red flag with an *eight* pointed sun in 1995 (which with a little imagination could be argued to constitute the core of the sun of Vergina) (see Figure 3.6). Two years after this controversy and according to the FYROM flag law of 1997, the use of 'foreign' flags was restricted on public buildings. This, in effect, limited the use of Albanian flags in the FYROM (FOTW, 2009g).

76 *Symbols of Nations and Nationalism*

Figure 3.6 The flag dispute in Macedonia, FYROM
Note: Flags of FYR of Macedonia (FYROM) in use 1992–95 (left) and as altered from 1995.
Sources: (Embassy of the Republic of Macedonia, 2005; Flagmaster, 1995a, 1995b, 1995c; FOTW, 2009b). Flag images courtesy of: (FOTW, 2010b).

Post-historical and counter-nationalist flags

However, historical material is not always useful as symbolic material. On the contrary, golden ages, victories, defeats and sacrifices condensed in flag symbolism may invariably become a challenge for territories in which history remains undefined, contested and divisive. Few territories have a straightforward singular history but the role of official history is to narrate the past along these singular lines and on the expense of marginalized groups. With the embellished historical theme in the European flags it is noteworthy that a new post-imperial flag-type has emerged, which in this sense is atypical. In its infancy, conclusions must be drawn with caution, but a new type of flags has been adopted along non-hereditary principles and claimed as flags of the future.

The likeness between the European Flag and the flags of Bosnia-Herzegovina and Kosovo is striking as far as flag-symbolism is concerned (see Figure 3.7). These flags are elite-imposed without much

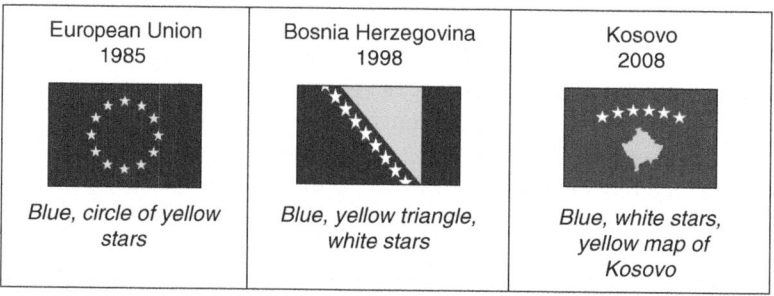

Figure 3.7 Post-historical and counter-nationalist flags and Europeanization
Sources: (European Flag. History of the Flag, 2010; Ž. Heimer, 2004). Flag images courtesy of: (FOTW, 2010b).

endorsement from the populations they claim to represent. In comparison it is interesting to note that the European Commission looked to the nation for inspiration when it introduced a number of 'symbolic measures' (Shore, 2000) including not only a European flag but also a European anthem and a Europe Day. These measures were taken to raise awareness among Europeans of their European heritage. The EU flag, however, in representing the whole of Europe had to avoid the symbols usually connected with European ancestry such as Christian imagery, heraldic designs or images related to democracy or republicanism that are associated with the many European flags. Instead, the European Flag (1985) displayed a circle of 12 gold stars on a blue background as the circular layout denoted the union. This image with 13 white stars in a blue field was used in the canton of one of the early flags of the United States (adopted 1777). However, in 1985, the stars of the flag were allegedly referring to a number of symbols linked to the European perception of civilization:

> Twelve was a symbol of perfection and plenitude, associated equally with the apostles, the sons of Jacob, the tables of the Roman legislator, the labours of Hercules, the hours of the day, the months of the year, or the signs of the Zodiac. (Shore, 2000, p. 47)

The references to Christian imagery were thus subtle since the EU flag was to be politicized, despite its references, as multinational, multi-ethnic and inclusive. It was never officially adopted because of the rejection of the European Constitution in 2008, which would have formalized its use and status as a union symbol. Jean Monnet allegedly once remarked that 'if we were to do it all again we would start with culture' (Shore, 1993, p. 785). The ways in which Monnet would have 'started with culture' are unclear but existing symbolic material could easily become divisive in one way or other. Given the complexity of Europe, its rival histories and narratives, finding meaningful, uniting and non-contested symbols would constitute a challenge. The European entourage of symbolism may not have inspired the loyalty intended and has become associated with controversy in many countries.

The emergence of the flag in Bosnia-Herzegovina, discussed previously as a long and complicated affair (1992–98), concluded with the enforcement of a flag that turned away from rival and divisive historical narratives by avoiding any of the heraldic devices and colours previously used. As noted, the United Nations intervened and the High Representative in Bosnia imposed the design that had received the most votes in the Bosnian parliament and it is inspired by the EU flag. In the case of

78 *Symbols of Nations and Nationalism*

Bosnia-Herzegovina, the stars resemble an infinite number of cantons (*Economist*, 1997; FOTW, 2004a, 2009a; Poels, 1998; Westendorp Commission, 1998). Similarly, the flag of an independent Kosovo is said to reaffirm 'our wish to become fully integrated into the Euro-Atlantic family of democracies' (Kosovo Declaration of Independence, 2008). The stars reflect the multi-ethnic character of Kosovo and represent its different communities – the Serbs, the Bosniaks, the RAE (Roma, Shkali and Egyptian Communities), the Turkish and the Goran communities (Constitution of the Republic of Kosovo, 2008; Numerical representation of the Kosovo Assembly, 2010). As argued, 'EU policy makers always realized that the way to manage the problem of Kosovo in the long-term was to bring Serbia and Kosovo within the European Union. This would, or so it was hoped, render the problem meaningless in the context of Europe's open borders and shared sovereignty' (Ker-Lindsay, 2009, p. 124). However, according to recent reports on human rights, Serbian education text books continue to describe Kosovo as the 'cradle of the Serbian nation' (Organization for Security and Co-operation in Europe, 2009). Thus, the Dardanian flag in use in Kosovo before independence was understood as a provocation, displaying at its centre the Albanian double-headed eagle (see Figure 3.8). Two recent books on Kosovo (Judah, 2008; Ker-Lindsay, 2009) highlight the use of divisive symbolism with covers illustrating the competition between Albanian and Serbian flags in Kosovo before independence. Thus, the new flag of Kosovo is especially noteworthy as an authentication of contested boundaries visualizing that Kosovo is not part of either Albania or Serbia.

The foundations of the flags of Bosnia-Herzegovina and Kosovo are claimed to be multi-ethnic flags of the future. That which distinguishes them from other national flags is their avoidance of historical symbolism. This does not suggest that history, nationalism

Figure 3.8 The Dardanian flag
Sources: (Kosovo before the declaration of independence. Kosovo under United Nations administration. Dardania (flag of uncertain status), 2010). Flag images courtesy of FOTW.

and ethnicity have played no part in the formations of these flags – clearly the potentially divisive agents of these phenomena have been main considerations – as the flag-symbolism adopted expresses the necessity to move beyond these and display symbolism of a post-historical or counter-nationalist character. This form of representation is unique and knocks, to a degree, on the door of post-modern understandings of communities as they highlight the complexity and fragmentation of identities in avoiding references to national oneness and sameness, understanding that such notions will be contested. The symbolic representation of Bosnia-Herzegovina and Kosovo does also express dependence on the European Union for military security and economic survival. Comparatively, the former British dominions reproduced British flags with variations (Australia, New Zealand, British Columbia, etc.) as did the former flags of the former Soviet Socialist Republics, such as the flags of Soviet Estonia, Soviet Latvia or Soviet Lithuania, etc. Flags of dominions or protectorates are derivative and express dependence on the powerful Centre.

Flagging and politicizing boundaries

National flags provide groups with the means to express complex concepts such as independence, liberation and freedom, and flags are easily reproduced or purchased. Having dealt with divisive flags, one may think that all flags are politicized, waved or saluted, which they are not. Whereas waved flags clearly mark the inclusion of members in national ceremonies or the exclusion of non-members during demonstrations, the taken-for-granted character of flags unwaved and hung outside public buildings is not to be underestimated (Billig, 1995). The latter mark boundaries and encapsulate the nation as a marker of 'in' and 'out' (A. Eriksen, 2007). Again, it is useful to look at contrasting examples illustrating the degree to which flag practices and reverence for the flag vary. This becomes increasingly clear in flag practices in America (Pledge of Allegiance) and varied flag practices within Scandinavia (Denmark, Sweden and Norway).

The 'Pledge of Allegiance to the American Flag' can rightly describe an identity-learning ceremony, the first version of which was written in 1892 for the 400th anniversary of Columbus's discovery. In 1943, the Supreme Court reversed its decision (1940) that the pledge of allegiance to the flag should be mandatory and thus avoided it becoming an easy target or rallying point for opposition (Kolstø, 2006). As it stands, the pledge is recited by students every morning in schools all over the

80 *Symbols of Nations and Nationalism*

United States and there can be no ambiguity as to its meaning and function: 'I Pledge Allegiance to the flag of the United States of America, and to the Republic for which it stands, *one* Nation under God, indivisible with liberty and justice for all' (Flag of the United States of America Website. The Pledge of Allegiance, 2005) (emphasis added). The key of this pledge is made to the *one* community:

> Many of the pupils participating in the ceremony no doubt could not care less about the words they are uttering, or even worse, while uttering them continue to believe that 'no, our nation is *not* one of liberty and justice, it is *illiberal* and *unjust*'. But through such a rejection of the official ideology such rebellious youngsters reveal that they nevertheless have taken on board the notion that there *is* one specific nation on earth called the American nation and they have internalized their membership in it (Our nation is not...). By rejecting the specific positive *attributes* ascribed to this nation, they confirm and reinforce the most important message of the school pledge: the *essence* of the nation, which is its oneness. (Kolstø, 2006, p. 678)

Clearly, the intention with practices such as this is to communicate and reinforce the imagination of *oneness*. The flag facilitates this process as it focuses the community on a tangible expression of their collectiveness (Cerulo, 1995) of its commonality represented by the *one* sign. Flags acquire different associations in the process of (re)making boundaries. As illuminating contrasts are the varied significance of the national flags in Scandinavia (see Aagedal, 2002). The significance of the Norwegian flag during the struggle for independence was explored in Chapter 2. However, overt forms of nationalism and flag waving are rejected as vulgar in Sweden (Eriksen and Jenkins, 2007). The Swedish flag, on the contrary, has achieved the status of a party-symbol and appears on birthdays and anniversaries, at Midsummer and Christmas but with little reference to the nation and has given Swedish nationalism and expressions thereof the description 'party-nationalism' (Aagedal, 2002). The use of the Swedish flag at parties does not contradict the lack of enthusiasm for public display of flags in ceremonies. Public display is still connected to the use of the Swedish flag by extremist and right-wing groups in the 1980s (Löfgren, 2007). Thus, the Swedish flag remains unwaved, but cannot be disregarded as meaningless as it continues to raise boundaries in a number of ways. Instead, unwaved flags provide 'banal reminders of nationhood' through 'flagging' the nation 'unflaggingly' (Billig, 1995, p. 41). The practice of displaying the Danish flag is, again, different from Norwegian and Swedish practices. The Danish flag, is connected with the 'good life' and is used to encourage consumption. Thus, the Danish flag hangs from ceilings in shopping centres and appears on beer bottles, on tins of ham, and so on. This has led Jenkins (2007) to conclude that the flag wants you to 'enjoy yourself through consumption'. Chosing the Danish flag in order to sell merchandise speaks for itself and has clearly been chosen in view of favourable associations to the nation. In a comparative light:

> in Sweden, the Danish practice is seen as slightly cheesy, in Norway as profaning a sacred symbol. There is, in other words, no single recipe for creating an efficient unifying symbol in a complex society, where the inhabitants are in most respect quite different from each other. Both the unwaved flags of Sweden, the noisily waved Norwegian ones and the commercialised Danish flags seem to bolster and confirm the sense of identification among most of the inhabitants. (Eriksen and Jenkins, 2007, p. 4)

Regardless of varied enthusiasm for flags in Scandinavia, the flags continue to validate membership. The appeal of nationality is further confirmed by the figures of national pride in Northern Europe as 93 per cent of Danes, 89 per cent of Norwegians and 87 per cent of Swedes claim to be either 'very proud' or 'quite proud' of their nationality. Corresponding figures for Iceland and Finland are even higher with 98 and 94 per cent (European Values Study Group and World Values Survey Association, 2006).

The unwaved flags stand in clear contrast to the reverence shown for the American and Norwegian flags or, for example, to those flags that raise attention in the Catholic or Protestant districts of Belfast in Northern Ireland. In the last few decades the usage and manufacturing of flags have been commercialized. This means that their usage today encompasses the many diverse spheres of art, advertising, literature, architecture and entertainment. The proliferation of flags in all kinds of social areas – sporting events, private organizations, cities, political units, businesses, labour unions – illustrates the extent of their usage. Their flexibility means that they can be adapted to new circumstances but remain compact and manageable symbols of expressing new notions of nationhood by endorsements or protests. Having said this, national flags are also treated with utmost respect and as if they were sacred objects.

The ritualization of flags as 'sacred' objects

Modern nations direct the usage of their flags to guarantee that the relationship between the flag and the nation is protected. Turning to the explanations of why the flag has remained the protected property of nations in a global age, this relationship and the separation of the flag from daily life must be explored and with this the statement that 'in every country where loyalty to the Fatherland (or Motherland) has become a religion, the flag is its chief symbol' (W. Smith, 1969, pp. 111–12). The symbolic disjunction between the piece of cloth and the underlying meaning of nations and their associated rituals, is illustrated by the image of the dying soldier in battle protecting the flag or by practices that regulate that flags fly at half-mast as a sign of mourning. Moreover, national flags are not allowed to touch the ground when lowered in official ceremonies or if they do they must be burned in a 'dignified' manner (United States of America Flag Site, 2005). Flags are also lowered at dusk, as flying in the dark or being left for days on end are against the flag rules of many nations. Codified according to flag etiquette or flag laws it is also, as a rule, illegal to burn the national flag and thus 'its "sacredness" is an officially imputed quality' (Firth, 1973, p. 365) so that the flag has in fact become a modern totem (Cerulo, 1995; Firth, 1973; W. Smith, 1975a) Thus, 'national flags tend to be assigned a quality of special reserve, removing them from the more sordid aspect of common handling. They represent 'society' much more, in its broadest political aspect' (Firth, 1973, p. 340). As a brief comparison, the totem, as the chief symbol of the clan or family identified the clan's ancestry, its qualities and traits through a particular animal or plant. Once adopted, totemic plants and animals, in turn, ultimately shaped the perception of society, its divisions, hierarchies and relationships (see e.g. Durkheim, 1976; Evans-Pritchard, 1965; Levi-Strauss, 1962). The totem gradually lost its religious character with the separation of the political, religious and economic spheres and with the division of labour. Totems of traditional kinship thus started to represent people of certain geographical areas as groups maintained signs that represented them. We are reminded that the clan has been described as 'a reunion of individuals who bear the same name and rally around the same sign' and that groups are only possible on this condition (Durkheim, 1976, p. 233). In this fashion, totems correspond to the heraldic emblems (coat of arms, banners and flags) of modern nations and lead to Durkheim to conclude that social life is made possible only by vast symbolism: 'Collective sentiments can just as well become incarnate in persons and formulæ: some formulæ are flags, while there are persons, either real or mythical, which are symbols' (Durkheim, 1976, pp. 231–2). The link between sacredness and the flags of the Middle Ages is especially clear with the saints and crosses painted on these in order to protect the armies that hoisted them justifying the cause of battle.

National flags, however, continue to be officially infused with sacred meanings according to the sacrifices in the name of the nation. Marvin and Ingle's (1999) study highlights nationalism as a civic religion and as one that is in continual demand of sacrifice, violence and war in order to guarantee renewal and unity. It is the myth of justified violence that ultimately holds society together. Violence is thus the fuel of the totem myth and the flag totem is central in justifying this sacrificial process:

> The flag symbolizes the sacrificed body of the *citizen*. This label has meaning only in reference to the group that defines it, the *nation*. Blood sacrifice links the citizen to the nation. It is a ritual in the most profound sense, for it creates the nation from the flesh of its citizens. The flag is the sign and agent of the nation formed in blood sacrifice. Still, raising a piece of cloth and calling it a flag will not declare territory and form groups, at least not territory that will be respected, or groups that will endure and fight to produce borders. The power of a flag must be sacrificially established. (Marvin and Ingle, 1999, p. 63)

Thus, nations send their nationals to die but sacrifices are given willingly and has clear links to 'the messianic sacrifice of the insider – turned – outsider is a sacred mystery that involves leaving the group through dying' (Marvin and Ingle, 1999, p. 75). These sacrifices define and defend borders and reproduce nations by establishing sacrificial boundaries and the nation may simultaneously condemn violence but require soldiers to kill in its name. Moments of greatest uncertainty are therefore marked by the greatest display of flags to make groups more certain of their identity. Vladimir Zhirinovsky, who challenged Boris Yeltsin in the first parliamentary elections after the disintegration of the Soviet Union, opposed the recently established flags of the 'new' nations, associating such changes in symbolism with war and bloodshed. He stated: 'They don't understand that you have to pay with blood for this process' (Marvin and Ingle, 1999, p. 63).

However, communication is not as one-sided as suggested and whereas sacrifice may strengthen moral communities they can also challenge them to the very core. The Star-Spangled Banner has been described as 'the most recognizable and holiest of all American national symbols' (Madriaga, 2007) but has also been related to the axiomatic relationship between American-ness and 'whiteness', which informs a rather different interpretation of the American Flag. Multi-ethnic societies are thought to be undermined by ethnic solidarity in providing a rival focus for nation building as other totems are worshipped. Official flag-related practices therefore continue to reinforce the sacred status of the flag. In the American flag-folding ceremony, the sacred relationship between the nation and the flag is made explicit. This demonstrates in no uncertain terms that the nation sanctifies itself through its flag and is in form similar to the Declaration of Faith read aloud by the congregation at a Sunday mass: the links between the ceremonial forms of religious groups and the national community are not subtle. The folding of the flag is an army and navy custom but is also performed in schools and only especially sanctioned individuals are allowed to fold it into a 'neat bundle'. The American flag is lowered and folded 12 times into the shape of a tricorne hat, associated with the soldiers who died fighting during the war of Independence, during which the following is read:

> The first fold of our flag is a symbol of life. The second fold is a symbol of our belief in the eternal life. The third fold is made in honor and remembrance of the veteran departing our ranks who gave a portion of life for the defence of our country to attain a peace throughout the world. The fourth fold represents our weaker nature, for as American citizens trusting in God, it is to Him we turn in times of peace as well as in times of war for His divine guidance. The fifth fold is a tribute to our country, for in the words of Stephen Decatur, 'Our country, in dealing with other countries, may she always be right; but it is still our country, right or wrong.' The sixth fold is for where our hearts lie. It is with our heart that we pledge allegiance to the flag of the United States of America, and to the republic for which it stands, one nation, under God, indivisible, with liberty and justice for all. [...] The eleventh fold, in the eyes of a Hebrew citizen, represents the lower portion of the seal of King David and King Solomon, and glorifies, in their eyes, the God of Abraham, Isaac, and Jacob. The twelfth fold, in the eyes of a Christian citizen, represents an emblem of eternity and glorifies, in their eyes, God the Father, the Son, and Holy Ghost. When the flag is completely folded, the stars are

uppermost, reminding us of our national motto, 'In God we Trust'.
(US Defense Department (Uniformed Services))

Related to the use of flags and the sanctification of nations are a number of practices heavily imbued with meaning, such as the lowering and rising of flags at memorials and funerals, flags flown at half-mast and covering coffins as a mark of respect linking the individual to the nation. In the Armed Forces at the ceremony of retreat the flag is lowered and folded in a triangle and kept under watch throughout the night as a tribute to those who sacrificed their lives. The next morning the flag is brought out at the ceremony of reveille and run aloft as a symbol of the resurrection. The general prohibition against burying national flags with the dead must be seen in light of the symbolism of the reveille where the flag (nation) is used as a promise of resurrection.

Flags bring solemn associations as memorial tokens in military processions, on memorial days or on coffins. The Union Jack embraced the coffins of the soldiers who recently returned from Afghanistan. In the United States, the flags are given to family members of servicemen and soldiers who have died in service. When involved in funerals, as is the case in Scandinavia, the national flag is at half-mast as the mourners arrive at church and is raised when they leave. The flag here, thus, represents the nation by connecting the past to the future but also to the notion of death and Christian resurrection. The use of the Swedish flag was seen in the aftermath of the Indian Ocean tsunami in which 543 Swedes died – half of whom were children – and 1500 were injured (BBC, 2005). The coffins with bodies being returned to relatives in Sweden were covered with Swedish flags as a mark of mourning and respect (Lichfield, 2005).

Furthermore, the flying of national flags at half-mast demonstrates the emotional charge of the flag, such as on official flag days of mourning. The Dutch lower their flags on Memorial Day (4 May) and the Belgians in 'Homage to the soldiers deceased during peace-keeping missions' (7 April) (FOTW, 1998b, 2005b; Roede, 2002). In Latvia, flags fly at half mast on the Commemoration Day of Victims of Communist Terror (25 March and 14 June), on the date of the Occupation of the Republic of Latvia (17 June) and on Commemoration Day of Victims of Genocide against the Latvian People by the Totalitarian Communist Regime (7 December) (FOTW, 2004d). The emotion invested in the practice of flying flags at half-mast becomes blindingly obvious when practices and codes of collective mourning are broken. For example, the offence caused when, after Diana, Princess of Wales, died, the Union

86 *Symbols of Nations and Nationalism*

Jacks on all public buildings had been lowered to half-mast except for the one flown atop Buckingham Palace. The associations of the flag flying at full-mast was understood as a sign of disrespect and caused outrage, whereas royal tradition stipulates that the flag fly at full mast when the Queen is in residence. Tradition had to give way to public pressure and the flag was finally lowered at the Palace under intense media coverage. The process did not stop there; to mark the first anniversary of Diana's death (31 August 1998) the Queen ruled that all flags at the royal residences should be lowered and half-masted as a special mark of respect. As a result, upon the announcements of the deaths of Princess Margaret (9 February 2002) and Queen Elizabeth the Queen Mother (30 March 2002) the flag was immediately lowered at all royal residences even if the Queen was in residence (BBC, 23 July 1998).

These are examples of the ceremonial contexts in which flags appear to provide a religious structure that activates the flag. Related to flag-related contexts and the division of the sacred and profane spheres are the violations or protests against the flags in the profane sphere that fundamentally do not challenge its sacred status. Flags also require less exaggerated respect in the mundane sphere where their sacred meaning is ignored (Stanner, 1963) (Firth, 1973), as in the case with the commercialized practice of the Danish flag. Flags can therefore also be used as decoration on clothes or be painted on the face of supporters on sporting occasions – associated meanings completely unrelated to the flowing of the same flag at half-mast. Historically, the Union Jack of Britain has moved between these spheres. Before 1939 the flag was associated with an official and/or royal context and its usage was restricted: 'It was the view of the King in Council 5th November 1800 that the Flag of Union could be flown on land only from His Majesty's forts and castles, and from His Majesty's ships at sea. It is the national official flag' (Gatty, 2009). This has changed with time and the Union Jack is today used as decorations, as cushions, on pieces of clothing, on teacups and in various forms of artwork.

The symbolic regimes of Europe: flags and counter-flags

We return to exploring national flags systematically and as distinct pockets of reference that transcend expression of nationhood and forms for Europe a specific symbolic pattern. With the attempts to change the socio-political structure after 1789, the usage of national flags spread over Europe and then to South America and finally to Asia, Africa and the Pacific. The 'syntactic structure' of flags (Cerulo, 1995), their associations, relationships, designs, configurations and structures are significant in understanding these. 'It is not simply the content of the flags that is important, but their form and the combination of their elements' (Firth, 1973, p. 46). In this study, time and context have been particularly important for classification of symbolic regimes with corresponding flag types. It would not be an exaggeration to state that symbolic 'truth' is set apart from reality with reference to the territorial claims made through most flag types.

Clearly nations cannot be dated in a precise manner. The periods when the flags appear, however, relate to historical events and circumstances that have much to tell us about the complexity of the nation-building processes. Table 3.2 aligns the symbolic regimes (pre-modern, modern and post-imperial) with flag-types (cross flags, tricolours, heraldic flags and post-historical flags) in accordance with the discussion in Chapter 2. These flag types originate in different periods and are linked by common traditions identified by the designs of successful symbolic codes, the reaction against these, and have become transferred into lasting symbolic institutions. National flags can thus be described as 'graphic demonstrations of political programs' (W. Smith, 1975a) but also as political counter-programmes as they emerged in reaction to their closest preceding symbolism.

(*Type 1*) The retained cross flags are tied to Protestant dissent from papacy and Roman Catholicism in effect becoming symbols of defiance. The Protestant Church developed along national lines in England, Denmark and Sweden as a dissenting religion tied to the monarch as head of the national church. Protestantism came to define these states and their flags and, as a result, expressed such Protestant loyalties through their designs. The growth of the state and the nation also coincided here. Catholicism, as a contrast, is transnational, which would explain why the *many* medieval cross-flags used by Catholic states, some of which also had to overcome bitter religious divisions, did not survive. Most of these Protestant countries are still monarchies and a complete revolution has not taken place, which was a major incentive for the introduction of the tricolours. For example, the Civil War in England, 1642–45 was followed by the Restoration of 1660. (*Type 2*) The tricolours demonstrate a clear entry into modern and secular times by being non-cross flags. The modern tricolours became symbols of revolution against monarchical or religious powers. Vertical tricolours were adopted in France, Russia, Italy, Romania, Ireland, Slovenia and the horizontal tricolours established in Germany, Hungary, Bulgaria, Lithuania, Estonia, Slovakia and Belgium (square).

Table 3.2 Symbolic regimes and flag categories in Europe

Symbolic Regimes	Type 1 Cross flags	Type 2 Tricolours	Type 3 Heraldic flags	Type 4 Post-historical
Pre-1789 Age of pre-modern nations	**Denmark England Scotland Switzerland Sweden Northern Ireland Britain**	The Netherlands Russia	Spain	
1789–1913 Age of modern nations	Greece Finland Norway	**France Belgium Italy Germany Hungary Romania Bulgaria**	Portugal	
Post-1914 (WW1) Age of post-imperial nations	Iceland Faroe Islands	Ireland Lithuania Estonia	**Austria Poland Latvia Czech Republic Slovakia Wales Croatia Slovenia Moldova Albania Ukraine Belarus FYR Macedonia Montenegro Serbia**	Bosnia-Herzegovina Kosovo

Note: This table demonstrates the particular association between flag types and symbolic regimes. The countries in bold highlight this trend and link cross flags to the age of pre-modern nations, tricolours to the age of modern nations and heraldic flags to the age of post-imperial nations. In the case of the last row, the past is embellished and contributes to justifying nation- and state-hood in the present. The post-historical flags constitute illuminating exceptions in this context in their avoidance of corresponding historical and identity-related symbolism.

(*Type 3*) The heraldic flags recycled historical material and staked out claims for independence in wars, against various empires with use of historical devices, colours and emblems often originating in the middle ages or often made in such an image. Above flags of states have been listed but several flags discussed in relation to the Spanish case would belong to this category. (*Type 4*) In sharp contrast to all the other flags, the post-historical and counter-nationalist flags have avoided references to historical identities and potentially divisive narratives pointing solely to the ambitions of the future and, as a symbolic type, have developed in reaction against the claims made by competing heraldic flags. Thus, golden ages, victories, defeats or sacrifices are not always appropriate to draw upon, especially not in nationally or ethnically divided territories. Flag-symbolism, invariably, becomes a challenge as a source of conflict for territories in which history remains undefined or contested. The likeness between the supra-national EU flag and the counter-nationalist flags imposed in Bosnia-Herzegovina and Kosovo is striking in this context. The flags of BiH and Kosovo demonstrate the extent to which flag-related symbolism also reflects new political realities and elite aspirations as these flags have been aligned with ambitions superseding the imagined oneness of nations and dependency on the Centre.

Symbols of conflict: warfare, revolution and independence

Intimately linked to the development of flags and counter flags, as described above, is the role of conflict for flag and nation making. The European flags became attached to their national communities mainly as symbols of warfare, revolution, independence and state reconstitution. Thus, the appearance of the flags is connected to the political context in which they appear as they display through their colours and design claims of lineage, continuity and rights to a designated territory. More specifically, the European flags can be categorized in accordance with their origins as symbols of warfare, revolution, independence or state-reconstitution. These origins are not mutually exclusive.

First, the earliest flags are symbols of warfare (some of which appeared as Cross flags or as naval flags) as in the cases of Denmark, Sweden, England, Switzerland, the Netherlands and Russia. Secondly, the flags of revolutions (and transformations) are those of France, Italy, Germany, Portugal, Spain, and the former Communist countries (variations on the Red Flag for the latter). Thirdly, the flags of independence include those of the Netherlands, Belgium, Greece, Hungary, Finland, Bulgaria, Norway, Ireland, Poland, Lithuania, Estonia, Latvia, Iceland, Croatia, Slovenia, Ukraine and Belarus. Fourthly, several flags appear as flags of state-reconstitution with the formations of unions and with the dissolution of the empires as with the United Kingdom (the Union Jack), Romania, Finland, Austria, the Federal Republic of Yugoslavia,

Czechoslovakia, Germany, Russia, the Czech Republic, Slovakia, Bosnia-Herzegovina and Kosovo.

The role of the flag in politics leads us to consider symbolic discontinuity as a sign of political instability. Flags are introduced and promulgated during, or after, significant national events and are also changed, contested and challenged. The major changes in flag-related symbolism are thus connected to revolutions, occupations, attainment of independence, formation of unions; transformations from monarchies to republics and vice versa; the communist domination and anti-communist transformations; and fascist and anti-fascist transformations. So the changes take place with ruptures between the symbol and the nation.

Nations among other nations – a system of communication

Nationalist symbols such as flags are distinguishable by their particular characteristic as they identify the nation alongside other nations in the international arena. However, differentiation with regards to symbolic form is not maximized through flag designs as there are vast similarities between these. Their standardization expresses the wish to claim a place among other nations and states, especially so in the cases of flags of nations without states.

It is noted that flags have become more embellished with time and that the core-flags utilize less content than their recent equivalents. Colour-combinations and flag designs also take a stance as they are employed to express loyalties and affiliations (but also dissociations) to neighbouring territories or to ideological narratives, for example, in the choice of designs, as with the Scandinavian cross-flags, the adoption of the Tricolour Flags or the flags displaying the Pan-Slavic colours. In terms of colours, a high proportion of the European flags display 'red' originally to symbolize bloodshed in battle, military valour, courage, readiness to sacrifice, revolution, struggle for independence and the necessity to defend the nation from the aggressive ambitions of other nations. Blood-related symbolisms are common and ancient but have retained their hold over the contemporary world and continue to be influential in contexts of religion and culture (Dillistone, 1986). Among the European flags mentioned 34 out of 43 use 'red' on their flags. It is only the flags of Scotland, Sweden, Finland, Greece, Ireland, Estonia, Ukraine, Bosnia-Herzegovina and Kosovo that do not. Many modification has taken place since Weitman noted that, internationally, eight out of ten flags display 'red', which makes this colour by far the most frequently utilized colour in national flags (Weitman, 1973). However, the latter still stands for Europe. The second most used colour is 'white' and conveys, not surprisingly, the opposite message of peace. 'White' appears on 30 out of 43 flags in Europe and is officially attributed to purity and peace but also stands for justice, truth, unity, prosperity or even the national landscape in the case of Slovenia's 'snowy peaks'. In the tricolour flag of the Republic of Ireland (green, white, orange), green is for Catholics, orange for Protestants and 'white' is for the wish for peace between them (W. Smith, 1975a). In this fashion, national flags provide information about the properties of the nation-state and their engagement in self-advertising, of presence, uniqueness and connectedness. Notably, half of the European nations display both 'red' and 'white' on their flags (21 out of 43) and as has been noted: 'It is as though, having rattled their sabers [sic] to show how much violence they are capable of unleashing, nations now hasten to let it be known that they really are, by nature, peaceful, friendly, oozing with good will' (Weitman, 1973, p. 353).

Successful flags and the politics of identity

It is the self-referential quality of flags that make them influential symbols. This is enforced by the ritual contexts in which flags are displayed and imbued with meanings elevating them as objects of self-worship. The ritual contexts in which flags appear provide them with an 'active' role: 'there is something fascinating in the seemingly endless and unassisted movement of a flag in the wind, much as there is something fascinating in the perpetual motion of flames and of ocean waves' (Weitman, 1973, p. 336). In Durkheimian terminology, a national flag is a reality *sui generis* and the flag is flown above us, forcing us to look up, which is further enhanced by pledges of allegiance and salutes to the flag. National ceremonies in which flags are used are especially effective as they involve motion and participation. The 'constant flaggings ensure that, whatever else is forgotten in a world of information overload, we do not forget our homelands [...] It is a form of life in which "we" are constantly invited to relax, at home, within the homeland's borders. This form of life is the national identity, which is being renewed continually, with its dangerous potentials appearing so harmlessly homely' (Billig, 1995, p. 127).

Since flags are protected by law against violation they can also be turned into powerful political tools for elites as well as peoples. Precisely because flags are instruments of state control they are also burned,

92 *Symbols of Nations and Nationalism*

defaced, corrupted or hung upside down in order to insult and protest against authority since an insult to the flag has transcendent meaning as an insult to the nation and its representatives. The flag used as a counter-instrument makes it a double-edged political tool against official or dominant views of the nation. The idea that the flag can be desecrated implies a number of things. The flag's relationship to the nation guides the state's treatment of it: when the flag is treated as an object worthy of worship and respect so will its associations.

The flags of Europe express different narratives some of which survived from the age of pre-modern nations, whereas others were fought over in revolutions, independence struggles and new state-formations. Because the Golden Age is a matter of interpretation and definition, their symbolic expressions may be contested and even divisive as their meanings are challenged. National flags may contribute to nation building and motivate action if they strike a carefully cultivated chord with populations. In the many adoptions and re-adoptions of flags accounted for in this book it is difficult to reach any other conclusion than that successful flags remain meaningful 'through the successful communication of their message' (Cerulo, 1995, p. 33), a message embellished and appropriated by national elites over time.

Flags in the capacity of political symbols have come to indicate some achieved success in the politicization of identities. Leaving aside, for a moment, nations and states, flags have been created for groups against the traditional national imagery as with the flags of Greenland (1985) and the Sami people (1986) which steered away from any form of heraldic tradition as well as the Scandinavian cross designs. These flags thus claim to have withstood the forces of imperialism. The symbolism of these flags is of *timeless* links to nature, whereas the majority of

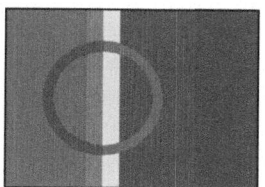 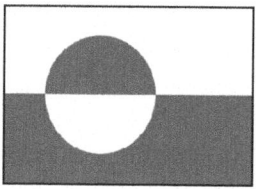 

Figure 3.9 Flagging identity beyond traditional territories
Note: The Sami flag on the left (red, blue, green and yellow) and the Greenland flag in the middle (red and white) are examples of timeless designs as is the Rainbow flag (red, orange, yellow, green, blue, purple) on the right.
Sources: (FOTW, 2009d, 2009f). Flag images courtesy of (FOTW, 2010a, 2010c) (FOTW, 2010b).

European flags usually refer to a point of departure and a significant past. The colours of the Sami flag are said to constitute traditional Sami colours, whereas the design with the half rings of blue and red represent the moon and the sun, also seen in the flag of Greenland (see Figure 3.9).

The evolving nature of flag-related symbolism confirms that flags are effective symbols in the politicization of identities also seen in the development of the Rainbow flag (1978) and corresponding Gay Pride festivals. This flag is yet another example of the reinvention of a political symbol to increase awareness within and without, here using the revolutionary stripes echoing values of equality, liberty and diversity with a multitude of colours. In these terms, flags such as these raise awareness of and represent groups spread over many nations.

4
National Days in Nation Building: Similarities and Differences

National days constitute a comparatively younger stratum of the nation. Whereas flags have been used to signal the presence of states and nations among other states and nations for some time, the nature of the national day is different as the in-group constitutes the focus for its celebrations, although 'others' and 'enemies' are much part of celebratory origins and establishment. National days enact institutionalized notions of *sameness* and *oneness* and contribute to making nations visible and are in this capacity intimately linked with nationalism. As part of official historical narratives appropriated by national elites, national days are usually officially recognized events that celebrate founding myths. As such they are socio-political in content and although they can appear as consensual they are often outcomes of long periods of struggle and conflict between various elites or between elites and peoples. In fact, little remains uncontroversial about national celebrations and commemorations and their (ongoing) formations, despite honouring events of an often distant past. Former British Prime Minister Gordon Brown learned this the hard way after he forgot to bow placing the wreath at the Cenotaph in honour of the fallen soldiers on Remembrance Sunday in London in 2009. In the following two chapters we trace the development of national days, their established patterns and their contributions to nation building.

Ceremonial statistics: national days and overview

The affinity between the nation and the state produced a new type of official festivity. As a rule, national and state elements of the national day are conflated and express official narratives. We are concerned either with the day recognized as the national day or, if there is no such officially recognized day, with the day operating as one, in which *one* national memory connected to *one* dominant culture is promoted. European national celebrations are not identical, but share common characteristics and general features. Some nations celebrate several days in honour of the nation, one of which is usually the paramount national day. This is not always the one acknowledged by the state. It is also a misconception that national days must be celebratory, as with the British Remembrance Sunday, which is a commemorative occasion but the only day honoured in all the nations within Britain.

National days must be explored systematically in order to form an understanding of *national day design*. First, we need information about the event that is being honoured and relate this to the socio-political context in which it emerged as a national narrative. National days tend to celebrate historic events related to the foundation of the state, such as the signing of a constitution, the beginning of independence or the proclamation of a republic. Secondly, ceremonial choreography, character and participation must be assessed. Who are the participants? Are they civilians or do they mainly represent the state or the military? Thirdly, is the national day a popular mass-participatory event, or is it mainly marked by elite participation? Fourthly, what does the use of national symbols tell us about the 'shortcuts to nationhood' used in the ceremonial context? The use of rallying symbols is, as a rule, used to highlight the nation in a varied manner and to promote national pride such as with the waving of national flags, the singing national anthems, and the wearing of specific costumes and other signs of membership. Music constitutes an integral part of choreography and design as it sets the tone, whether provided by military units, massed bands or individuals. Procession or parades – military or civilian – are also central features of national celebrations. Ceremonial routes constitute ways in which historical claims to grandeur, glory, loss and sacrifice are integrated into the present and materialized in architecture and monumentality, and as such connected to the design of the national day. Finally, most national days have been declared public holidays and are free from work but the degree of state sponsorship varies. With these questions in mind, some key features of national days can be identified at the outset. *National days honour, as a rule, founding myths and official national narratives that glorify nationhood in terms of oneness. National days are designed in such a way that they perpetuate notions of sameness and of a shared experience.* As will be demonstrated, the degree of success with reference to the latter varies.

National days emerged with the age of nationalism and the majority appeared during the 1800s and 1900s and were formalized in the 1900s.

96 *Symbols of Nations and Nationalism*

Exploring their origin and identifying dates of first celebrations, official adoptions and formal establishments lead us to events of national assertion. Few nations have uninterrupted celebrations and development of their current national day. Ireland, Greece, Denmark, Sweden, Switzerland and Britain are exceptions to this rule, some of which have national days that were adopted relatively late and some of which, in turn, are not characterized by mass-participation. Considering the role of national days in justifying political regimes, it is duly noted that national days are altered in similar fashion to national flags; many were altered during the twentieth century and have a relatively recent date of institution signalling interruption in sovereignty or political repositioning. The current national days in Europe are categorized below in chronological order according to their appearance. The dates provided in the tables below are approximate dates but demonstrate ultimately that (re)establishing national days are complicated and contested affairs.

National days with pre-modern origins

National days with pre-modern origins were originally religious holidays that either survived into modern times or were combined with national days or transformed into national holidays, notably in the cases of Ireland, Hungary and Spain (see Table 4.1). The annual saint days provided a ceremonial prototype for national days as these were combined with national calendars. These turned into nationalized religious holidays or religious holidays transformed into national civic holidays generally much later on. As an example, the cult of St Patrick in Ireland has been dated to the eleventh century. These religious celebrations turned, in time, into a St Patrick's Day (17 March) aided by the resistance to British rule. It has been described as taking off as a national holiday after Irish independence, one of the first large parades was arranged in 1931. In fact, the first parades were arranged outside Ireland by the Irish diaspora in the United States (Freeman, 2004; Hopkin, 1989; McCormack, 2000; RandomHistory, 2010; Nagle, 2005). Significantly, St Patrick's Day was first promoted during the early nineteenth century to bridge religious cleavage and remained a religious holiday until the 1970s. However, the Day, described as 'shared' between Catholics, nationalists, Protestants and unionists, is not characterized by consensus as clashing narratives are promoted. The Day became a source of conflict and exclusion already in the 1960s, triggered by the prohibition of Irish nationalist symbols in Northern Ireland, which included the ban on Patrick's Day parades because of the nationalist symbols

Table 4.1 National days with pre-modern origins

Country	Name of day	Dates*
Ireland (Northern Ireland)	St Patrick	(11th c. religious) 1922–31
Hungary	St Stephen	(1038, 1100 religious) 1764–1848, (1848) 1860–91 (1948–56) *1991*
Scotland	St Andrew	1320, *1687 Order of Thistle*, 2007
England	St George	*1348 Order of the Garter*
Wales	St David	12th c. 18th c. *2000 (Welsh Assembly)*
Portugal	Dia de Portugal, de Camões e das Comunidades Portuguesas	1595, 1880, *1910*, 1933–74, *1978, 1982*
Spain	Día de la Hispanidad, combined national day in honour of Virgin Mary and Columbus discovery	1613 (Virgin of El Pilar), 1892 (Columbus Anniversary), 1913, *1918*, *1958, 1982, 1987*

Note: * Dates are subject to availability and interpretation and presented in the following order: date of first claimed origin followed by any periods not officially recognized/celebrated (in parentheses) and/or the year established by decree or law in *italics* if available.

used in these (Nagle and Clany, 2011). The related saints' days of Scotland, England and Wales are explored in the case study on Britain below.

In turn, St Stephen's Day in Hungary (20 August), originally named after the monarch and after canonization commemorated as a saint, is celebrated today as the founder of the Hungarian State. As a celebration it was acknowledged as early as 1038 and celebrated from about 1100 onwards when the Hungarian kings held royal assizes by listening to complaints from their subjects. The celebrations developed out of the assemblies that used to gather annually to pay homage to St Stephen. The continuity claimed with reference to this national day must thus be questioned as St Stephen's Day was abolished following the reforms of Pope Benedict XIV (1675–1758) but re-appeared and decreed a holiday by Empress Maria Teresa in 1764 when the Order of St Stephen was founded. It remained an official day until the Revolution of 1848 when it was abolished again. It re-emerged as an act of defiance in 1860 and was declared a national day in 1891. The communist regime after the Second World War again abolished St Stephen's Day when it was known as Constitution Day from 1950. St Stephen's Day was officially adopted as the national day in 1991 and in line with its origins a church service is given in honour of St Stephen all over Hungary on this day (Ministry of Foreign Affairs, 1992, 1996; Morgan, 1993; Osvalds, 1996; Santarsieri, 2004).

Portugal Day (10 June), is a tribute to the national poet Luís Vaz de Camões (died 10 June, 1580) who wrote the epic description of Vasco da Gama's voyage to India (*Os Lusíadas*). As with many celebrations of ancient statures it is claimed to have been honoured in 1595; however, the transformation into Portugal Day with celebrations of the Portuguese communities internationally took place in modern times. It was first celebrated in 1880 but emerged as national festival first from 1933 onwards. The republic of 1910 established the national holidays they found ideologically aligned and abolished a number of religious holidays. During 1933-74, and with the formation of the new state, the national day become known as the Day of the Portuguese Race and 10 June was understood as a strategically close to the religious festival of St Anthony on 13 June. Portugal Day has been celebrated on different dates over time and with different emphasis. The current date (10 June) was re-established in 1978 as the original *Dia de Camões* was declared a public holiday in 1982 (Costa, 2004; Cravo, 2000; Guerra, 1999).

The Spanish national day (12 October) constitutes an interesting example of the merging of the national and religious calendars and the combination of two separate national holidays. The celebrations in honour of the Virgin Mary (Virgin of El Pilar) constitute one of many devotions to the Virgin. The cult of the Virgin in Saragossa honoured on 12 October was developed in the context of the Counter-Reformation and as such institutionalized by the Council of Saragossa in 1613 and after 1640 worshipped outside this area. During the twentieth century the Virgin became patron of the Hispanidad and, from 1913, also of the Civil Guard (Guardia Civil, created in 1855) (Alvarez Junco, 2001; Barrachina, 2000; Serrano, 1999; Vernet i Llobet, 2003). Thus, 12 October was also the date chosen for the celebrations of the fourth centenary of Columbus's arrival in the Americas in 1892. The Day was re-launched in 1913 and recognized as Fiesta de la Raza (Day of the Spanish Race) in 1918, a description that changed in 1958 and again in 1982 but identified as the national day in 1987. As a national day it was politicized in the context of the Civil War and Francoism (Cenarro Lagunas, 1997; Humlebaek, 2003, 2004) and, with the latter in mind, is a not uncontroversial day in all parts of the Spanish state.

Modern national days, republics and constitutions

National days that originated in the modern period reflect the justifications of nationalisms and claimed rights associated with the historic births of nations and independent rule in the present. These days provided at the outset a comparatively secular framework for the celebrations (see Table 4.2). The era of modern nationalism commenced with the early celebrations of Bastille Day (14 July) in France, originally commemorating the storming of the Bastille in 1789, the Revolution that followed and the forming of the first Republic. As such it was first celebrated in 1790 and was honoured as a national holiday in 1792 but did not turn into a mass-celebration before it had been drained of its turbulent historical references in the 1880s (see case study below).

Several countries celebrate their constitutional frameworks as a function of independence or state (re)constitution as seen below in Poland, Norway, Denmark, Switzerland and Sweden. The Polish case is representative of the many countries that have experienced significant changes in their symbolism following the territorial acquisitions of the European empires and those during the First and Second World Wars. Russia, Austria and Prussia partitioned Poland in 1772. The Constitution was proclaimed on 3 May 1791 and followed by celebrations in 1791–92.

Table 4.2 National days and the age of nationalism

Nation	Name of national day	Dates*
France	Bastille Day, Republic	1790–92, 1872, *1880*
Poland	National (Constitution) Day	1791–92, *1918* (1939–56) 1956
Norway	Constitution Day	1827 (WW2) *1905*
Greece	Independence Day (Feast of Annunciation)	*1838*
Denmark	Constitution Day	*1849* (WW2)
Bulgaria	Liberation Day	1878 (1944–89) *1990*
Belgium	Independence Day	*1890* (WW1) (WW2)
Netherlands	Queen's Day	*1891* (WW2)
Switzerland	Confederation	*1891*
Sweden	(National) Day of the Swedish Flag Constitutional reform and Gustav Vasa's accession to the throne	1893, 1916, *1983, 2005*

Note: *Dates are subject to availability and interpretation and are presented in the following order: first claimed to have originated followed by any periods not officially recognized/celebrated (in parentheses). The year established by decree or law in *italics* if available.

The constitution was abolished again in 1792 and the second partition, conducted by Russia and Prussia, took place in 1793. The third partition of Poland took place in 1795. Polish sovereignty was thus declared again in 1918. Constitution Day was officially re-adopted in 1918 with Polish independence but celebrations were forbidden during the Second World War and the Communist era and were invoked after the revolt of 1956. During the time of the latter the celebrations of 1 May constituted a main holiday. Today, there are two other significant public and national holidays, namely Independence Day (11 November), in honour of 1918, and the Anniversary of the Battle of Warsaw (15 August 1920), commemorating Polish victory over Russia. The latter is celebrated with large military parades and also referred to as Army Day (Embassy of the Republic of Poland, 2004; Polish Cultural Institute, 1974; Polish Government Official Website, 2004; Zahorski, 1991).

Constitution Day was celebrated in Norway long before the other Scandinavian countries attempted to create similar events (see case study below). Denmark commemorates becoming a Constitutional Monarchy on 5 June 1849 (Adriansen, 2003), whereas Sweden's national day – originally known as Day of the Swedish Flag (6 June) – ambivalently celebrates the constitutional reform of 1809 as well as the election of Gustav Vasa as king in 1523. First celebrated in 1893 and adopted as a national day in 1983, 6 June became a public holiday only in 2005 (Magnergård, 2003; Olsson, 2002; Östros, 2004) at a time when most other nations had had a recognized national day for some time.

The Swiss also celebrate a date from an ancient past and that which is perceived of as the beginning of the original Confederation – Die Ur-Kantone – in 1291. The first celebration, however, was held in 1891 to commemorate the 600th anniversary of that which was claimed as the origin of the Confederation (Santschi, 1991; Schneiter, 2004; Zimmer, 1999). Emerging at a similar time is Liberation Day (3 March) in Bulgaria, first celebrated in 1880 as the Day of the Ascension of Emperor Alexander II, but since 1888 as the Day of Liberation from Ottoman rule. Under Todor Zhivkov (1954–89), Bulgaria followed the cycle of Communist celebrations and liberation from Nazi rule was celebrated (9 September). The Bulgarian parliament reclaimed 3 March as a public holiday in 1990.

National days emerging in the age of modern nationalism are usually narrated around revolutions, independence and liberation. Here, the Greek, Belgian and Dutch national days have a slightly different focus. Independence Day in Greece (25 March) combined from the outset the national and religious agendas as the Bishop Germanos of

Patras was connected to raising the Greek flag of resistance against the Ottomans in 1821, later identified as the beginning of the war of independence. The Decree on Independence Day was signed by King Otto in 1838 and the first celebration took place in 1838. The Church plays a central role here as the Feast of the Annunciation is also celebrated on the same day (25 March) with colourful religious ceremonies (Ross, 1999a, p. 3, 1999b). The Belgian Independence Day (21 July), established in 1890, also has an indirect focus as it officially commemorates the date when the first Belgian monarch, Leopold I, swore the oath of allegiance to the Constitution in 1831 and thereby formalized the state of Belgium with independence from the Netherlands. Adding to the competition of national days in Belgium, the Flemish community celebrates Flanders Day (11 July) and the victory of the Battle of Golden Spurs in 1302 whereas the French community celebrates Wallon Day (Fête de la Communauté française, 27 September) (Belgian Information Service, 2005; Devoldere, 2005; Dimrilieri, 2005; Embassy of Belgium, 2004; Meyeux, 2005; Site officiel du Parlement de la Communauté Française, 2004). In the neighbouring Netherlands, the popular Queen's Day (Koninginnedag, 30 April) stands out as a national holiday emerging towards the end of the nineteenth century but remaining royal in its focus. Queen Wilhelmina (reigned, 1890–48) celebrated her official birthday on this date (Queen Wilhelmina from 1891, Queen Juliana from 1949, and Queen Beatrix since 1980). Queen Beatrix reaffirmed 30 April as Queen's Day to honour her mother as she was installed as queen on this date (Netherlands Government National Archief, 2004; Royal Netherlands Embassy, 2004). Celebrations on 30 April could of course be understood as a highly strategic date as the day after, 1 May, was emerging as a political day of reform and protest.

Post-imperial national days and independence

As seen in Table 4.3 below, considerable change has taken place with reference to the post-imperial national days established after the First World War. Interruptions in celebrations happened, as a rule, during the Communist and Nazi occupations. Many of the former Central and Eastern European countries under Communist rule followed the cycle of Communist celebrations including Liberation Day or Victory Day (liberation from and victory over Nazism or Fascism), Constitution Day (new constitutions), May Day or Labour Day. Independence, as may be expected, is a main theme and celebrated in Finland, Lithuania, Estonia, Iceland, Slovenia, Ukraine, Macedonia, Albania and Belarus.

102 *Symbols of Nations and Nationalism*

Table 4.3 National days and the age of post-imperial nations

Nation	Name of national day	Dates*
Finland	Independence Day	*1917, 1937*
Lithuania	Independence Day	1918 (WW2) *1990*
Estonia	Independence Day	1918 (WW2) *1989*
Latvia	National Day	1918 (WW2) *1990*
Britain	Remembrance Sunday	*1919*
Czech Republic	National/ Statehood Day	1919 (WW2) (1948–89) *1989, 2000*
Iceland	(National) Independence Day	*1945, 1971*
Italy	Republic Day	*1946, 2003*
Faroe Island	St Olav Day/Opening of Parliament	1948
Austria	National Day of the Austrian Flag	*1955, 1967*
Romania	National Day	*1918* (1944–89) *1989*
Belarus	Independence Liberation Day	1944, 1991, *1995*
Germany	Unification Day	*1990*
Slovenia	Independence / Statehood Day	*1991*
Ukraine	Independence Day	*1991*
Macedonia FYROM	Independence Day	*1992*
Slovakia	Constitution Day	*1992*
Moldova	Independence Day	*1991–92*
Albania	Independence Day	(1912) *1991–92*
Croatia	Statehood Day	(1991) *2003*
Russia	Russia Day/Independence Day	(1991) *2004*
Serbia	Constitution Day	*1992, 2004, 2007*
Montenegro	Independence Day	*2004, 2007*
Kosovo	Independence Day	2008
BiH	*In process*	–

Note: * Dates are subject to availability and interpretation and presented in the following order: year of the first celebration/commemoration, followed by any periods not officially recognized/celebrated (in parentheses) and/or the year established by decree or law in *italics* if available.

In Finland, national heroes and champions of Finnish national identity, such as Runeberg, Lönnrot (compiler of the *Kalevala*) and Snellman, were the focus for the ethno-cultural celebrations that took place before independence from Russia and the founding of the Republic in 1917 (6 December). Similarly, the Baltic States, as expected, commemorate independence after 1918: independence and restoration of the Lithuanian State (16 February); the proclamation of the Republic of Estonia (24 February); and the restoration of the sovereign power of Latvia (18 November). These days were later re-adopted in Estonia in 1989 and in Lithuania and Estonia in 1990 (Karjalainen, 1997, 2004; Pellinen, 2004). The Czech Republic, Croatia and Slovenia honour Statehood Day and celebrate their states' challenges throughout history. For example, the Czech Republic used to commemorate the founding of the Republic (28 October 1918) after the fall of the Austro-Hungarian Empire but this was forbidden during 1939–44 and was later turned into the Day of Nationalization (1948–89) during the Communist era, a period when Victory Day (9 May) commemorated the liberation from Nazi rule and the end of the Second World War. The celebrations of 28 October were reinstated in 1989 and have been a public holiday since 2000 (Czech Republic Official Website, 2004; Frous, 2004; Parliament of the Czech Republic, 1992). Likewise, the Second Austrian Republic of 1955 began celebrating the Day of the Austrian flag and sovereignty (26 October) and it became a public holiday in 1967. Previously, Austria's national days reflected the pursuits of the ruling regimes. Thus the birthday of the Emperor Franz Joseph (18 August) had been celebrated from 1867 onwards, Republic Day from 1918 (12 November) and Constitution Day (1 May) from 1932 onwards. In 1934, 1 May became Labour Day, Youth's Day and Mother's Day and in the Nazi era, from 1938 onwards, the National Day of the German People (Beaufort-Spontin, 2004; Bichler, 2004; Federal Ministry for Education and Cultural Affairs, 1990; Virtual Vienna, 2004).

There is much to say about the long list of national days that emerged and/or re-emerged after the First World War in the twentieth and the twenty-first centuries. A few interesting examples can be mentioned in terms of Independence Day in Montenegro (13 July) that commemorates the date of the Berlin Congress recognition of Montenegro in 1878, as well as the uprising against Nazi occupiers in 1941, the latter a theme that constituted a central part of the cycle of communist celebrations. In Kosovo and Bosnia-Herzegovina, contrasting developments as regards their national days are reported. In Kosovo all parties, apart from representatives of the Serbian community, supported the establishment of Independence Day (17 February) in 2008, a day emerging as a day of celebrations. The situation has been described as being characterized by ever-declining Serb protests on Independence Day (Krasniqi, 2010). Alongside Independence Day, specific memorial days are commemorated among Kosovo's ethno-national communities (Krasniqi, 2010). In contrast, and in view of the complicated process of agreeing on a flag for Bosnia-Herzegovina (1992–98) and the many years (1999–2009) it

104 *Symbols of Nations and Nationalism*

took to find suitable words for the national anthem, it was inevitable that it would be even more problematic to agree on a narrative for a national day of celebration. At the time of writing, a national day for Bosnia Herzegovina is subject for debate in parliament and has not been agreed upon (Turajlac, 2010). Bosnia-Herzegovina is thus the only country in Europe that does not have a national day, something which highlights its status as a political symbol with divisive propensities and also ongoing internal disunity. Thus the national day transpired as a proxy for a number of related issues with regards to membership and territory. We turn now to three illuminating case studies that describe the role of the national day in nation building.

National days and nation building: case studies

In order to explore in detail the contribution of national symbols to nation building and the symbolic layering of nations (national days and anthems usually follow the institutionalization of flags) we turn to the three significant cases of national day design and remember that the cases previously discussed briefly hide similarly interesting stories of nation narration through national days and their design. The military national day of France (Bastille Day on 14 July), the popular celebration of Norwegian national identity (Constitution Day on 17 May) and the commemoration of the fallen (Remembrance Sunday on 11 November) in Britain.[1] These cases chosen for closer examination have become part of different nation-building strategies and represent various ceremonial types and designs. In terms of the official celebrations, the military French Bastille Day, the child-oriented and joyful Norwegian Day and the sombre British commemoration of the fallen of Remembrance Sunday constitute sharp contrasts.

Bastille Day or 14 July in France

The reference to Bastille Day is not used in France, where the national day is described by its date 14 July (Fête Nationale). The Bastille, state prison and symbol of the *Ancien Régime* and arbitrary rule was stormed on 14 July 1789. The Bastille has since become a symbol of the Republic and of liberty, democracy and equality. For the anniversary in 1790, citizens and delegates arrived from all over France to proclaim their allegiance to the new Republic by their participation in the Fête de la Fédération as it was first called. The cult around 14 July was the first true celebration of modern France and the need to commemorate the Republic was intimately linked with justifying the break with the past. A number of ceremonial activities and public events were adopted by the Republic in order to justify its existence and course of direction but these were ultimately unsuccessful in its attempt to create a lasting revolutionary calendar (Ozouf, 1988). Bastille Day is an exception, but it took a hundred years before it became a mass celebration. As an official national holiday of the Republic, 14 July was reinvented in 1880 and celebrated in memory of the capture of the Bastille and the Fête de la Fédération (1790) (Ministère de la Défense de France, 2002b). At this time, the Day was national and ecumenical in character, which facilitated the shift of attention away from the violent reality of 14 July in 1789 and the Revolution in general. Thus, the sceptics of the Republic were reassured at little cost to the republicans and Bastille Day was turned from a *dies irae* to mass national holiday (Amalvi, 1996).

It was the Third Republic that made Bastille Day an official feature of the public calendar (1880) and a day that glorified and defined the rebirth of France in increasingly nationalist times which coincided with rivalry over colonies in Africa. Several dates were considered in the 1870s before the decision was reached that 14 July was the most appropriate revolutionary event to celebrate as it capitalized on the rupture with the *Ancien Régime*. The choice of 14 July remained contested. For the enemies of the Third Republic the day remained a model of 'revolutionary saturnalia' that reminded of the bloody reality of the Revolution:

> Each party does what it can. Christianity celebrates the holidays of its God, its heroes, its saints, and its martyrs; the monarchy had its splendid national calendar: Tolbiac, Bouvines, Taillebourg, Marignano, Arques, Ivry, Rocroi, Fontenoy, Marengo, Austerlitz, Jena, Algiers, Sebastopol, Magenta. *The Republic celebrates cowardice, treason, and murder.* (Amalvi, 1996, p. 129) (Emphasis added)

In effect the Republic institutionalized a practice that already existed, as the Republicans had taken up these celebrations again in 1872 in more public form, and a link to the ideals of the first Republic thereby could be established. Moreover, the heroic capture of the Bastille, *the* symbol of tyranny, moved references away from the 'terror' that followed the Revolution. The only Day that ever rivalled the celebrations on 14 July was Armistice Day in 1918 (11 November) which remembered the war dead. The Remembrance ceremony in 1920 had been especially significant commemorating the second anniversary of victory in 1918 and the fiftieth of the founding of the Third Republic (a direct consequence of the French defeat in 1870) (Inglis, 1993, pp. 7–31). The Unknown Soldier was hereby (re)buried at the Arc de Triomphe in the ceremony on 11 November 1920 with the inscription *Ici repose un soldat français mort pour la patrie*. In this way the Arch gained much significance as a focal point for the nation's sacrifices adding to this the eternal Flame of Remembrance that was introduced in 1923. Bastille Day regained its place as the primary national holiday as the cult of the Fallen in effect was integrated in the 14 July celebrations. Already in 1919 a temporary Cenotaph had been raised inside the Arc de Triomphe and was honoured by the military parade passing the Arch on 14 July (Inglis, 1993, pp. 14, 23–4). Thus, Bastille Day from this perspective is the result of a successful combination of 14 July and 11 November, two poignant national ceremonies clearly outlining the boundaries of sacrifice and heroism. Armistice Day (1918, on 11 November) and Victory Day (VE Day, Victory in Europe, 1945, 8 May) are also linked to the nexus of politicized and militarized commemorations in France.

The military parade

The 14 July celebrations are divided into two different parts: the morning, which is characterized by official ceremonies such as the military parade in central Paris, and the afternoon by various forms of entertainment, sports and festive activities. The latter is followed by festivals, neighbourhood dances and fireworks all over France. In terms of the official national day ceremonies the capital celebration in Paris, the military procession, is central to 14 July. The parade commences at the Arc de Triomphe surrounded by Haussmann's boulevards, and continues down the Avenue Champs-Élysées and reaches the Place de la Concorde (see Illustrations 4.1 and 4.2). For the significance of the ceremonial route see Chapter 5. Briefly, the Arc de Triomphe was commissioned by Napoleon in 1806 in honour of major victories during the Revolutionary and Napoleonic periods but was transformed to commemorate the fallen after 1830, enforced by the installation of the Tomb of the Unknown Soldier in 1919. The Arc thus provides a significant backdrop of French military success and sacrifice for the ceremony and spectators are provided with a historic frame of grandeur linked to its contemporary equivalent in French national defence. Thus the survey of military strength includes mounted decorated guards as well as modern artillery and transport. Geometry is central and the procession is carried out with impeccable precision. The level of organization is key, as may be seen in a typical programme: troops and motorized vehicles are in position (09.10) and inspected by the officers commanding the parade (09.20). The detachments of honour of the Republican Guard are in position (09.45). The President of the Republic arrives at Place de l'Étoile to review the troops before being escorted in an open car to

Illustration 4.1 Arc de Triomphe, flypast Champs-Élysées, Bastille Day, Paris
Jets fly over Paris for the military parade on Bastille Day, leaving blue-white-red vapour trails. Photo courtesy of Ammar Abd Rabbo (2008), Balkispress, France.

Illustration 4.2 The military procession, Place de la Concorde, Bastille Day in Paris
All military units divide as they approach the Presidential Podium located in the middle of the Place de la Concorde. The President, with honorary guests, follows the military procession together with millions of television viewers. Photograph courtesy of Ammar Abd Rabbo (2008), Balkispress, France.

Place de la Concorde (10.00). The latter is followed by musical entertainment (10.15) by various units (10.20). The military parade commences with a fly-past (10.30) followed by foot soldiers (10.35), police officers on motorbikes, an aerial parade of army light aircraft and a parade of armoured-vehicle troops (11.00). A fly-past and parade of mounted troops (11.25) conclude the ceremony before the departure of the President of the Republic (11.35) (Ministère de la Défense de France, 2002a, 2002b; Week's Newsflash, 2004).

As the fly-past commences the 14 July parade, jets fly over Paris leaving vapour trails of blue, white and red. The President travels in an open car from the Arc de Triomphe, the Champs-Élysées to the Place de la Concorde and the presidential podium. He is met by the Prime Minister and the Military Governor of Paris; the national anthem is played with the Republican Guard standing to attention. The flag, the anthem and the honorary companies of the infantry are national elements of honour bestowed on the President. The 'presentation of the colours' was introduced once 14 July had been adopted officially in 1880 and technically consists of the national flag being raised as the President reviews the military unit, while music is played. As an tribute to the guest of honour, a guest detachment opens the military parade. For instance, a Spanish detachment began the parade in 2001 and, in 2009, 400 soldiers from the Indian armed forces led the parade to the backdrop of concert music. This was followed by 4100 French military personnel including detachments of officers and soldiers from the army, the navy, the marines, the air force, special squads (such as the paratroopers), the Gendarmerie and other units, about 300 military vehicles, 83 motorbikes, 280 horses, 68 planes and 37 helicopters (Joshi, 14 July 2009). A final fly-past follows as does a parade of mounted troops, the French Guard, on horse and in ceremonial dress, accompanied by fanfares and music from military bands, constituting the Grand Finale (see Illustration 4.1).

One of the last detachments on foot is in this context remarkable, namely the Foreign Legion. The Foreign Legion was created by Louis Philippe in 1831 and took part in the conquest of Algeria. Its symbol – the Legion Flag – is associated with the battle of Puebla in Mexico in 1863 when three officers and 62 legionnaires resisted 2000 Mexican soldiers and has thus remained a symbol of missions carried out to the bitter end. The symbol of the battle of Puebla therefore adorns every Legion flag. The special uniforms of the Legionnaires and their solemn marching-pace in parades, which is much slower than any other unit – 88 steps a minute (La marche Le Boudin), compared with the normal marching-speed of 115 steps a minute for all other units – have given them with a special place in the parade. Within the Legion, the pioneers, the Sappers, march at the comparatively majestic speed of 80 steps a minute (La marche de la Légion étrangère) in order to emphasize their significance (ENDirect, 2009; Ministère de la Défense de France, 1992). This is further highlighted by their uniform: a leather apron and the 'path-breaking' axe. Controversially, the Foreign Legion carries foreign insignia captured in battle, which precede the different units within the Legion (TV5 Monde, Juli 2007). One description of the legionnaires defines them as 'volunteers of any nationality, race or creed, always ready to serve France [...] Foreigners by birth, the legionnaires have become Frenchmen by the blood they have spilled' (French Foreign Legion: What is the Foreign Legion, 2010).

Guests of Honour and the politics of recognition
The meaning of Bastille Day is increased by the presence of foreign Heads of State and Governments (Wray, 14 July 2008) and belongs clearly to the politics of recognition, reconciliation and state business. The politics of bestowing honour has developed along complex lines in what today constitutes a hierarchy of guests with terms such as Chief Guest of Honour and Guest of Honour, etc. The choice of Guest of Honour is also followed intently and has been known to be controversial as when President Francois Mitterrand decided to invite Chancellor Helmut Kohl in 1994 together with members of the Euro Corps, the mainly German and French force in Strasbourg, to participate in the parade with soldiers from Belgium, Luxembourg and Spain. Instead of interpreting this as part of a wider reconciliation process, French newspapers wrote that German troops would once again march on the Champs-Élysées as the international press noted that 'Bonn's troops drum up storm for Bastille Day' (Nundy, 13 July 1994). In clear contrast to such ambitions of reconciliation, Bastille Day of 2000 evoked the victory of the First World War and reproduced the grand Victory Parade of 1919, an hour long itinerary which included Allied troops. The following year, in 2001, the King of Spain was guest of honour at Place de la Concorde. One could imagine this to be somewhat sensitive, considering that the honorary delegation is positioned close to the place that was once the stage for the guillotine and the decapitations of the aristocracy, a matter seemingly uncontroversial.

The President of Syria, Bashar al-Assad was together with the United Nations itself guests of honour in 2008 when the UN flag presided with the French Tricolour over the parade (FOTW, 2009c; Penketh, 22 August 2008). In 2009, the Prime Minister of India, Manmohan Singh, was Chief Guest of Honour, together with Horst Koehler, the first German President ever to be invited to Bastille Day (DeutscheWelle, 2009). At the

110 *Symbols of Nations and Nationalism*

head of the 400 Indian soldiers leading the parade down the Champs-Élysées was the prestigious Maratha Infantry Brigade described as the oldest Indian regiment with 240 years of illustrious history, recognized for their influence in North Africa and in Italy during the Second World War (France 24, 12 July 2009). As reported, state business is part of the agenda and the signed arms deals between France and India and, on this occasion, the Indian wish to purchase 126 French fighter jets (DD News (Doordarshan News), 2009) may allegedly have influenced the proceedings. The French Prime Minister, Nicolas Sarkozy, later received an invitation to attend India's Republic Day. The latter suggests that national day design contributes to showcasing and promoting technological sophistication and, although the national day is perceived as a celebration of national virtues, it may be turned into a national veranda for the armed business of states. Bastille Day in 2010 saw the military parade open with troops from 13 of the former sub-Saharan colonies, 50 years after having achieved independence, and their Heads of State, for example of Burkina Faso, Cameroon, Congo, Madagascar and Senegal, presiding as Guests of Honour (ENDirect, 2010a, 2010b). Particular ceremonial care was taken with regards to the flags of the former colonies which were recognized in an especially designed ceremony alongside the French Tricolour.

Ceremonial structures, foci and meanings

In terms of symbolic embellishment we find thousands of Tricolours on display. One extremely large Tricolour hangs from the vaulted ceiling of the Arc on all national holidays and state occasions and four large Tricolours surround the Arc and in this manner highlight it as a shrine of sacrifice. Tricolours decorate both sides of the Champs-Élysées and are flown outside all official buildings. The presentation of the national colours constitutes a ceremonial moment and indicates the high status associated with the flag, raised not only as a signal to the troops but also in honour of the Head of State.

However, there can be no uncertainty about the original aim of Bastille Day as it gained official forms towards the end of the nineteenth century, in contexts of domestic and international rivalry when it was deemed necessary to display the strength of French defence. Although reinvented for contemporary France, the atmosphere continues in more ways than one to provide a testimony of the past. The military parade and the associations of victory have been at the centre of the 14 July celebrations from the beginning. Meaning is also attached to the performance of the parade, with geometric perfection and discipline, providing the image of efficiency and dedication of the soldiers willing to sacrifice their lives for France, qualities paraded also in front of foreign Heads of State. The geometric precision of the parades are predominantly military although emergency services also demonstrate how equipped France is to deal equally with natural and civil disasters. The official version of the celebrations on 14 July stresses its republican roots (rather than its revolutionary origin and anachronistic message within a context of European integration):

> Bastille Day today means, for all in France, the solemn military parade up the Champs Elysées in the presence of the head of state. It is also a holiday on which each commune holds a local dance and fireworks. But above all, Bastille Day, or the Fourteenth of July, is the symbol of the end of the monarchy and the beginning of the Republic. The national holiday is a time when all citizens can feel themselves to be members of a republican nation. It is because this national holiday is rooted in the history of the birth of the Republic that it has such great significance. (Republic Symbols: Bastille Day 14 July, 2010)

The live coverage of Bastille Day's military parade reaches roughly three million spectators annually (Simon, 2008). It is clear that the Revolution is no longer a stake in official history writing and the national holiday has effectively 'been drained of its historical and political substance' and aspires to constitute a Day of Unity rather than a day of controversy and discord (Amalvi, 1996, p. 118). Many nations have deserted military parades altogether but Bastille Day military focus remains. The link between the military procession and war-ridden French history stand unambiguous (Ozouf and Furet, 1989) and is embedded in a nexus of national symbols and ceremonies within the overall ceremony. The military parade is also part of a televised framework that has grown enormously in the last decades and is marked by a breakthrough at the time of the Bicentenary of the Revolution in 1989 when viewers also became integrated in the televised coverage. Increasingly, in recent years, television coverage has also influenced the parades in adapting to the cameras, especially obvious with the aerial views and special effects prepared for the celebrations in 2009 and 2010. For the latter, parachutists were dropped over Champs-Elysee carrying the flags of the guests of honour so that these could be presented at the presidential podium at Place de la Concorde. Seen in this context, the military procession is appropriate to be viewed on screen rather than at the location itself.

There is a contrast between the highly organized parade and the communal celebrations in the afternoons and evenings of Bastille Day when Bastille Day Bashes, street parties, dances and fireworks are organized all over France. In fact, it has been argued that the unofficial dances and fireworks, without state involvement, have overtaken the importance of the military parade and have become separated from the latter (Ory, 1980). Interestingly, the absence of official and critical debate opposing the military parade demonstrates that ceremonies of nations are not easy to criticize or change – something we will see also in the cases of Norway and Britain below. The nature of televised coverage and loyalty to ceremonial message, the attention to ceremonial routes and coverage of military life that follow the military parade disempower those who remain critical to the military display in that it can be seen to constitute 'an anachronistic ritual in an epoch of European Integration' (Simon, 2008, p. 617; see also Elgenius 2005b) True, arranged protest against the French nation and state commence precisely at the beginning of the celebrations of Bastille Day and demonstrates growing discord. In recent years, car-burnings in run-down suburban areas have become regular occurrence at the outset of the celebrations of Bastille Day. In 2009, police claimed 240 people were arrested and that this figure had doubled from the previous year (DeutscheWelle, 2009).

Constitution Day in Norway (17 May)

Norway has a long-standing tradition of celebrating its national day, known as Grunnlovsdagen (Constitution Day), in honour of the Norwegian constitution. Large-scale celebrations and processions are organized by and involving all schools throughout the country. A survey on national identity in 1998 concluded that 78 per cent of the population participate in some kind of celebration on Constitution Day (Blehr, 1999a) and related figures indicate that this number may be even higher. The main procession takes place with school units and massed bands under a sea of flags in central Oslo on Karl Johann Gate (Karl Johan's Avenue) (see cover).

In order to understand the development into a flourishing national day, the contributing historical complexities must be explored. The building of modern Norway began with the Treaty of Kiel (14 January 1814) signed towards the end of the Napoleonic Wars. Denmark had sided with France against Sweden and the victorious alliances against Napoleon and as result lost Norway to Sweden. The imperial approach of transferring Norway from one neighbour to another caused outrage among the Norwegian elite and a popularly elected National Assembly was convened at Eidsvoll (ca. 60kms north of Christiania (Oslo)) to provide Norway with a constitution of its own. The main political groups were represented here: those expressing loyalty to Denmark, those who found the union with Sweden strategically beneficial and those who aimed for independence. The constitution was established on 17 May 1814 when Prince Christian Fredrik of Denmark was also elected King of Norway. Sweden was provoked by these events and embarked on a military campaign in July when the king was forced to abdicate at the Convention of Moss in August. Norway was hereby forced into a union with Sweden that lasted until 1905, as noted in Chapter 2. However, Sweden accepted Norway's separate constitution as King Karl XIII was declared King of Sweden and Norway in November. Although, the foundations of Norwegian nationalism had already been articulated in the eighteenth century by the elite in Copenhagen and later in Christiania, the 'national movement was not a prerequisite of 1814, but a product of what happened. Within a few months, a fellowship had arisen and a national movement was created' (Østergård, 1997; Østerud, 1987; J. Seip, 1974, p. 52).

To clarify this point, there was no strong nationalist movement before this event but Norway had suddenly acquired its own constitution, parliament and – at the time – the most democratic election system in Europe, the vote being granted to all propertied men. It was within the enforced union with Sweden that an assertive form of nationalism emerged and the celebration of the constitution expanded during the nineteenth century in leaps and bounds. This happened in opposition to two significant others, Sweden whose king was also King of Norway and Denmark whose culture remained influential in Norway after centuries of rule from Copenhagen (Elgenius, 2011).

The day of the adopted Constitution came to mark the date of rebirth of an ancient state, immortalized by Wergeland who described 17 May as 'the most special and salvationary of all the days that God had let shine over the mountains of Norway'. This day linked Norwegians to 'all free peoples' who wished for independence after the 'four hundred years' night' of Danish domination (Thorsen, 2000). The quest for a *suitable* past (Hobsbawm and Ranger, 1992) justifying the right to independence in the present, was crucial for a nationalism that attached such significance to the constitution. The need for a heroic Norwegian past was urgent in the nineteenth century during the struggle for independence. A period of *greatness* in the Middle Ages provided such a past (Myhre, 2006) and served as inspiration for the re-birth and explained the unfortunate decline of the original Norwegian state (Bagge, 1995a, 1995b). A common point of departure was the unification of Norway in 900, leading to an independent kingdom by the early fourteenth century. The decline of an independent medieval Norwegian state intrigued historians as they attempted to explain the transition from the golden age to the loss of independence. Many agreed that a Norwegian identity already existed in the Middle Ages but slumbered in Norway's fjords and valleys during the long age of Danish rule (Grimnes, 2007; Lunden, 1995). Most contemporary scholars remain critical of this idea (Bagge, 1995b; T.H. Eriksen, 2002). Moreover, scholars of the day argued that Norway was settled by free peasantry. Whereas Swedes and Danes had immigrated from the south and subdued indigenous populations, Norwegians allegedly arrived from the north to an empty territory which they made their own. Following this leitmotiv of independence: 'The Norwegians were seen as descendants of *one* race, with a common language, a legal people with its own "national character" an "undiluted Norwegian spirit (*Volks-geist*)".' (A-L. Seip, 1995, p. 42, italics in original)

This national revival was also marked by the study of linguistic and the construction of new Norwegian language also went under way. Danish had constituted the main written language in Norway but was replaced with two written languages: Bokmål and Nynorsk (New Norwegian) that competed in attaining the status of national language (Østergård, 1997). Bokmål was modelled on Danish and modified in line with a Norwegian character and remained the dominant written language in Norway, whereas Nynorsk was constructed from the dialects of south-western Norway and Old Norse. Here nationalists turned to Nynorsk when naming their national institutions, which were given medieval names such as the parliament (Storting) and its two chambers (Lagting, Odelsting). The first king of independent Norway, who came from the Danish royal family and whose name was originally Karl, was renamed Haakon (VII), a name linking the monarchy with the ancient kingdom and ruling dynasty before 1350. The continuity between the medieval Norwegian state and its nineteenth century successor has been described as 'completely fictional' (T.H. Eriksen, 2002).

The Norwegian independence movement was shaped out of different hopes as some groups wanted reunification with Denmark whereas others were pragmatic unionists. The third group, small but growing stronger later in the century, was that of the nationalists opposed both to the union with Sweden and to the cultural remnants of Danish domination. Whatever the objections, these groups were united in the wish to restore the image of the reduced Norwegian kingdom (Mykland, 1996), which resulted in celebrations of the anniversary of the country's constitution on 17 May (1814) which identified Norway as an independent nation. The budding celebrations of the constitution and the adoption of a national flag helped emphasize commonality and sameness and thus overriding regional differences and diversity. Participation in the celebrations under the same flag claimed that the urban and rural parts belonged to one and the same culture and shared the same interests (T.H. Eriksen, 2002). Significantly, the national independence movement commenced its battle for the recognition of Norway by celebrating the constitution and by adopting a Norwegian flag (and an anthem) during the 1820s – crucial symbols that raised boundaries against the Swedes. The king attempted to outlaw the early celebrations of the constitution and the Swedish parliament refused to recognize the Norwegian flag in the 1890s on similar grounds.

Ceremonial design and the rhetoric of freedom and equality

In highlighting the importance of ceremonial style and choreography the appeal of national celebrations must change over time if they are to continue to appeal to the imagination of citizens. The celebrations of Constitution Day have been dominated by three recurring strands of rhetoric over time. These relate to 1) freedom 2) equality and democratization and 3) inclusion. The first two narratives were part of the formative processes that established the celebrations of the constitution for the first celebratory decade and a half. The matter of membership, belonging and inclusion is also a recurring theme but has particularly claimed ownership of the debate related to multiculturalism explored in the subsequent section.

The first known private celebrations of the constitution started in Trondheim in the early 1820s. By 1823 they had turned more public and newspapers reported the event as *Grunnlovsdagen* (Constitution Day) and a year later university students proceeded to organize celebrations in Christiania (A-L. Seip, 1995). Constitution Day was officially celebrated in the capital in 1827 as a way of resisting Swedish encroachments. As one may imagine, Constitution Day was originally celebrated in defence of the constitution. The motto on the banners of the first citizens' or people's parades (*Borgertog* or *Folketog*) called on the people to 'Guard the Constitution' (Mykland, 1996). The celebrations were perceived as a provocation in Sweden whose parliament proceeded to outlaw them in 1828 when the king went to Oslo with the intention of preventing them. This, however, had the opposite effect and the students at the University of Oslo continued their resistance (A-L. Seip, 1995). Expressions of Norwegian nationalism continued to develop successfully in the 1830s and the king and the Swedish parliament realized that the Norwegian constitution could not be suppressed without a war. The King of Sweden and Norway, Karl Johan, (quite correctly) regarded the celebrations as demonstrations against the union. It was not until after his death in 1844 that 17 May was celebrated to the full (Mykland, 1996). Notwithstanding attempts to intervene in early 17 May celebrations, Swedish dominance can be described as relatively mild. As the Norwegian parliament grew in power in the nineteenth century, there was no attempt to make Norway 'more Swedish' and the ruling classes remained Norwegian (although often with Danish and/or German origins) (Tønnesson, 2009). Thus, when the Citizens' Parade was introduced for the 17 May celebrations in 1844 this was not officially contested (Thorsen, 2000). The rhetoric of 17 May developed along the lines of democracy, equality and class-associated rights. From the 1870s to 1890s the liberal urban citizens and the farmers stood against the old ruling elite. Conflict between these groups turned Constitution Day into a day of discord with separately organized processions during the 1890s when the 'unmarked' flag also became a highly politicized symbol with the intensification of the struggle for independence (Grimnes, 2007). The emerging democratic claims became embedded in a nationalistic language that described the king as a foreign ruler (Stråth, 2005).

In the (re)negotiation of the political sphere '17 May' became a recognized arena for political battles in which the political groupings competed about being the 'true defender or heir of the *Eidsvoll* legacy' (Thorsen, 2000, p. 346). Before the dissolution of the union, independence became the focus for all 17 May celebrations and the population appeared united under this overall narrative. The main disputes between Norway and Sweden concerned the king's right to veto, the wish for a separate Norwegian foreign policy and consular services. The disputes within these areas led Norway and Sweden to prepare for military action and the union-friendly Prime Minister Francis Hagerup of Norway resigned in March 1905. The sentiments towards the Union can be illustrated by the words of the anti-unionist, Fridtjof Nansen, in a significant speech in Oslo on 17 May in 1905, celebrations of which have been described as 'emotional' (Scott, 1988):

> A tiger will fight for its young as long as it can move a limb; and a people is surely not poorer spirited than a tiger. It will defend its independence and its hearth to the utmost of its abilities. Of this we are sure: come what may, we must and shall defend our independence

and right of self-determination in our own affairs. *On these rights we must now stand or fall*. (Sørensen, 2004) (Emphasis added)

The day after these celebrations, 18 May, a separate consular law was passed in the Norwegian parliament only to be vetoed by the king in Stockholm. The king had vetoed the establishment of a separate Norwegian consular service on three occasions but could legally only do so twice and was thus in breach of the constitution. As a result the ministers of the Norwegian government resigned and by so doing prevented the king from fulfilling his royal obligations exercised through the government only (Sørensen, 2004). The Norwegian Parliament declared on 7 June, without a dissenting vote, that the union with Sweden under one king was to be dissolved. In consequence the king was to cease to function as king of Norway (Scott, 1988, p. 331) and was thereby effectively written out of the Norwegian constitution. The Swedish government demanded a referendum in Norway, held in August and which overwhelmingly supported the break up of the Union. The votes were counted 368 208 in favour to 184 against and Norway was recognized as an independent kingdom on 26 October (Sørensen, 2004; Steine, 2003). It is noted that Norwegian ship-owners came to constitute a significant pressure group in the conflict over representation for diplomatic missions abroad as they found their interests neglected by the Swedish 'stations' and serves as one indication of the instrumental motives behind Norwegian nationalism contributing to rapid separatism in the late nineteenth century. Norway's secession, however, did not lead to war and territorial disputes were non-existent (Vedung, 2001). Peaceful secession also had the support of the relevant international powers at the time (England, Germany and Russia) and of the Stockholm-based monarchy. Moreover, Norwegian unity stood against Swedish disunity as the Swedish soldiers could not be relied upon to attack. In Swedish historiography, the union and its breakup has a modest status. However, at the time, even the Norwegian-friendly quarters in Sweden described the proceedings leading to the breakup in terms of 'betrayal', 'deceit', 'crime' and '*coup d'etat*' (Stråth, 2005).

The Norwegian constitution survived, in other words, unaltered in contrast with many other European constitutions established in the revolutionary years following the Napoleonic wars, which contributes to our understanding just how the celebrations managed to become such an integral element in the rise of nationalism in the nineteenth and twentieth centuries despite also becoming a high profile forum for the negotiation of internal conflicts. The celebrations turned into central battlefields during periods of political mobilization. Rather, domestic disunity was channelled through demonstrations for independence, democracy and class-associated rights.

After independence was achieved, the 1920s and 1930s brought new conflicts on the agenda, this time between the middle and working classes. The middle classes participated in the processions but protested against the internationalism of the working classes, whereas the working classes were encouraged by their leaders to keep the class struggle alive and ignore 'the bourgeois celebrations' as they held alternative celebrations on 17 May (Mykland, 1996, p. 4) and organized rival events on International Labour Day and on 1 May in the weeks before the national day (17 May) (Kolstø, 2006). The freedom-rhetoric of the 17 May celebration was from the beginning positioned against the neighbouring countries and later in the union era of the nineteenth century specifically directed against Sweden representing a threat to Norwegian independence. The experiences of Nazi occupation (April 1940–May 1945) gave the celebrations of 17 May a deeper meaning in the Cold War years. The national poet Nordahl Grieg wrote at the time: 'Now stands the flagpole bare behind Eidsvoll's budding trees. But in such an hour as this we know what freedom is' (Mykland, 1996). The significance of the occupation for national identity in Norway must not be underestimated. A period of reconciliation between the left and right is described as having taken place during the occupation of Norway 1940–45 and thus also a period of considerable significance for nation building.

Whereas, the post-war years again turned the focus towards democratic rights and fellowship on 17 May, disunity with reference to membership in the European Community was manifested on Constitution Day (Kolstø, 2006). With two referenda in 1972 and in 1994 and a majority voting against the EEC/EU, the national celebrations were politicized and the national colours used in the campaigns for as well as against membership of the European Union (Mykland, 1996). As an example, the campaign 'No to EU' was excluded from the Peoples' Parade (with political assemblies, branches of national voluntary associations interspersed with brass bands) in the early 1990s. However, the organization was allowed to participate in Bergen (in 1992 and 1993) under the banner 'Defend the Constitution'. As a result, 'Movement for Europe' also wanted to participate in 1994 but both organizations were refused permission to take part. To fuel the controversy, 'No to EU' broke the ban and marched in any case under the banner 'The Constitution is 180 years old: Happy Anniversary!' (Blehr, 1999b, p. 182). The main point is that both political opponents had acknowledged Constitution Day as an important arena for the debating of political ideas in view of its encompassing participation and media coverage.

The Children's Parade, national day design and inclusion

The avenue Karl Johan (Karl Johann Gate) has from the beginning been a centre for the celebrations. The avenue was named after King Karl XIV Johan of Sweden and Norway (reigned 1818–44) who was, ironically, against the celebrations of the Norwegian constitution. The originally guarded celebrations, however, transformed with time into jubilant parades. Significantly, Constitution Day has remained popular long after the establishment of a constitution that is no longer threatened. The Children's Parade held in all Norwegian cities, towns and villages is the striking feature of the national day (see Illustration 4.3). Its introduction must be understood as a strategic move considering the discord that characterized the processions towards the end of the

Illustration 4.3 Ceremonial focal point and the Constitution Day Parade in Oslo
The parade is greeted by the Royal Family on the balcony of the royal palace, Karl Johan's Avenue in Oslo. The palace and the Royal Family provide the ceremonial focal point by design of the parade (above from the direction and perspective of the crowds). The statue of King Karl Johan of Sweden and Norway stands in front of the royal palace seen above. Photography by Gabriella Elgenius (2010a).

nineteenth century and contributing to the building of a nation. A flag parade of schoolboys was first introduced in the 1870s on the initiative of Bjørnson who was one of the nation builders on the left. As part of the general process of democratization, girls were invited into the processions in 1889 after which it became known as the Children's Parade (Barnetoget) and women also joined in subsequent years (Blehr, 1999b; A. Eriksen, 2007; Mykland, 1996).

Constitution Day commences with local flag-hoisting ceremonies, church services, speeches, the singing of the national anthem, the laying of wreaths at memorials commemorating the original members of Eidsvold. In Oslo the gatherings at memorials include those to Henrik Wergeland, Bjørnstierne Bjørnson, Henrik Ibsen and the first fallen during the Nazi occupation (Viggo Hansteens and Rolf Wickstrøms) (Oslo Kommune, 2010). The large-scale parades and festivities (public and private) which follow are organized in all towns and villages in cooperation with local schools. In fact, the parades are coordinated by the primary and secondary schools in Norway and every family is in effect included in the celebrations (Aagedal, 2002). The involvement of the schools highlights the significant role of teachers in the interpretation of 17 May but also as directors and organizers of the parades and festivities. In Oslo thousands of school children, forming units in a section of their own, walk in the main parade. For reference, 109 school units took part in the 2010 Olso parade. Each unit is preceded by two main flag-bearers carrying large national flags, by their special school banners and by school bands as they walk towards the royal palace. Special radio and television programmes cover the celebrations all over Norway and portray loyalty to the overall narrative of the festivites as postitive and joyful celebrations of Norwegianess. The festivities in Olso, Bergen, Tromsø and Trondheim follow a similar pattern: parades with school children, massed bands and national music.

> The children march as representatives of their school. Their collective identity is presented by a banner with the name and the year of establishment of the school. Along with this banner, those up front carry large Norwegian flags. Most schools have their own brass band with banners of their own. Thus, a complete manifestation of a school will consist of the banner of the school, [Norwegian] flags, the banner of the band, the musicians wearing uniforms, followed by lines of children, preferably in folk costumes [...] All children are expected to wave small Norwegian flags [...] Children are not compelled but are strongly encouraged to parade. (Blehr, 1999b, p. 178)

The other striking feature of Constitution Day, is the widespread use of regional festive folk dress (*bunad*). The *bunad* is a double-shuttle woven woollen skirt or dress with a jacket and scarf for women, and for men a colourful embroidered three-piece suit. The use of this festive and regional festive folk dress emphasizes regional diversity but constitutes at the same time a supra-regional or national symbol. Hulda Garborg systematized (and nationalized their use within one system of communication) the regional *bunad* traditions in *Norsk Klædebunad* from 1903 onwards and 'never denied the syncretic and partly invented character of the new, traditionalist folk costumes but emphasized their role as a marker of rural, Norwegian identity' (T.H. Eriksen, 2005, p. 12). Some of these festive costumes, as in the case of the *bunad* from Bergen which dates from 1956, were clearly invented recently. It is interesting that regional symbols have come to be visible at a supra-regional event such as this and demonstrate how the *bunad* continued the process of politicizing culture that started in the Norway of the 1820s. More than 60 per cent of Norwegian women today own a *bunad*, which equals around 30 per cent of the population. The corresponding figure for Sweden is less than 6 per cent. The total value of the 1.5 million Norwegian *bunad* in existence is estimated at around 30 billion NOK (*ca.* 3 billion GBP) (Aagedal, 2002; T.H. Eriksen, 2005). In other words, the *bunad* industry constitutes a significant business, the success of which is displayed on Constitution Day.

> The 17th of May, Norway's Day of Constitution, brings everybody in Norway back to pre-industrial times, and they dress up as if they have just arrived from the country side [...] People pay anything between fifteen to fifty thousand Norwegian kronor, or the equivalent of £1200 to £4000, in order to decorate themselves with this particular outfit on this particular, once-a-year event. (Nielsen in Aagedal, 2002)

The participation in the parades, the waving of the Norwegian flags, the singing of national anthems, the wearing regional costumes formalize as well as authenticate boundaries of nationhood and provide visual codes to membership. With an increasing multicultural approach to celebrations in mind, 17 May was brought into the political-moral arena once again. The rhetoric of inclusion has resurfaced in order to address the encouraged participation of the 10.6 per cent of the Norwegian population with immigrant backgrounds (Statistics Norway, 2009). Eriksen argues that 'the 17th of May as an ethno-cultural and national ritual has within a few years, at least in Oslo, turned into a cosmopolitan ritual of inclusion' (T.H. Eriksen, 2008). We discuss this further in Chapter 5. Children of immigrant backgrounds participate in the parades under their respective school banners and in cases where they appear in clusters this represents in effect segregated residential areas (Blehr, 1999b). However, the rhetoric of 17 May presents national identity in traditional terms of oneness and sameness.

Remembrance Sunday – a British affair?

It is a misconception that national days must be celebratory. Renan argued early to the contrary and that 'sorrows have greater value than victories; for they impose duties and demand common effort' (Renan, 1939, p. 203) True, it is relatively unusual not having a public holiday day of national celebration. The day that attempts to bring together the nations of Britain is commemorating fallen soliders on Remembrance Sunday (Elgenius, 2007a, 2007b; Heath et al., 2007). This is not an official national day in the sense of the many Independence Days in Europe, but in its forms and functions aims to provide a focus for Britain as a whole in honour of *its* fallen. Commemorations also take place all over Britain and are for many free from work as Remembrance Sunday is commemorated on the Sunday nearest to 11 November. Originally thought of as Armistice Day, the ceremony at the Cenotaph in Whitehall in London had such an appeal after the First World War that another ceremony or memorial was not deemed necessary after the Second World War. Instead, remembering the fallen was extended to include all British and Commonwealth servicemen and women who died in the two world wars and other armed conflicts. On this basis Remembrance Sunday is considered the unofficial national day of Britain (Elgenius, 2005a, 2005b; Heath et al., 2007; Poulter, 2009). National days as a rule are contested as they claim to represent the whole country and all groups within it. Remembrance Sunday is no exception. The commemorations in Northern Ireland, as one example, have become associated with the Protestant and Unionist community leading to less participation by the Catholic community and the British origin of the ceremony has been abhorred by nationalists (Robinson, 2010). The main Remembrance ceremony in London, however, is portrayed as if representing the multinational and multi-ethnic territory that is Britain.

Before we begin, it is noted that the situation of public commemoration and celebration is complicated in Britain. While the English have had the privilege of defining the concept of 'Britishness' historically, nationhood within Britain is claimed through the legendary celebrations of St Andrew in Scotland, St Patrick's Day in Northern Ireland (within which there are further competing celebrations) and St David in Wales. These are days of national (political or cultural) promotion and pride and constitute important national symbols (in more recent decades used as part of marketing strategies), whereas St George's Day in England passes by comparatively quietly. There has been a growing interest in England since the 1990s (Skey, 2009) and in order to encourage celebrations English Heritage has produced a *St George's Day Guide* (English Heritage, 14 April 2008) (StGeorgesDay.com, 2010; Telegraph.co.uk, 2010). The lack of celebrations in England compared with those in Scotland, Wales and Northern Ireland has been discussed in terms of loss for the English: 'The Scottish, the Welsh, and, and the Irish to an extent, seem to cling on to their identities much *better* than the English do. [...] I think the result is, that the English have sort of lost, lost a little bit of that, and, and I think we need to get a bit back' (interview ESRC project on Identities see Heath et al., 2007). The process of cultivating national days is ongoing not only in England but also in Scotland where St Andrew's Day as a popular day was declared a national day in 2007. The history of St Andrew as Scotland's patron saint – and one of the apostles – is linked to the declaration of independence in 1320 (the Declaration of Arbroath) (McCrone, 2009). In terms of governmental involvement, the Leader of the Scottish National Party and First Minister of Scotland from 2007, Alex Salmond, had declared already in 2005 that: 'I want all of Scotland to take part in celebrating our national day. The *One* Scotland, *Many* Cultures theme will allow us to celebrate our national identity in a positive, diverse way, not just in an exclusive, traditional Scottish way' (Scottish Parliamentary Corporate Body, 2005) (emphasis added). As an emerging theme for national day design, inclusion is discussed in depth in Chapter 5.

Now, the competing national days in England, Scotland, Wales and Northern Ireland make the study of a Remembrance Sunday for Britain illuminating on many levels. Most communities in Britain erected a war memorial after the First World War and it is around these that commemorations take place on Remembrance Sunday (National Inventory of War Memorials, 1997). Church services and ceremonies are also held all over Britain precisely at 11 a.m. in order to mark the signing of the Armistice in 1918. The main televised coverage is of the ceremony that takes place in London at the Cenotaph, on Whitehall. The main representatives of the state are involved as sponsors and chief participants as are representatives of the different nations. Thus, at least in official terms, Britain stands united in remembering the fallen, which has something interesting to tell us about the construction of nations as communities of sacrifice and illuminate the perceptions of such corresponding boundaries.

The Glorious Dead

The Cenotaph refers to an empty tomb raised in memory of the war dead whereas the actual resting place for the Unknown Soldier is Westminster Abbey (Inglis, 1993; Winter, 1995). The building of a Cenotaph was suggested in response to the need for a dignified focal point for the Victory March on 19 July 1919. More specifically, it was after learning that the French would include such a 'saluting point' and that French troops were to salute a catafalque under the Arc de Triomphe on 14 July, that a similar focal point ought to be planned for the Victory March in London (Mosse, 1990). Since Britain did not have an Arc de Triomphe, Sir Edwin Lutyens was asked to design a non-denominational focal point – a Cenotaph – and redirect the notion of a (French) Catholic catafalque. This was unveiled in 1920 and was visited by 400 000 people in three days (Mosse, 1990; Winter, 1995). The ceremony was from the outset designed as an exclusively British affair. The Cabinet decided, as reported by *The Times* (10 November 1920) that 'in view of the strictly national character of the memorial ceremony, [...] *there will be no foreign representation*' (Uzelac, forthcoming) (emphasis added).

The connection between patriotic and religious feelings constituted a general background for the cult of the Unknown Soldier at the end of First World War. Commemorations took place all over Britain and memorials for the fallen were built in most communities in order to console the bereaved. Most families had been touched by death in war in one way or the other and all their million war dead lay in foreign graves. The government had as early as 1915 decided that the dead were not to be transported back to Britain (a subject that relates to a more complicated legal framework of body ownership) which 'caused a rupture in long-established patterns of grieving, which had traditionally taken place around the dead body and the grave' (Moriarty, 1991, p. 63). Thus, the return and burial of the Unknown Solder became of utmost significance. The pomp with which he was brought back to Britain and the care with which the final resting place in Westminster Abbey was chosen, testify to the significance to the cult of the fallen, a context in which the Cenotaph became the memorial to all fallen soldiers:

> The return and burial of the Unknown Soldier was accompanied by a riot of symbolism, for all the symbols present in the design of military cemeteries, and in the mythology which surrounded the fallen, were compressed into one ceremony – indeed, into one symbol. This

now became the focus not only of Armistice Day, but of various other national ceremonies as well [...] During the war, several Englishmen had put forward the idea of constructing a Tomb for an Unknown Soldier, and when he was finally exhumed and selected in 1920, once again the emphasis was placed on symbolic action. The bodies were collected from the most important battlefields like Ypres and the Somme, and the one to be buried in London was selected not by a wounded soldier of the rank and file but by a high-ranking officer. The Unknown Soldier was transported over the channel by the French destroyer *Verdun*, so that this battle was included by name in the ritual. The coffin itself was made of British oak from a tree at the Royal palace at Hampton Court (a palace with many historical associations). Together with a trench helmet and a khaki belt, a Crusader's sword was placed in the coffin. The Unknown Soldier was brought to the Arc de Triomphe and the Cenotaph, situated in the middle of Whitehall, a broad avenue, was unveiled (Mosse, 1990, pp. 94–5).

Ceremonies in honour of the nation's war dead commenced in 1919, in London by the temporary Cenotaph in Whitehall, a construction made permanent in 1921. No less than 15 000 troops, led by their commanders, took part in the Victory March on Armistice Day in July 1919. They marched past all the main state buildings in London, after being reviewed by the king at Buckingham Palace, continuing via Trafalgar Square, Whitehall, the Houses of Parliament and Westminster Abbey. The march was followed by peace celebrations, entertainment and fireworks in London's parks (Homberger, 1976; King, 1998). By the following day, the Cenotaph had become the focus of attention and part of the newly established symbolism of collective mourning. Lutyens' monument was understood as being so evocative that it was transformed into a permanent British war memorial in Whitehall (Winter, 1995). Whereas the Cenotaph in London became a permanent feature, the catafalque in Paris was removed after the ceremony on 14 July. When the Armistice was commemorated in November 1919 and the wreaths of poppies placed at the Cenotaph (and at 11 a.m. in town squares and on village greens) the Great Silence (two minutes' silence) was introduced after Big Ben had struck the eleventh hour (Homberger, 1976; Inglis, 1993) when all activity was interrupted as a mark of respect: 'Commemorating the war dead was regarded as a sacred act. The 11th of November became known as "Armistice tide", giving it the air of an ancient religious tradition' (King, 1998, pp. 20–1). After the construction of the permanent Cenotaph in 1920 the Unknown Soldier was also reburied in Westminster Abbey. The king made the connection between

126 *Symbols of Nations and Nationalism*

the Cenotaph and the tomb in Westminster Abbey by unveiling the Cenotaph and then walking behind the gun carriage which bore the coffin of the Unknown Soldier into the Abbey (Mosse, 1990). Great crowds followed the procession with the coffin to the Abbey and the inscription on the tomb stated: 'A British Warrior who fell in the Great War 1914–1918 for King and Country'. More than a million people visited the Cenotaph after 11 November in 1920 (Inglis, 1993, pp. 22–3).

The Cenotaph ceremony

The televised Remembrance ceremony takes place at the Cenotaph in Whitehall in London and consists of three main sections: the laying of wreaths by state representatives, the service led by the Bishop of London and the march-past (see Illustration 4.4). The following elements form the structure of the ceremony: (a) units that are to constitute the parade rally around the Cenotaph before the ceremony starts; (b) procession of official state representatives; (c) the two minutes' silence, the sounding of the Last Post and the Reveille; (d) the placing of wreaths of poppies at the Cenotaph by officials of the State; (e) a religious service led by the

Illustration 4.4 Ceremonial focal point: the Cenotaph in London
Participants are preparing for the march past the Cenotaph in Whitehall in London on Remembrance Sunday. The Cenotaph is seen in white marble off centre. Spectators line the street. Photograph by Gabriella Elgenius (2009b).

Bishop of London; (f) placing wreaths of poppies by the participants of the parade. Musical pieces are performed during different stages of the ceremony. At the beginning of the ceremony the Cenotaph is undecorated apart from the Union Jack and the flags of the Royal Navy, the British Army, the Royal Air Force and the Merchant Navy (since 2007), and the carved wreath on either side and the words *The Glorious Dead* (chosen by Rudyard Kipling).

The representatives that gather around the Cenotaph in a hollow square before the ceremony starts include a number of military units (the Royal Air Force, the Royal Navy, the Territorial Army, the Household Cavalry, the King's Troop, Royal Horse Artillery, the Horse Guards, the Scots Guards, the Royal Gurkha rifles and the Royal Logistics) the Merchant Navy, the Royal Corps, the Royal Women Volunteer services, the Red Cross and the police, the fire brigade, the ambulance and prison services. The Cenotaph ceremony commences with *Rule Britannia*, followed by the musical entertainment of different massed bands. Traditional pieces are performed: the *Mistral Boy*, the *Isle of Beauty*, *David of the White Rock*, *Oft in the Stilly Night*, the *Flowers of the Forest that Withered Away* and *Nimrod* from Elgar's *Enigma Variations*. As the procession of official representatives approaches the Cenotaph, they are accompanied by John Arkwright's *Supreme Sacrifice*. Headed by a boys' church choir and the Bishop of London, carrying the insignia of the cross and a crucifix of poppies, the procession includes representatives of the state (the Prime Minister, former Prime Ministers, Opposition party leaders, the Leader of the House of Commons, the members of the Cabinet, a representative for Northern Ireland, the Welsh National Party and the Scottish National Party; representatives of the military: Air Force, Army, Navy, and of the Merchant Services; the High Commissioners of the Commonwealth and representatives of different faith communities (representing the Baptists, Buddhists, Free Churches, Greek Orthodox, Hindus, Jews, Methodists, Muslims, Reform Movement for Judaism, Roman Catholics, Salvation Army, Sikhs, Unitarian and Free Christian Churches, United Reform Church). Finally, the monarch, today Queen Elizabeth II, escorted by the Duke of Edinburgh, the Prince of Wales, the Princess Royal, the Duke of York and the Duke of Kent.

The Royal party arrives at the Cenotaph just before the two minutes' silence at 11 a.m., marked by a salute when all movement comes to a halt. As Big Ben strikes 11 a.m., it is to recall the eleventh hour on the eleventh day of the eleventh month when the guns were silenced and the Armistice came into force in 1918. The two minutes' silence ends with another salute, and trumpeters positioned around the Cenotaph then play a fanfare in order to mark its significance. The silence is followed by the Last Post, sounded by buglers of the Royal Marines and the Reveille. With the Last Post, the Unknown Soldier is committed to earth and the Reveille calls him to awaken. This ceremony has clear Christian references and promise of resurrection. It identifies the Unknown Soldier at the core of the nation at this point – through his sacrifices for his community. Beethoven's Funeral March accompanies the placing wreaths at the Cenotaph. The Queen lays a wreath on behalf of the nation, dedicated to all who have suffered and died in war and she bows as a mark of respect. The other members of the Royal Family, also laying wreaths, follow the Queen. After the Royal Family follows the Prime Minister, the leaders of the opposition and the representatives of Northern Ireland, the Scottish and Welsh nationalist parties. Thus all the nations and rivalling parties are represented at the Cenotaph. After the politicians, the High Commissioners on behalf of the Commonwealth volunteers, the Chiefs of Defence (Royal Navy, Army, Royal Air Force) and the representatives of the Merchant Fleet place wreaths.

The ceremony continues with prayers led by the Bishop of London that combine patriotic and religious ideals. The short service concludes with a hymn (*O God, Our Help in Ages Past*) and the Lord's Prayer. The participants standing around the Cenotaph to place wreaths at the Cenotaph are called to attention with the national anthem, *God Save the Queen*. After the national anthem the official representatives, including the monarch and her family, retire to the Foreign Office. The president of the Royal British Legion and representatives of the Legion (organizers of the parade) start the parade by placing wreaths of the British Legion at the foot of the Cenotaph. Music such as the *Trumpet Voluntary* marks the pace. All the parading units march, by tradition six abreast, saluting the fallen as they pass the Cenotaph. A large number of people (10 to 13 000) participate in this parade from Whitehall towards Parliament Square, accompanied by marching music and massed bands. Considering the thousands of people that gather in central London it is respectfully quiet. The gathered crowds represent many generations, not only (ex-)military but also those who have lost relatives and friends. The official BBC commentator David Dimbleby (10 November, 2001) interpreted the ceremony in the following manner:

> It is the feeling of duty and of respect and the hope to rekindle the unique spirit of comradeship fostered by war and hardship that make the vast numbers of people turn up to commemorate Remembrance Sunday at the Cenotaph.

According to official figures, around 9000 people took direct part in the march past the Cenotaph in 2009 (David Dimbleby, 8 November 2009). Naturally such numbers demand careful planning and organization and have from the beginning been controlled by government offices, first by a Cabinet committee presided over by the Foreign Secretary (1921–23), then the Home Office (1924–2001) and the Lord Chancellor's Department (2001–). The ceremonial activity prior to the Cenotaph ceremony is considerable as the 9000 participants and the official representatives attend remembrance services in churches all over London beforehand. Similar remembrance services take place all over Britain. All church services include an Act of Remembrance repeating 'We will remember them' from Laurence Binyon's poem 'For the Fallen', the two minutes' silence, the Lord's Prayer and the National Anthem. Daily newspapers report that 'tens of millions in the UK stopped what they were doing to pause and observe the two minutes of silence' (Knight, 2005) on Remembrance Sunday. In terms of the Church as an important actor on this day, a special Remembrance Service ritual was commended for general use since 1968 and updated by the Archbishops of Canterbury, York and Wales, and the Cardinal Archbishop of Westminster and the Moderator of the Free Church Federal Council in 1984. The BBC commenced its live broadcast in 1928 and the first televised coverage took place in 1937 and then annually from 1946 onwards and is as such claimed to be one of the longest running live televised event. In recent years television screens are put up in central London since movement is restricted around the Cenotaph.

The Poppy (Poppy Day)

The respect to the fallen is expressed and visualized by the wearing of a poppy (see Illustation 4.5 on fields of remembrance) in the weeks leading up to Remembrance Sunday. The poppy has become a distinct symbol of remembrance and affiliation and was originally inspired by McCrae's poem 'In Flanders' Fields', written on the battlefield of Flanders on 3 May 1918: 'In Flanders Fields the poppies blow/ Between the crosses, row on row/[...] If ye break faith with us who die/ We shall not sleep, though poppies grow/ In Flanders' Fields.'

The British Legion was formed in 1921 and sold poppies to raise funds for the victims of war, ex-Servicemen and their dependants. In 1921 the Legion sold 8 million poppies, by 1926 the number reached 30 million, the exact funds raised unknown (Homberger, 1976; Inglis, 1993). The amount raised for the Poppy Appeal in 2009 reached more than 30 million GBP when more than 26 million poppies were sold (Howse,

130 *Symbols of Nations and Nationalism*

Illustration 4.5 Fields of Remembrance in London
Fields of Remembrance at Westminster Abbey in London. Crosses with poppies are planted in honour of fallen soldiers in current conflicts. The death toll of British servicemen in Iraq amounted to 179 dead by 2009 and in Afghanistan reached 364 by spring 2011. (iCasualties.org). Photography by Gabriella Elgenius (2009a).

30 October 2009). According to the British Legion as many as 57 per cent of the adults in Britain were reported wearing a poppy in 1995 a number that increased to 73 per cent in 2001 (Royal British Legion (Official Website), 2004). Funds are also raised through the annual Remembrance concert at the Royal Albert Hall (since 1927) which concludes with a shower of poppies from the dome – each poppy representing a dead soldier, known or unknown (Inglis, 1993) – living and dead thus symbolically joined.

The British Legion is one of the largest membership organizations in Britain and recognized as the custodians of remembrance. The British Legion organizes the march past the Cenotaph in London, remembrance services all over Britain, the two minutes' silence in Trafalgar Square on 11 November at 11 a.m., the Fields of Remembrance at Westminster Abbey and St Paul's in London, the Cardiff Field of Remembrance, the Garden of Remembrance at St Paul's, the Field of Poppies in Flanders (at the Menin Gate in Ypres) as well as pilgrimages to war memorials outside Britain. During the Poppy Appeal and the festivals of remembrance, the London Eye turns red in support of the cause and poppy projections were shown on the Shell Building by the Thames. At the Fields of Remembrance at Westminster Abbey (Illustration 4.5) red crosses with poppies are planted as 'a solemn reminder of the ongoing human cost of conflict and reminds us of the importance of remembering the generations we as a nation have lost' (Royal British Legion (Official Website), 2010).

More than 60 000 crosses were planted at Westminster Abbey in 2009 and included for the first time the crosses of soldiers who died in Iraq and Afghanistan. The queues where extensive and the practice transformed the official ceremony into a private commemoration.

The contours of a pattern

The forms, functions and expressions of national days will be analysed in subsequent chapters on the basis of the cases discussed here. For now, we may say that national days appear as annually repeated complexes of national symbolism and ceremonials. They provide by their design a framework for the imagination and expression of nationality in terms of commonality and oneness. As seen, the national days of Europe span a spectrum of variety in terms of ceremonial statistics, cause and character and ways in which official narratives are cultivated and are expressed. Having said this, the contours of a pattern is formed by the fact that national days honour founding myths linked to political events such as independence, liberation, unification, the constitution and the forming of a state. Monarchs, saints, heroes and golden ages are also part of this nexus, especially with regards to celebrations that emerged in pre-modern times but in reinvented forms reappear as national day celebrations with historic claims to modern territories.

Most national days are linked to events and circumstances relating to the rebirth of the nation or to the pursuits of personifications that lends the nation its virtues and justifications, as well as aspirations, so references to the past and future become interlinked. The founding of states, their sovereignty and constitutions are constitutive elements of free nation-states as are independence or liberation, the latter emerging as a forming trend of post-imperial times. As seen, national days are adapted to political change and modernized notions of nationhood, including their suppression in periods of occupation. The adoption of national days, much like that of national flags, expresses the ideals of surviving historical narratives. This means by default that some voices, stories and narratives remain unacknowledged, a matter to be discussed in the subsequent chapter.

National days comprise a younger stratum of the nation and the development of national days in France, Norway and Britain illuminate the process of nation building in various ways, responding to different dilemmas and achieving different results, but all continue with their developments the process of nation building. The modern French nation was founded with the new Republic and the ideals of 1789 and the military style of the official 14 July parade is understood in the context of the conflict-ridden French past. The celebrations of Bastille Day today have, however, developed far beyond the reality of the Revolution. In Norway, too, the struggle for independence against foreign domination overshadowed the formative years of honouring the Constitution that declared Norway independent before statehood had been achieved. A unique national day design has thereafter contributed to the transformation of guarded celebrations into celebrations of Norwegian identity. In Britain, the honouring of the war dead commenced after the First World War, first as a Day of Victory with victory parades and, following this, with claims to righteousness as well as glory. British virtues remained in this fashion, with the transformation into Remembrance Sunday, closely linked to the sacrifices of the citizens and the commemoration of their losses. Through these commemorations, boundaries are redrawn annually between those sacrifices that are remembered and those that remained unacknowledged. The solemnity of the British Remembrance Sunday could not be more different to the joyful flag-waving on Constitution Day in Norway, which, in turn, does not have much in common (at least on the surface) with the militaristic Bastille Day. The next chapter will explore difference and similarity in more depth in consideration of these cases and the many national days in Europe.

Note

1. The descriptions of the national days in this chapter are based on first hand observations and recordings of official TV broadcastings 2001–10 and of secondary material, such as recordings and photographs available on the web. I am grateful to John-Paul Stonard (Courtauld Institute of Art, London), Anna Dezeuze (Courtauld Institute of Art), Dr Gordana Uzelac (London Metropolitan University) for recorded material and to Antonie Kraemer (SOAS) and Ammar Abd Rabbo (Balkispress) for photographic illustrations.

5
National Day Design: Towards a Typology of Successful National Days

The relative standardization of national days, their similarities with regard to expressions and imaginations, calls for an investigation of national day design. There are many themes related to this concept, some of which will be explored in this chapter. First, the syncretic nature of national days must be explored by comparing claimed origins to first celebrations and their transformations into national holidays. Moreover, ceremonial choreography, ceremonial routes and the creation of moral federations must be assessed in terms of ways in which nations authenticate their boundaries. Related to the nexus of national day design are national anthems – and the singing of nationalism – that constitute yet another building block of the nationalist parcel. Nation builders have continued to operate from the assumption that national days contribute to the maintaining of nations and these continue therefore to be introduced, abolished and re-introduced but also modernized, transformed and reinvented with changing circumstances. The extent to which national days contribute to community building is hard to assess in absence of adequate and comparative data, as is the actual influence of ceremonial structures that justify the official historical narratives. An examination of the European cases confirms that national days are generally popular events but that that they do not by default contribute to cohesion. On the contrary, many current national days are the outcomes of conflicts and some have not been able to produce consensus about what is being celebrated. All of them are presented as community occasions that capture the essence of the nation formation process. However, a number of criteria can be identified as contributing to the participation and success of national days and also make it possible to assess whether they are exportable to other nations. Recent national day initiatives in multi-ethnic and multinational nations are of particular interest here and also call for a discussion on the related issues of ceremonial transformation, inclusion and reconciliation.

Ceremonial foci: new traditions and beginnings

National days emerge, as a rule, after a perceived or constructed break with the past as seen in the cases of France and Norway but also in the many examples of Independence/Constitution Days celebrated in Europe. Out of the 42 national days accounted for 12 are older than 1870, five appear during 1870–1914 and 25 are introduced after 1914. The elites were clearly at work during the period of mass-production of inventions 1870–1914 (Hobsbawm and Ranger, 1992). These figures suggest that a new successful tradition had been invented and was established by the end of the nineteenth century. Most national days appear, as would be expected, following the redrawing of the map after the First World War.

> [T]he symbolic descriptions of *Heimat* [homeland] were familiar phenomena throughout Europe in the age of 'mass-producing traditions'. National individuality was articulated in *a European symbolic language of similitudes*. Among these similitudes were the mixture of pride stemming from traditions and from innovation in the representation of the nation, the mixed reactions to modernity as agent of progress and producer of anxiety and nostalgia, and the emphasis of national uniqueness. (Confino, 1997, p. 211) (Emphasis added)

According to this language of similitude, there are two overall types of recognized national days in Europe that honour (type 1) national personifications (saints, monarchs and heroes) and (type 2) significant political events (republics, constitutions and independence). Celebrations of national personifications and saints originate in an early form – as a rule – in the age of pre-modern nations. Celebrations of political events (independence, liberation, unification, state formation, constitutions) appear during the age of modern nations. Tables 5.1 and 5.2 account for ceremonial content and their claimed origins whereas Table 5.3 identifies the time of the first officially recognized celebrations/commemorations after taking a national form.

Celebrations of national personifications honour perceived characteristics, pursuits and enterprises of specific historical epochs as ways of bringing the heroic past into the present. National heroes and golden epochs provide a tangible form of national enterprises, heroism and

Table 5.1 National personification and golden ages (type 1)

Saints	Monarchs	Heroes
Ireland and Northern Ireland (St Patrick) (*ca.* 11th c) England (St George) (*ca.* 14th c) Scotland (St Andrew) (*ca.* 14th c) Spain (Virgin Mary) Wales (St David *ca.* 12th–18th c)	Hungary (*ca.* 1100) (King/St Stephen) Netherlands (Queen's Day) (1891) Faroe Islands (King/St Olav) (*ca.* 11th c)	Spain (Columbus, 1492 discovery) Portugal (Luis Vaz de Camões, death in 1580) Britain (fallen soldiers, 1919)

Table 5.2 Political events (type 2)

Republics (R), Unions (U) Confederations (C)	Constitutions	Independence (I), Liberation (L), Sovereignty (S)	
Switzerland (1291, C) France (1789, R) Czech Republic (1918, R) Iceland (1944, R) Italy (1946, R) Romania (1918, U) Germany (1990, U)	Poland (1791) Sweden (1809) Norway (1814) Denmark (1849) Faroe Islands (1948) Slovak Republic (1992) Serbia (1804, 1835)	Greece (1821, I) Belgium (1831, I) Finland (1917, I) Estonia (1918, I) Lithuania (1918, I) Slovenia (1991, I) Ukraine (1991, I) Macedonia (1991, I) Montenegro (1878, 2006, I) Kosovo (2008, I)	Bulgaria (1878, L) Albania (1912, L, I) Belarus (1944, L) Latvia (1918, S) Austria (1955, S) Russia (1991, S) Croatia (1991, S)

values as did the religious saints or the celebrations dedicated to Virgin Mary for religiously sanctioned communities. The commemorations of the sacrifices of fallen soldiers ultimately honour a nation for which it is worth dying and are integrated in the ritual year of the nations involved in the First and Second World Wars and often integrated as part of national day design.

European nations mainly honour political events such as unification, forming of republics, declaration of sovereignty, signing of constitutions, constitutional reform, independence or liberation. Thus,

Table 5.3 National days and symbolic regimes

Symbolic regimes	National personifications	Political events	
	Saints, Monarchs and Heroes	Constitutions, Republics (R) Unions (U)	Independence, Liberation (L)
Pre-1789 Age of pre-modern nations	*Originally religious days*: Ireland, St Patrick (*ca.* 1000) Hungary, St Stephen (*ca.* 1100) (1764) Scotland, St Andrew (1320) England, St George (1348) Spain, Virgin of El Pilar (1613) Wales, St David (*ca.* 18th c.)		
1789–1913 Age of modern nations	Portugal, Dia de Camões (1880, 1933) Netherlands, Queen's Day (1891) Spain, Columbus (1892)	France (1789, 1880, R) Poland (1791) Norway (1827) Denmark (1849) Switzerland (1891, U) Sweden (1893)	Greece (1838) Bulgaria (1878, L) Belgium (1890)
Post-1914 Age of post-imperial nations	Britain (1919) Ireland, St Patrick (1922) Faroe Islands, St Olav (*unknown*), (Opening of Parliament) (1948)	Czech Republic (1919, R) Iceland (1945, R) Italy (1946, R) Romania (1989, U) Germany (1990, U) Slovakia (1992, R) Serbia (2007)	Finland (1917) Estonia (1918) Lithuania (1918) Latvia (1918) Belarus (1944) Slovenia (1991) Croatia (1991) Ukraine (1991) Albania (1991–92) Macedonia (1991) Russia (2004) Montenegro (2006) Kosovo (2008)

'others' continue to figure in ceremonial foci. In establishing these national days, national elites demonstrate a wish to stretch the birth of the nation as far back as possible. Some nations have 'collected' historically significant events to the same celebrations on the same date (e.g. Spain and Sweden). The Spanish national day (12 October) combined one of the many celebrations of Virgin Mary – Virgin of El Pilar – a celebration that developed during the Counter-Reformation (1613), and the fourth centenary of the arrival of Columbus in the Americas (1892) on the same date. As a national holiday it was later politicized in the context of the Civil War and Francoism. Similarly, Sweden's national day celebrates Gustav Vasa I being elected King (in 1523) and the constitutional reform of 1809 but celebrations started first in 1893, and became a public holiday as late as in 2005.

Thus the dates claimed as the ceremonial foci (Tables 5.1 and 5.2) will in many cases differ from the first celebrations. Table 5.3 correlates the time of the first known celebrations of the current national days to that of ceremonial foci. For example, the Swiss celebrate the perceived date of the first Confederation (1291) (Table 5.2) a celebration dated to 1891 (Table 5.3), and Portugal Day commemorates the nation's poet who died in 1580 (Table 5.1) although the day was first celebrated in 1880 and nationally in 1933 (Table 5.3). In the Faroe Islands the celebrations of St Olav or King Olav (who died at the Battle of Stiklestad in 1030) provides the national day with a golden age whereas St Olav has been celebrated together with the Opening of the Parliament since 1948. Serbia's established national day (2007) commemorates the uprising against Ottoman rule in 1804 and the constitution of 1835. Thus a clear pattern can be seen (Table 5.3) when aligning symbolic regimes with national narratives and the ceremonial content of national days in Europe.

National day design and ceremonial choreography

Ceremonial foci constitute one contributing reason for the popularity of national days, especially in the formative years. However, a crucial factor to popularity and survival over time is the style of the celebrations and national day design will here be understood as contributing to the appeal and success of national days, especially when many national days are honouring events of a distant past. National day celebrations or commemorations demonstrate a continued appeal of nations imagined as *one* community, despite the overwhelming evidence against the reality of such notions.

Parades and processions

There are a number of significant variables to consider in terms of choreography as European national days vary. Some national days are popular, others not, and celebrations range from speeches given by government officials in public spaces to the participation of the military or whole nations in processions, parades, carnivals and street parties. The main character of national days can in this regard be classified according to whether they are official state or popular celebrations and whether they are military and civilian. When described in such a manner it is the character of the processions and parades that are noted. As we are concerned with nation building and the strategy of national day design the official ceremonies are categorized as seen in Table 5.4, which shows a majority of the selected national days are popular and civilian.

The diagram is an approximation of ceremonial styles but demonstrates that national day design vary significantly although the information is subjective to interpretation and also to change. On the one hand the state-led military celebration of Independence Day in Belgium can be contrasted to the popular civilian celebrations of Portugal Day or Constitution Day in Norway. The military as well as popular celebrations of Liberation Day in Bulgaria or Bastille Day in France stand against the state-led civilian national days in honour of constitutional

Table 5.4 National day design and ceremonial variety

	Military	Civilian	
Elite (State)	Britain Belgium	Poland Austria Denmark Sweden Germany Slovakia Croatia Russia	
Mass (Popular)	Spain France Greece Bulgaria Finland Estonia Latvia Ukraine	Ireland Hungary Scotland Wales Portugal Norway Netherlands Switzerland	Lithuania Italy Iceland Romania Slovenia Macedonia Faroe Islands

reform in Sweden or Unification Day in Germany. Again, national days fall in between these categories and celebrations are mixed. It is noted that several of the designs marked by military parades also incorporate civilian and children parades as in the cases of Spain, Greece, Bulgaria and Belarus to mention a few diverse examples. Some national days are described as relatively popular but honoured primarily by the state, notably in the cases of Austria and Belgium where they are characterized by official elements (Beaufort-Spontin, 2004; Belgian Information Service, 2005; Bichler, 2004).

Elite events: military and civilian
Military celebrations involve carefully orchestrated, executed and precisely timed parades. Military involvement is by nature elite-led and state presence is significant. However, these can easily be transformed into civilian festivities after the official ceremonies as is the case in France. On account of the origins of the national days in Spain, France, Greece, Bulgaria, Belgium, Finland, Estonia, Latvia, Britain and the Czech Republic, the armed forces have continued to play a role in the official celebrations. It is also noteworthy that the Spanish and Greek celebrations constitute a combination of military and religious traditional festivities; in Spain of the Virgin Mary and in Greece the Feast of the Annunciation. The military plays a role also on related days such as Polish Army Day (15 August) remembering the defeat of the Red Army in 1920 whereas Victory Day (9 May) in Russia celebrating victory of 1945 has remained the unchallenged national celebration in Russia, commemorating the 'vast reservoir of past suffering [...] and the horror of its collective sacrifice' (Ignatieff, 1976, p. 159). The commemoration of the Second World War, or the Great Patriotic War, and the Moscow Victory Day parade on Red Square has remained important in Russia. As an example, over 70 cities organized Victory Parades for 2010 and the anniversary that marked the 65th anniversary of the defeat of Nazism and Fascism in 1945 (RussiaToday, 2010a, 2010b).

Official national days that are mainly marked by the state do not, as a rule, commemorate historical events that have acquired the status of being a symbol of the nation. This seems the case in Denmark and Sweden (Adriansen, 2003; Neuman, 2004; Royal Danish Embassy, 2004) which officially celebrate constitutional reform. Other examples of elite-led ceremonies are Unification Day (Germany) and Russia Day with little public participation (Confino, 1997; Embassy of the Russian Federation, 2004; Schulze, 2002). In Germany this can be explained by the complex associations of nationhood and unification. In the case of Russia (but also in Slovakia and Croatia) the public national holidays were established recently and a pattern not yet formed. In the Russian case, we note that some national days do not create consensus about what is commemorated. Here, the former national day (the Day of the Great October Socialist Revolution) became known as the Day of Accord and Reconciliation in 1991 after the collapse of the Soviet Union, and was exchanged for Russia Day in 2004 (12 June) on the grounds of the former being 'ideologically outdated' (Ria-Novosti, 2004a). The Russians are said not to celebrate any of the days (Russia Day, the Day of the Fatherland or the National Unity Day) that were established by the state elites. A poll conducted by the Yury Levada Analytical Centre in Moscow also showed that 68 per cent were against replacing the Day of Accord and Reconciliation (7 November, the Anniversary of the October Revolution in 1917, celebrated before 1991) with a Day of National Unity (4 November) (Ria-Novosti, 2004b).

Mass events: military and civilian

National day design is linked to content and performance and most national days are popular celebrations notably in Norway, Greece, Spain, Portugal, Ireland, Lithuania and the Netherlands. The celebrations in Greece combined holidays as well as ceremonial forms: Independence Day and the religious holiday of Annunciation are celebrated on the same day with a large armed forces parade in Athens, school flag parades in every city and village and religious services. The involvement of children in the parades in Norway, instead of soldiers or state representatives, makes emphasis on timing and precision redundant. The commemoration of the war dead in Britain at the Cenotaph, however, combines military, religious and civilian elements of the nation and commands representation of most major British institutions, government and opposition in England, Scotland and Wales. Elite-led in terms of organization and design, there are strong elements of participation through the many ceremonies of remembrance that take place all over Britain as the only supra-national occasion in which the whole country is involved.

The role of television has emerged as an influential partner to national day design in the narration of public historical culture and communication over the last 20 years: 'More than any other educational institution, television plays a role in the formation of political opinions and the diffusion of historical knowledge' (Simon, 2008, p. 616). Television coverage can make a profound impact on the presentation of parading ceremonies in particular as it is able to provide sophisticated overhead views. Televised coverage reaches a larger proportion of the population and contributes to a sense of shared experience. Watching the military parade on Bastille Day it is clear that this ceremony has been adapted for television with views from the sky that are not seen from the ground. Remembrance Sunday in Britain is another example since movement is restricted around the main ceremonial area as is the Victory Parade in Moscow's Red Square.

Singing nationalism

National day design is closely connected to a variety of national symbolism that provides shortcuts to the nation. All processions and parades include music performances, whether provided by military units, massed bands, civilian corps or school bands, as these move the parades along the ceremonial routes. The performing of nationhood – the waving of flags, the singing of national anthems – contributes to visualizing commonality and membership. National(istic) music forms a central part of such performances. National anthems were systematized as part of the vehicle of symbolism, with modern nationalism and mass-politics in the nineteenth century when rhythmic elements were introduced in national ceremonies in similar ways to flags and national days appropriated to encourage the undivided loyalty of its citizens. National anthems spread beyond Europe and were often adopted akin to established musical traditions. Again, a successful symbolic code had been invented and was adopted as part of national communication.

It may seem somewhat anachronistic with the aspirations of European integration in mind that many of the European anthems are anything but peaceful. It may therefore come as a no surprise that many of them were shaped by the Napoleonic Wars and are about the waging of war. As noted, 'The flag, the anthem, and most national festivals always retained something of the nation-in-arms about them, even in times of peace' (Mosse, 1993b, p. 14). In fact, references to war, conflict, death and brotherhood became one main theme. Interestingly, many national anthems containing such references have not been altered and indicate that they have been drained of their original meanings and contexts.

Table 5.5 below is not exhaustive of changes and alterations but indicate the claimed dates that anthems (as text and/or lyrics) appear, as a rule, *after* national flags are in use. Additionally, many national anthems

Table 5.5 National anthems of Europe

Country	National anthem	Dates*
England Britain	God Save the King (Queen)	1745, 1808, *1825*
Spain	The Royal March (La Marcha Real) Today Himno Nacional Español	1770
France	La Marseillaise	1793, *1795* (1815–, 1852–70) *1879*
Netherlands	The William (Wilhemus)	1815, *1932*
Denmark	There is a Lovely Country	1835
Switzerland	Schweizerpsalm	1841, 1961, *1981*
Hungary	Anthem	1844
Sweden	Thou Ancient, Thou Free	1844
Wales	Land of my Fathers (Mae Hen Wlad Fy Nhadau)	1858
Belgium	The Song of Brabant (La Brabançonne)	1860
Norway	Yes, we love this country	1864
Greece	Hymn to Liberty	1865
Finland	Our Land	1867
Portugal	The Portuguese Song	1910
Albania	Hymn to the Flag	1912
Ukraine	Ukraine's Glory Has Not Perished	1917
Lithuania	National Song	1919
Estonia	My Fatherland, My Happiness and Joy	1920
Latvia	God Bless Latvia	1920
Poland	Dabrowski's Mazurek	1926, *1927*
Ireland	The Soldier's Song	1926
Italy	The Song of the Italians	1946, *2005*
Iceland	Hymn, O, God of Our Land	1944
Austria	Land of Mountains, Land on the River	1946
Faroe Islands	Thou fairest land of mine	1948
Belarus	We, the Belarusians	1955, 2002 lyrics
Germany	Deutschlandlied (verse 3) originally (verses 1–3)	1848 (1922–45) *1952, 1990*
Bulgaria	Dear Motherland	*1964*
Scotland	Flower of Scotland	1965, 1974
Romania	Awaken Thee, Romanian	1989
Slovenia	A Toast	1989
Macedonia	Today over Macedonia	1945, *1991*
Croatia	Our Beautiful Homeland	1991
Czech Republic	Where is My Home?	1918, *1993*
Slovakia	Lighting over the Tatras	1993
Moldova	Our Language	1994
Russia	State Hymn of the Russian Federation	2000
Montenegro	O, Bright Dawn of May	*2004*
Serbia	God of Justice	1904, *2004*
Bosnia-Herzegovina	National Anthem of BiH	1999, 2009 lyrics
Kosovo	Europa	*2008*

Note: * Dates are subject to availability and interpretation and presented in the following order: first claimed origin, followed by periods not officially recognized (in parentheses) and/or the year established by decree or law in *italics* where available.
Sources include: (Bristow and Reed, 1993; Hang, 2003; Leonard, 1996; National Anthems website, 2010).

appear *in between* the establishment of flags and national days. Interestingly, some anthems have never actually been officially adopted and the overwhelming majority were introduced in the twentieth century.

God Save the King and the *Marseillaise* are two European prototypes that inspired many other European anthems (Nettle, 1967). The British anthem, written in a warlike context to a soothing piece of music with a singular message sets a path for the anthems to follow connecting a singing message to the nation. *God Save the King* was first performed in the presence of the king at the Drury Lane Theatre in 1745 by actors wanting to show loyalty to Charles Edward Stuart (Bonnie Prince Charlie) the claimant to the English throne during the Jacobite rebellion (1745–46). The music was distributed via a Gentleman's Magazine and the anthology *Thesaurus Musicus* in 1745 (Cerulo, 1995, p. 19) and authorized by the government as the official national hymn in 1825 which makes it one of the oldest official national anthems. The warlike verse two 'O Lord our God arise, scatter his/her enemies, and make them fall: confound their politics, frustrate their knavish tricks, on Thee our hopes we fix: God save us all' has been cause for some debate but there has not knowingly been any serious discussions to change it. However, today verse three has been found more appropriate in the context of church services on Remembrance Sunday: 'Thy choicest gifts in store, on her be pleased to pour, long may she reign: may she defend our laws, and ever give us cause, to sing with heart and voice: God Save the Queen'.

Many of the war-like European anthems were modelled on the revolutionary *La Marseillaise*, first known as *Le Chant de guerre pour l'armée du Rhin*. It was written and first performed in Strasbourg in April 1792 (by Rouget de Lisle) upon the news that France had declared war on the King of Bohemia and Hungary (Vovelle, 1998). Clearly a war song repeating its theme after each of the seven verses, it is characteristic of the time: 'To arms, oh citizens! Form up in serried ranks! March on, march on, may their impure blood flow in our fields'. These lines were directed against foreign armies but also against counter-revolutionary forces: 'Arise children of the motherland, our day of glory has arrived! Over us, the bloodstained banner of tyranny holds sway'. Regardless of these references, the *Marseillaise* became known as the hymn of liberty of the Republic, invoking freedom and devotion. The minister of war, Servan, argued in 1792: 'the national anthem known as *La Marseillaise* is the *Te Deum* of the Republic, the song worthiest of the ears of free France' (Vovelle, 1998, p. 37). In 1793 the Convention ordered the anthem to be sung at all Republican events and from 1794 it was allegedly 'sung at every show and on every street corner in Paris' (Vovelle, 1998, p. 39).

In 1795 it was established by the Convention as the national anthem, which makes it the first officially adopted national anthem in Europe. The *Marseillaise* was part of a cultural revolution and a central feature of the revolutionary process. In contrast to the Tricolour, it never been altered. However, it was together with the Tricolour banned by Napoleon and his Empire, by Louis XVIII in 1815 (the second restoration) and by Napoleon III (1852–70). It was again reinstated in 1879 and transformed from a revolutionary song into a national anthem during the period of conflicts that followed (1879 to 1919).

The *Marseillaise* forms an integral part of Bastille Day to this day and its chorus is played at the presentation of the national colours. President Giscard d'Estaing attempted to have it played at a slower tempo for greater solemnity, following the nineteenth century conservatives who preferred an *oratorio Marseillaise* but the suggestion caused a storm of protest (Vovelle, 1998). Serge Gainsbourg sang a reggae version of the anthem in the 1970s and allegedly received death threats from war veterans (Lindblad, 2010). The official view below:

> Some people are offended during national ceremonies, when they hear such vengeful verses as 'these ferocious soldiers who slaughter our sons and wives' or demanding 'that impure blood flow in our fields.' But the majority of French people do not wish to change so much as a comma in their national anthem. Didn't the members of the Resistance in WWII sing it as a final and supreme challenge to Nazi-occupying forces as they fell beneath the bullets of the firing squad? [...] One can not tamper with that which is sacred! (Embassy of France Official Website, 2010)

In contrast to the French *Marseillaise*, the national anthem in Germany has been changed on a number of occasions over the centuries. The imperial anthem *Heil dir im Siegerkranz (Hail to Thee in Victor's Garlands)* in use prior to 1919 and sung to the melody of *God Save the Queen* was changed with the republic to *Deutschlandlied* from 1922 to 1945. The ill-famed anthem *Deutschland, Deutschland über alles, über alles in der Welt* was originally directed against the rulers of the formerly independent principalities opposed to unification but later reinterpreted aggressively with the myth of the Battle of Langemarck a symbol of triumph and heroic youth becoming part of the Nazi programme of regeneration. The image of the young warrior dying for his country is present in many anthems and whereas *Deutschlandlied* took a more defensive posture at first it was brought to its peak during the Nazi regime which instituted 'a veritable cult of anthems' as part of national worship. The musical forms used were similar and the anthems were simple, plain and heroic. In view of the history of *Deutschlandlied*, it took Germany several years to settle on an anthem after the Second World War when it did not have an anthem for some time. Finally it was decided to keep the third verse of the original anthem calling for unity: 'Unity and rights and freedom for the German fatherland. Let us strive for it together, brotherly with heart and hand' (Bristow and Reed, 1993). Many critical voices wanted the anthem banned but the third verse was re-adopted as the anthem in West Germany in 1952 and later the anthem of a united Germany after reunification of 1990.

In terms of pastoral and peaceful hymns these have traditionally been confined to smaller nations such as Switzerland, Norway and Finland. Many of these have attempted to establish an analogy between the nation, its 'divine' foundation and nature. As in the first verse of the Swiss national anthem the *Schweizerpsalm* (1841): 'When the Alps glow bright with splendour, pray to God, to Him surrender, for you feel and understand, for you feel and understand, that He dwelleth in this land' (Bristow and Reed, 1993). In Norway, a competition was held in order to select a national anthem in the 1820s. The winning contribution in 1827 – *Sons of Norway the Ancient Kingdom* – was sung on the first celebration of Constitution Day. The current national anthem *We love this Country* (lyrics by Bjørnstjerne Bjørnson, melody by Rikard Nordraak) was introduced to mark the fiftieth anniversary of the adoption of the Constitution in 1864 when it was officially adopted (Bristow and Reed, 1993; National Anthems Website). The Norwegian anthem claims continuity with a golden age and links this to nature and family with the words: 'Yes, we love this country which looms up rocky and weathered above the sea with its thousand homes. [We] love it, love it and think about mother and father and the sagas that send dreams to our earth and the sagas that send, send dreams to our earth' (Bristow and Reed, 1993). Today, other national songs are included in the national day celebrations, with significant titles such as *We are a nation too* and *The land we inherited*.

An interesting anthem that breaks with the traditional content of national anthems is the anthem of Kosovo called *Europe*. Kosovo had adopted an instrumental national anthem in 2008. It was written by the Kosovo composer Mendi Mengjiqi and voted the winner in the competition in Parliament: 'The rules stated that the song should not imply loyalty to any particular ethnic group' (BBC, 11 June 2008). An instrumental anthem was also adopted in Bosnia-Herzegovina in June 1999 and was given lyrics in 2009, after ten years of deliberation as an agreement could not be reached. The final line of the current anthem states: 'We are going into the future together' (Balkan Insight, 23 February 2009; Website of the Office of High Representative, 1999). Thus, in line with the flag-related symbolism discussed earlier, Kosovo and Bosnia-Herzegovina break existing patterns also with regards to their adopted anthems. In this context, we remind ourselves of the reasons why the European anthem *Ode to Joy* has remained instrumental.

Ceremonial and processional routes

National day design has also come to depend on the construction of public spaces such as Trafalgar Square and Whitehall in London, Arc de Triomphe and Champs-Élysées in Paris, Karl Johann's Avenue in Oslo, the Red Square in Moscow, Wenceslas Square in Prague, Vabaduse Plats in Tallinn, Hősök Tere (Heroes' Square) in Budapest, Piazza della Republica in Rome, Brandenburg Gate in Berlin, Puerta del Sol in Madrid or Senaatintori (Senate Square) in Helsinki. Ceremonial routes provide the framework for national day ceremonials and symbolic action made permanent through urban iconography symbolizing a shared history and golden age (A.D. Smith, 1986). The peak of the construction of European national capitals took place between 1850 and 1914, during one era of nationalist mobilization, mass migration, urbanization, mass education and class polarization. National monuments reinforce a feeling of permanence not only in terms of its material but because history is used as a mediator between past, present and future. Their significance may change over time but they reach an objective status as part of the national landscape (Bhabha, 1990; A.D. Smith, 1987, 1989). Thus it is as a vision of one collective identity expressed in public places and ceremonial routes that operates at the intersection of ceremony, urban design, capital architecture, art, imagery and monumentality. The referential framework of the iconographers of the *Belle Époque* was that of an historicism looking towards the future with a mass didactic purpose. Its architecture and sculpture drew inspiration from the Classicism of antiquity and the medieval Gothic and formed the monumental cornerstones of European capital cities (Therborn, 2002, 2006, 2007). Central and new institutions of authority were manifested in magnificent parliament buildings, palaces of justice or, where the monarchy was still significant, royal palaces. Religious devotion also left its imprints with architectural institutions such as Notre Dame, the Vatican, Westminster Abbey and St Paul's. The capital was hereby nationalized through the institutions of high culture and materialized also through operas, museums, libraries and universities, a process commencing in the eighteenth century and providing concrete forms of a *shared* national heritage. As such, national monuments and open places became an integral part of national festivals that had obtained a common national focus when rendered useful in creating bonds of loyalty.

Maps 5.1 to 5.3 constitute the ceremonial routes of Paris, London and Oslo and demonstrate that ceremonial space is standardized to a degree with historically significant places, avenues, monuments and institutions along the way but also in terms of logistics with a significant starting point via a nationally designed parading avenue leading to a ceremonial focal point.

The ceremonial route in Paris is part of the Grand Axe consisting of the Grand Arc de la Défense, the Arc de Triomphe (at L'Étoile), the Obélisque de Luxor in Place de la Concorde and the Arc de Triomphe du Carrousel (Palais du Louvre). The year 1789 marked the break with royal absolutism and left a lastingmark on Paris through symbolic investment in public space. Following the ceremonial route (see Map 5.1), the Arch of Triumph was commissioned by Napoleon in 1806 after his victory at

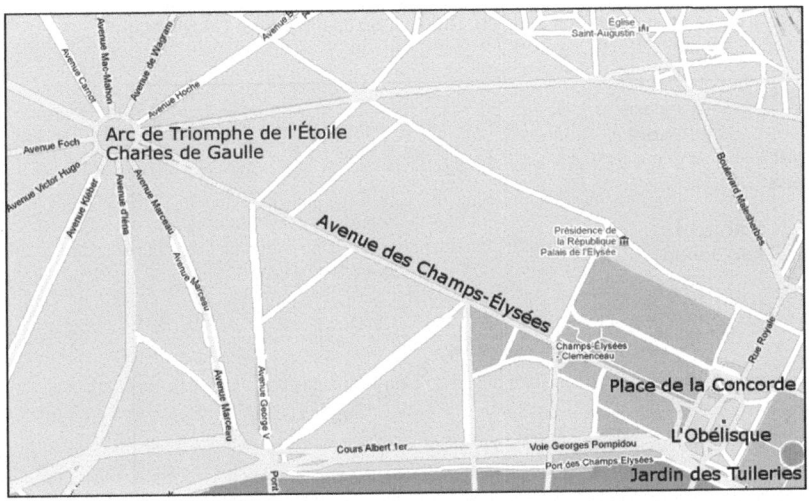

Map 5.1 Via Triumphalis of Paris
The ceremonial route commences at Étoile and Arc d'Triomphe (the Unknown Soldier) via Avenue Champs-Élysées to Place de la Concorde and the Tuileries. (Illustration adapted from Google Maps)

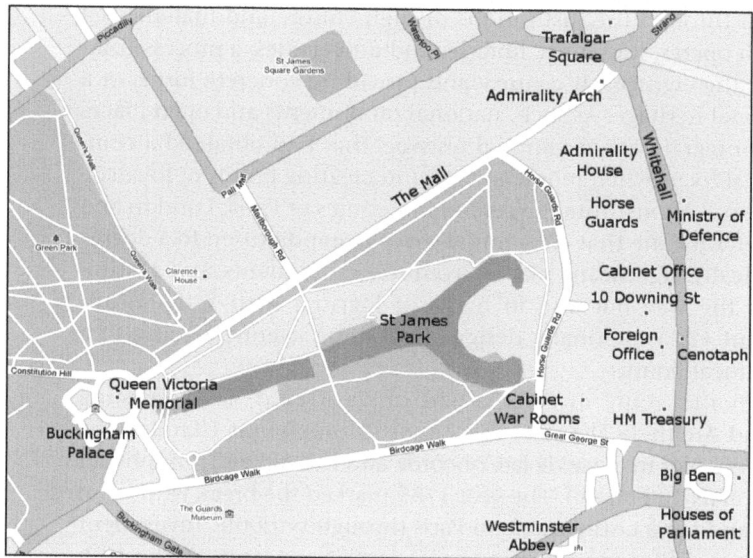

Map 5.2 The national and royal routes of London
The national route commences at Trafalgar Square via Whitehall and the Cenotaph towards the Houses of Parliament and Westminster (see Illustrations 4.4, 5.1 and 5.2). The royal processional route also departs from Trafalgar Square via The Mall towards Buckingham Palace (see Illustrations 5.3 and 5.4). (Illustration adapted from Google Maps)

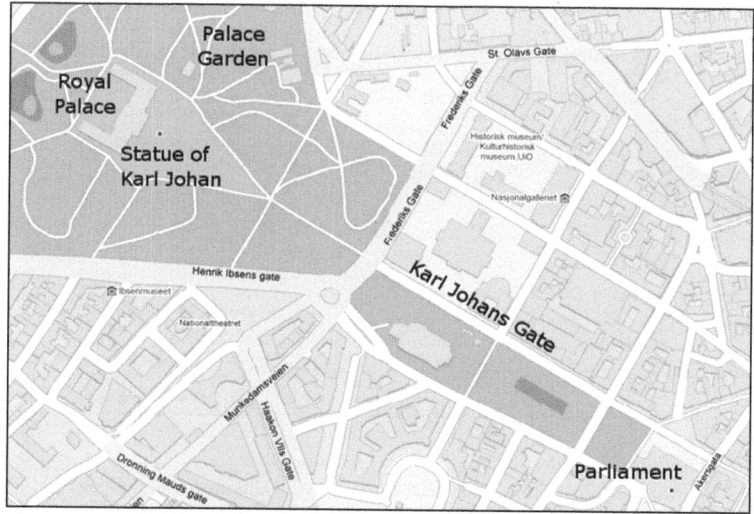

Map 5.3 Ceremonial route of Oslo
The royal and ceremonial route of Oslo via Karl Johan's Gate towards the Palace. (Illustration adapted from Google Maps)

Austerlitz and engraved atop are the names of major victories won during the revolutionary and Napoleonic periods. After 1830 the Arch was transformed to commemorate the fallen, later by installing the Tomb of the Unknown Soldier in 1919. The names of the smaller victories, and of 558 generals, are inscribed on the inside walls (A.D. Smith, 2003; Therborn, 2002). From the Arch leading to Place de la Concorde – the two kilometres long Avenue des Champs-Élysées – also called the Elysian Fields, a name evoking the mythical afterlife and the final resting place for the heroic and the righteous. Constructed in various phases during the seventeenth and eighteenth centuries, it is also named as one of the most expensive strip of real estate in Europe today. Moving to Place de la Concorde, this square was originally constructed (1754–63) under the rule of Louis XV and given the name Place Louis XV but became Place de la Revolution during the Revolution and location for Madame Guillotine or the National Razor (Agulhon, 1998). As all main squares in Paris were renamed and provided with suitable monuments of the new republic, Place de la Concorde has thus followed the turbulence of French history. As the largest square in Paris, representing France as a whole, it is the site for the statues representing the French cities of Lille, Strasbourg, Lyon, Marseilles, Bordeaux, Nantes, Brest and Rouen. The Bastille Day parade is televised from Place de la Concorde and provides hereby a view of the parade on Avenue des Champs-Élysées suitably framed with the Arch as a backdrop linking the parade to victory and sacrifice.

Britain's two main ceremonial routes depart from Trafalgar Square: the royal route via the Mall through Admiralty Arch to the Queen Victoria Memorial and Buckingham Palace, and the national route via Whitehall to Downing Street, Westminster and the Houses of Parliament. The chosen ceremonial route for Remembrance Sunday is a testament to the democratization of sacrifice. It should be noted that the Cenotaph was placed between Trafalgar Square (named after Admiral Nelson's victory and a tribute to Britain's naval history), the Houses of Parliament (site for governmental buildings since Henry VIII's court in the 1530s and current centre of British politics) and Westminster Abbey. The Abbey as the site of coronations and royal marriages is moreover replete with memorials to the heroes of the nation such as Newton, Livingstone, Chaucer, Johnson, Dryden and Browning. The placement of the Cenotaph in Whitehall was thus no coincidence, located as it was on the national spine of British history. A new anatomy of egalitarianism in ceremonial terms was hereby formed and this national route was intended to make the people and the state ritually egalitarian (Kapferer, 1988, p. 152). For this reason, the traditional royal route via the Mall was not considered appropriate and a Cenotaph was not intended for the Mall leading to Buckingham Palace. Instead, the Cenotaph was placed on Whitehall and among the institutions of the state that had called the soldiers to war in the first place.

In Oslo, the large-scale parade on Constitution Day begins beyond Karl Johan's Avenue (Karl Johan's Gate) and passes the Parliament (Storting) and moves towards the royal castle and royal gardens. Oslo's main avenue was built and named after King Karl XIV Johan of Sweden and Norway (reigned 1818–44) (Leiren, 2005). It may seem ironic that this street became integrated as part of the ceremonial framework as the King did not take to the expressions of Norwegian nationalism lightly. His statue still stands outside the royal castle overlooking the avenue and its inscription reads: 'Norway's and Sweden's King. The Norwegian People built this in his memory'. The statue was in place in 1875, several years after his death in 1844 and thus erected in the midst of the building of a new Norway by the then union-friendly forces. The monarch and royal family constitute *the* ceremonial focal point for the thousands of participants of the Constitution Day parade and provide *the* direction for the parade itself. The Norwegian monarchy is said to constitute a significant symbol of statehood achieved after a century-long struggle. Significantly, few publically critical voices are heard with reference to the large-scale celebrations. This is particularly interesting with reference to the homogeneous manifestations of Norwegian-ness but also to the central involvement of the royal family. The lack of critical public debate here demonstrates that national days and national day designs have received something of a sacred status and cannot easily be criticized, a subject we turn to below.

Creating moral federations and membership by sacrifice

National days are also means by which nations sanctify their acclaimed virtues, values and purposes in particular in reference to membership by sacrifice. Honouring war dead and national heroes remains a significant part of European national day design and constitutes in effect a way to re-establish sacrificial boundaries and membership. Many national days include a sombre start to the festivities with the laying of wreaths at memorials, commemorative ceremonies and church services. Reference to the community of sacrifice is also integrated through monuments as part of ceremonial routes and public places, such as the Arch in Paris and the Cenotaph in London. The celebrations of the Norwegian national day commence with the honouring of the nations' great and take place all over the country in the morning before the children's parade. Speeches are given in Oslo at the graves of Wergeland, Bjornson, Ibsen and the first men shot during the Nazi occupation of the Second World War. National sacrifice and righteousness is thus linked to membership and to the greatness of nations. Staged as part of the national day, commemorations have developed with new forms of iconography and sacred places.

As national festivals appeared, marked by the imaginations of the community as one, new materializations linked sacrifices to ceremonies. In fashion similar to Christian notions, the morality of the community was achieved through these sacrifices. Nations were to demand sacrifices by a body of citizens whose equality was both realized and reinforced through this manifestation of equality in sacrifice, the latter a prerequisite for the *oneness* of the community. Thus, nationalism in Europe has continued to depend on the ceremonial ways of the Christian world where hopes and fears are acted out within liturgical forms. Commemorative ceremonies are of particular significance with their contribution to the formation of moral codes and values. The justifying quality of history would be swept away unless events, places and heroes were materialized, honoured or consecrated. 'If we still dwelled among our memories, there would be no need to consecrate sites embodying these' (Nora, 1998, p. 2). A substantial bank of pre-existing motifs of 'sacrifice' and 'martyrdom' provided nations with a framework for myths of salvation and ideals of sanctity and heroism through the sacrifices of members of the community (Durkheim, 1976). The extensive use of symbols and ceremonies, contributes in these ways to a loosely defined 'secular' religion in which self-representation can become a powerful component referring to a notion of an *authentic* past and restoration of an *authentic* community (Mosse, 1975, 1993a). In the particular context of warfare (Hutchinson, 2009) this amounts to the construction of sacred and moral communities.

Revolutionary France constitutes an early example where the impact of nationalism in the building of the French state is unambiguous with the convocation of a national assembly, the drawing up of a national constitution and the choice of national symbols (Alter, 1994). The ceremonial activity in place gave form to the political religion in which the people, now deified, began to worship themselves as previous monarchical emblems sanctified by religious and aristocratic ceremonies and codes were 'replaced by *a national flag* (the tricolour), a stirring *national anthem* (the Marseillaise), and great open-air festivals of public dedication (oath-taking) to and *commemoration of the nation*' (Hutchinson, 1994, p. 39). With reference to Bastille Day, Victor Hugo argued that the overthrowing of Bastilles constituted the deliverance of humanity, as did Gambetta who identified the storming of the Bastille as the Day when 'we received our New Testament' (Amalvi, 1996, p. 122). They hereby challenged the Catholic Church that had had almost exclusive control over public space in France since 1815. With help of Bastille Day and careful planning (of public celebrations, dedications of statues, parades, processions and commemorations) this Day was intended as a shared experience for which the sacred character of religious ceremonies was to be transferred to a secular sphere. As an illuminating example we find that even *Pater Noster* was republicanized and recited on 14 July in 1880:

> Our father, who art in the nation's Élysée, glory be thy name. May Liberty, Equality, and Fraternity reign through thee on earth, and may the will of our forefathers of 1789, that man should be his own master, be done. Give us this day our Liberty, and forgive us our sins against the Republic. Give us the strength to defend the democratic Trinity and deliver us from the evil that we may involuntarily do to it. Amen. (Amalvi, 1996, p. 134)

Within such contexts the nation emerged as a 'sacred communion' that invited people into mass-celebrations (A.D. Smith, 2003). The display of such community-oriented enthusiasm transformed the symbols associated with the Republic – the Fatherland, Liberty and Reason – into sacred ideals. With the privilege of defining the public sphere, the republicans replaced Virgin Mary with Goddesses of Reason, transformed churches into temples of the nation, most notably with the Cathedral of Notre Dame which became the Temple of Reason and the Panthéon: Aux grands hommes la patrie reconnaissante. Thus, the French Revolution marked a transition of mass-celebration from the cult of the Church to the cult of the people, which was to continue into the twenty-first century and today expressed with the formalization of national days, the re-invention of old ceremonies and the introduction of new ones which are discussed towards the end of this chapter.

Nationalization of sacrifice – remembering the fallen

Days of Remembrance and victory have been transformed into de facto national days in the cases of Remembrance Sunday in Britain and Armistice Day in Belgium. Victory Day in Russia, today with somewhat different associations, also falls within this category. These days have provided a foundation for a supra-national narrative challenged by competing nationalities and ideologies. In Britain and also in Belgium, with separate celebrations by the Flemish and French communities, the days of remembrance have become supra-national days of reflection.

Remembering the war dead emerged with the age of mass politics and democratic awareness (Mosse, 1990; Winter, 1995) and developed as a ceremony to inspire and unite the living (A.D. Smith, 1996) that through the remembrance of sacrifices were authenticated by the dead. The scale of death was unprecedented after the First World War and *democratizing sacrifice* was a necessity in order to dampen resentment. The discontent in the army and industrial unrest had a great impact on the establishment of Remembrance Sunday in Britain. The Cenotaph ceremony helped transform the victory parade, a moment of high politics and potential protest, into a solemn occasion where millions contemplated the reality of death in war but also reinforced patriotic feelings justifying the sacrifices. It is noted that 'the government feared that Bolshevism might gain a foothold in Britain. Therefore, it was felt that everything possible should be done to use the victory to work up patriotic feeling' (Mosse, 1990, pp. 95–6). Traditionally, war monuments commemorated kings, emperors, generals and admirals and officers had their names inscribed and graves marked on the war memorials in Europe. Now nations constructed tombs dedicated to unknown soldiers, cenotaphs and mass cemeteries for the dead and turned mourning into a collective cult (A.D. Smith, 2003). The war cemeteries were easily distinguished from civilian cemeteries through the mass graves that 'left no doubt that the war dead were not only comrades but above all members of the nation rather than individuals' (Mosse, 1990, p. 85). Whereas mass cemeteries referred to national loss they simultaneously also glorified oneness and moral triumph. Counterparts to the Cenotaph in Whitehall, the Unknown Soldier's tomb in Westminster Abbey in London and Le Tombeau du Soldat Inconnu at Arc de Triomphe in Paris, were created in Rome and Berlin. In Rome the tomb was positioned after the First World War at the Vittorio Emmanuele monument (1910) honouring Italian unification, whereas the neoclassical guardhouse designated for the Unknown Soldier in Berlin was raised as late as 1931 and part of the reinvention of nationhood in a defeated Germany. In Italy a bereaved mother selected the Unknown Soldier by putting white flowers on one of 11 coffins, in Belgium it was a blinded veteran, in Romania a war orphan pointed to one of ten coffins and stated 'This is my father' (Inglis, 1993, p. 11).

Commemorations around empty coffins originated as an Athenian tradition during the wars against Sparta, a practice later adopted by the Roman Empire. In Britain, remembering the dead of the Boer War

(1899–1902) served as a model for Remembrance Sunday. Christian iconography played a vital part in the building of memorials and in the mourning process that helped sanctify the sacrifices (Moriarty, 1991). The cross is therefore a common type of symbol connected to memorials after the First World War: 'Without the biblical imagery purveyed through the Church, the men at the front and those at home would have had hardly any "containers" at all to help them through those four years of constant death and bereavement' (Wilkinson, 1978, p. 196). Thus, the Cenotaph in Whitehall became a civic crucifix and a symbol of resurrection testifying to the moral achievements of the dead and their significant contribution to the worthy cause of protecting the nation. A ceremonial *chronotope* was created by Lutyens' Cenotaph – anonymous and simple – providing a focus for collective mourning allowing people to ascribe their own meanings to it (Winter, 1995). Interestingly, the burial of the Unknown Soldier in London also involved Westminster Abbey. The Cenotaph was unveiled as the *empty* tomb of the Unknown Soldier whereas the body of the Unknown Soldier was carried through procession in London and was reburied in Westminster Abbey in 1920. However, the 'crucial image was not the tomb itself, but the story of the selection of the body from the cemeteries on the Western Front' (King, 1998, p. 139) and the circumstances that would make sure he was unidentifiable. The French followed the British example and reburied the Unknown Soldier at the Arc de Triomphe. The French, too, used the symbolic inscription 'warrior', chosen to emphasize the heroic sacrifice of a heroic age.

> Originally, there was no reason to expect that the events and memorials which constituted public reflection on the Great War would be so overwhelmingly concerned with death. The royal proclamation which instituted the two minutes' silence specified that it was to 'afford an opportunity' to 'perpetuate the memory of the Great Deliverance' as well as 'of those who laid down their lives to achieve it'. The committee which made the arrangements for the Armistice Day ceremony at the Whitehall Cenotaph in 1921 intended to set a tone to be copied throughout the country, and insisted in its recommendations that 'Armistice Day is not a day of national grief'. (King, 1998, pp. 216–17)

However, Remembrance Sunday became a day of reflection and mourning and by design more like a state funeral fusing civic and religious symbolism such as crosses, funeral music, funeral dress, the Cenotaph itself and associated symbols and practices (see Illustration 5.1).

Illustration 5.1 Nationalism, Christianity and sacrifice, Remembrance Sunday
The Cenotaph Ceremony on Remembrance Sunday in Whitehall, London. A crucifix is displayed on large screens and transmitted to viewers during the service led by the Bishop of London. Photography by Gabriella Elgenius (2009d).

Notions of destiny, the glory of self-sacrifice and transcending death were significant themes in the formative years of many remembrance ceremonies. The links between nationalism and Christianity, death and sacrifice are closely interconnected in the Western world and the persuasive power of nations manifested in the willingness to die for the imagined community (Anderson, 1991) and act against their self-interest (Reicher et al. 2007). Still today, as the cross is displayed on large screens and transmitted to viewers, the Bishop of London states at the Cenotaph: 'we who here honour those who died in the service of their country and the crown, may be so inspired by their spirit of love and fortitude that we, forgetting all selfish and unworthy motives, live to your glory and to the service of mankind through Jesus Christ our Lord.' The service closes with a blessing and ties the living with bonds of gratitude to the dead.

Is remembering the dead still important?

The collective function of commemorative ceremonies (remembering and honouring the dead) has been said to have gained a more individual character in a 'post-national era' (Gillis, 1994). In sharp contrast to the formative years of Remembrance Sunday and the periods of mass-loss of the First and Second World Wars, it is noted that visitors today pay in order to get into Westminster Abbey and the tomb of the Unknown Soldier. The Cenotaph, in turn, does not draw the same number of visitors as does Arc de Triomphe in Paris, the latter having become a landmark of the capital. This suggests that the importance of the Cenotaph and its symbolism is connected to its ceremonial context and also that as a national shrine its significance is expected to have decreased as the population directly involved in the wars aged. Research on British national pride indicates that the decline of Britishness is exclusively generational in nature and that younger generations have substantially lower levels of pride in being British compared with older generations (Tilley and Heath, 2007). However, a recent popular resurgence in significance and public profile is related to military engagements in Iraq and Afghanistan.

The extent to which Remembrance Sunday is sustainable in current ceremonial form is uncertain. Its aim to provide an umbrella for remembrance in a multinational, multi-faith and multi-ethnic society is ambitious and the ceremony was from the outset designed as a British affair. On a national level, Remembrance Sunday in Northern Ireland has remained contested owing to its British origin and has been abhorred by nationalists, most notably in the related IRA bombing of Remembrance Sunday in 1987 (Robinson, 2010). One major obstacle was 'the extensive use of British national symbols such as the union flags and the national anthem in remembrance ceremonies. In the rest of the United Kingdom this would generally not have been a problem, but in Northern Ireland such symbols were associated exclusively with the Protestant community and thus served to designate war remembrance as Protestant' (Robinson, 2010, p. 84). In consequence, wearing the poppy has become a complicated matter in Northern Ireland and a political statement with poignant political symbolism that cannot be avoided whether you wear it or not. In the context of the latter, avoiding wearing a poppy may refer to anti-British, anti-unionist or nationalist sentiments (Quilley, 2000). In Northern Ireland the 'history of war commemorations in Troubles-era Northern Ireland show the power of commemorative forms, but primarily suggests that commemoration and other rituals may be less about the events which they ostensibly remember' (Robinson, 2010, p. 80). Remembrance Sunday in Northern Ireland therefore had to be redesigned so that both Protestants and Catholics would be able to connect to it.

In terms of the related multi-ethnic and multi-faith representation, the first invitations to attend the Cenotaph ceremony were extended in 1924 and corresponded with the inclusion of the religious service by the Bishop of London. The faith leaders invited at the time represented the Baptist, Congregational, Presbyterian, Catholic, United Methodist, Wesleyan, Church of Scotland and the Chief Rabbi. The numbers of attendees varied in the formative years and the Department of Culture, Media and Sport (Green, 2010) notes that the Salvation Army was first invited and attended in 1933, the Unitarian and Free Christian Churches in 1945 and the Free Church Federal Council from 1947 onwards. A representative from the Catholic community was invited in 1924 but did not attend until 1967 (a matter that must be related to the issue discussed above) whereas the Church of Scotland did not respond to its first invitation. In 1972 representative changes corresponded to the formation of the United Reformed Church from the incorporation of the Presbyterian and Congregational Churches in England (Green, 2010). There has, in other words, been continual and significant discussion on the matter of faith representation since 1924. We note this and consider that the current faith representation at the Cenotaph was agreed as late as 1999–2000 following consultation with the Chaplains-in-Chief to the armed forces and the Cohesions and Faiths unit at the Department for Communities and Local Government. Altogether 14 faith leaders were invited to attend the ceremony in 2000 representing the Baptists, Buddhists, Free Churches, Greek Orthodox, Hindus, Jews, Methodists, Muslims, Reform Movement for Judaism, Roman Catholics, Salvation Army, Sikhs, Unitarian and Free Christian Churches and the United Reform Church. This initiative followed local initiatives of multi-faith representation in remembrance ceremonies, some of which, most notably in Southampton in 1994, had been criticized in local press and claimed to have turned 'the remembrance ceremony into a political farce' (Gilliat-Ray, 1999, p. 239). In order to combat such views and to take steps towards the modernizing of a ceremony steeped in protocol, representatives of long-established non-Christian faith communities in Britain were also to be acknowledged as were the sacrifices of voluntary and civilian services, also previously excluded. As an example of the latter, the First World War Pardon Association represented those shot for alleged cowardice or desertion during the First World War in 2000 (BBC News, 11 November 2000).

However, a ceremony described as the 'uniting of a nation' (BBC News, 2009) has remained contested among British Muslims. From a theological perspective, participation is complex because of the prohibition of participation in non-Muslim ceremonies and with the current format of the Cenotaph ceremony in mind there is a concern that there could be 'a hostile response at the ceremony in front of the world media' (Kaplan, 2010) in protest against recent wars. Moreover, anti-war sentiments and the lack of recognition for the suffering in Iraq and Afghanistan in such ceremonies pose a challenge and raise complex questions related to national identity and loyalty (Ansari, 2009; Field, 2010). Figures also confirm that the war in Iraq, for example, has damaged British Muslims' trust in political institutions (Heath, 2006). Awareness of such sentiments within its communities in Britain and the sensitivity of the issues involved made the Muslim Council of Britain produce a report on Remembrance Sunday (2009) in order to highlight Muslim contributions to Britain's armed forces (Field, 2010; MCB, 2009). The report concluded: 'Remembering the shared sacrifices of our armed forces who came from all faith groups and racial backgrounds can help us to unite around a "Britishness" that has optimism and confidence about the future while being rooted in the shared and divergent histories of our country' (MCB, 2009, p. 3).

Following this discussion of multi-ethnic and multi-faith recognition leads to the late official recognition of the role of women in the world wars. Today, female participation is noticeable in the march past the Cenotaph especially since 2000, but it is noteworthy that the contributions of women in the Second World War were recognized by a separate monument (in bronze) at the Cenotaph as late as 2005 (see Illustration 5.2). In fact, a war monument to animals that suffered and died alongside the British, Commonwealth and Allied Forces in the twentieth century was completed and unveiled the year before in 2004 (Park Lane, Animal in War Memorial Fund).

Ceremonial design operates as a proxy for related debates on membership and citizenship as traditionally marginalized groups have gained access to national ceremonies at an even slower pace than to other social institutions. There are a number of related and complex issues to explore here, among them the lack of acknowledgement of sacrifices of perceived current or former allies and/or enemies. There are also a number of ways in which the worthiness of sacrifice, the justification of death in war, continues to be perpetuated officially. In general, the official representation of Remembrance Sunday enforces a moral imperative and provides a loyal portrayal to dominant ceremonial messages. The nature of televised coverage of remembrance events and of Remembrance Sunday itself contributes to narrating the justification of sacrifice

Illustration 5.2 Women of the Second World War
Monument dedicated to the women who served Britain in uniform and on the home front. The monument, in bronze, unveiled by the Queen in 2005, is located on the ceremonial route of remembrance at the Cenotaph at Whitehall in London. Photography by Gabriella Elgenius (2009c).

and also to disempowering those who are critical. The sophistication of televised coverage provides a tidy and aesthetic package, far from the reality of sacrifice in war. It is also clear that the commemoration of sacrifice remains on the political agenda in warfaring nations. As an example, the Chancellor of the Exchequer, Gordon Brown, proposed that a Veterans Day would make a suitable addition to Remembrance Sunday in 2006. Inspired by the celebrations of Veterans Day in the United States, this day was to celebrate the British veterans and the worthiness of their pursuits. The 'Armed Forces Day', marking the commitment of all serving members, was later introduced and celebrated for the first time in June 2009. It takes place in a different city every year. About 1000 troops marched through Cardiff in 2010 and the military parade will take place in Edinburgh in 2011. A number of related initiatives have followed with the construction of this Day such as the creation of an Armed Forces Flag.

Remembrance ceremonies and monuments remain protected by law and those who break the rules of 'appropriate behaviour' are punished in one way or other. The emotional significance of sacrifice-related symbolism is noted as a student photographed urinating on a wreath of poppies at a war memorial in Sheffield in the United Kingdom only narrowly escaped jail. The photograph was reproduced by the British press and the student was told by the court: 'The image of you urinating over the poppy wreath on the war memorial in this city will make most people turn away in disgust, shock and sadness. It has undoubtedly distressed and upset many. The war memorial is a sacred and special place' (BBC, 4 November 2009; Metro, 5th November, 2009). Allegedly, one war memorial is desecrated in Britain every week. Figures released on the eve of Remembrance Sunday in 2009 claimed that 56 war memorials had been desecrated in 2008–9 (Shipman, 2009). Overall, it is noteworthy that few protests take place on the actual day of Remembrance Sunday. This is remarkable in view of the public outcry against the governments that commenced the wars in Iraq and Afghanistan.

The extensive wearing of poppies, as signs of remembrance, remains unique in Britain. This becomes a visible symbol in the weeks before 11 November and suggests that remembrance continues to be taken seriously. For our reference, 73 per cent of all adults allegedly wore a poppy according to the British Legion (Royal British Legion (Official Website), 2004) in 2001. Over 30 million pounds sterling were raised for the Poppy Appeal in 2009 when more than 26 million poppies were sold (Howse, 30 October 2009). However, emerging dissatisfaction is also visualized in this context by the production of a *white poppy* whose bearers protest against wars and the military associations of the red poppy but wish to honour the sacrifices of those who have died. The white poppy has been understood as a challenge to the perceived triumphalism and nationalism surrounding Remembrance Day.

Unsuccessful national days

The majority of national days constitute some form of community days and 'do not go unnoticed' (Geisler, 2007). However, they do not by default generate mass-participation and the lack of success also illuminates the complex nexus of nationhood building. The national days listed in Table 5.4 as elite celebrations, include those of Poland, Belgium, Denmark, Slovakia, Croatia and Russia. Significantly, all these nations have national holidays other than the officially named national day in which popular participation is evident. To clarify this point, besides its formal Constitution Day, Poland celebrates Independence Day (11 November 1918) and the Anniversary of the Battle of Warsaw

(15 August 1920) or Army Day. In Denmark, a national focus is provided for the royalists on the Queen's Birthday (16 April) and for many on Liberation Day (4 May) (i.e. liberation from Nazi occupation during the Second World War). In Belgium, Armistice Day (11 November) constitutes a community day. The Day of the Dynasty (15 January) is also celebrated as is Europe Day (9 May) at least in Brussels (Site officiel du Parlement de la Communauté Française, 2004). The Flemish community celebrates Flanders Day (11 July) in memory of the Battle of Golden Spurs in 1302 and the founding of the Flemish nation, as the French were defeated. This is a popular day of encompassing festivities, street parties, fireworks and concerts on Grande Place in Brussels. The French community in Belgium, likewise, celebrates Walloon Day (Fête de la Communauté française, 27 September) and the anniversary of the victory of the Walloon army over the Dutch invaders in 1830. Festivities last the whole of September. Some national days have been established so recently that a pattern is not yet established, including those of Slovakia, Croatia and Russia. However, Slovakia has two other popular celebrations: Victory Day (8 May 1945) and the National Slovak Uprising Day (29 August 1945), Croatia celebrates Independence Day (8 October) and the Day of Victory and Patriotic Gratitude (5 August) and Russia, as mentioned, commemorates Victory Day (9 May).

However, there are a few exceptions with nations that do not have popular national days. The state-led celebrations of the Swedish national day, the Day of the Austrian Flag and Unification Day in Germany cannot be considered popular days in comparison with other national days in Europe. In Sweden, although there has been some change in recent years, the contrast becomes clear when comparing the national day to the popular celebrations of Midsummer Eve, celebrated all over Sweden. These, however, are devoid of references to the Swedish nation or state. In Sweden, the mobilization of the population never reached the same level of participation as did Norway's call for independence. Sweden did not participate in the two world wars and remembrance of the fallen has thus never taken place. Two other examples are Austria and Germany. Popular participation is not evident on the Day of the Austrian Flag and Declaration of Neutrality (26 October 1955) nor on the German Unification Day (3 October 1990). Here additional factors must be taken into account. There are several potential founding moments in Austrian and German history, but the anxious approach to assertions of nationalism after the Second World War must be taken into account as one explanatory factor here. Below, an exploration of the German case sheds light in understanding these complexities.

National days in Germany

The history of German national celebrations is illuminating, characterized as it is by discontinuity and rupture, and the whole concept of a 'German national day' has given nation-builders considerable problems over time and highlights the difficulties involved in creating a national day in the past let alone in the present.

The end of French power in Germany and Poland and the War of Liberation gave rise to the first celebration in 1814 when nationalist forces declared with the decisive Battle of Leipzig (16–19 October 1813) 'the significant event of all Germans'. Significantly for a multi-religious state, these anti-French and anti-Catholic celebrations (19 October) coincided with the commemoration of the 'beginning' of the Reformation (31 October 1517) and were celebrated together (Mosse, 1990; Schulze, 2002). The Battle of Leipzig was seen as a celebration of freedom that throughout the nineteenth century helped revive anti-French feelings. The event was never officially recognized and did not survive nor engage the various political and religious groups in a divided Germany. As the German Empire was formed after the Franco-Prussian War (1870–71) the unchallenged annual festivity was the Birthday of the Kaiser, which was celebrated with a parade in his honour from 1871 onwards (Hattenauer, 1990, p. 137; Schulze, 2002; Zimmer, 1999). However, the celebrations of the conclusive defeat of the French army in the Franco-Prussian War Day of Sedan (*Sedan Tag*, 2 September) became cause for another divisive celebration in 1873 when proud declarations were made, for example, by the government of Rhein-Westphalia:

> The hand of the living God has visibly and forcefully interfered in history through the event of 2 September, and it will be easiest on this particular day of commemoration to remind the German people what great things the Lord has done for us. (Hattenauer, 1990, p. 142).

These conservative celebrations were never officially recognized, but enforced and highlighted existing divisions among: 'Kleindeutsche' against 'Grossdeutsche', pro-Prussians against anti-Prussians, rich against poor and Catholics against Protestants (Confino, 1997, p. 55). As an example of the emerging movement for class-associated rights, Kaiser Wilhelm II attacked the Social Democrats in Germany at the 25th anniversary of Sedan in 1895, describing them as 'that group of people, who are not worthy of calling themselves Germans' (Hattenauer, 1990, p. 143). This statement was provoked by protests against the involvement of the army in the celebrations. *Sedan Tag* also attracted protests from the Catholic Church that referred to Saint Sedan and a Satan's celebration. On behalf of the Catholic Church, the Bishop of Mainz prohibited his priests from taking part in the celebrations of military victories in 1874 with the rationale that 'the anniversary of every national holiday will tear open the old but continuously bleeding wounds' (Hattenauer, 1990, p. 145). By calling for celebrations of Sedan Day, the conservatives tried to take possession of the interpretation of the present.

Sedan Tag generated considerable political debate (between socialists and conservatives, republicans and monarchists) and alternative national days were continually being suggested. A national committee for German National Holidays was founded in Berlin in 1896 and sought to protect current national celebrations as the socialists mobilized the forces towards getting 1 May (Workers' Day) recognized as a national day. This day became an official public holiday in Germany in 1919 with the Weimar Republic but did not develop into a day of national unity. The Weimar Republic also established Constitution Day (11 August) with the hope of creating a generally accepted national day.

> Constitution Day (August 11) was supposed to induce loyalty to the new Republic. But even the official publication, published as a directive for the celebrations, displays an astounding ambivalence. Joy over the constitution is mixed with bitterness for the suffering of the German people. Nothing in the world is perfect, states the pamphlet, all is in flux, even the constitution. (Mosse, 1975, p. 124)

Constitution Day was designed as the chief Republican festival but was celebrated in August when all schools and institutions were on vacation. The Weimar Republic also introduced *Volkstrauertag* (Day of Mourning).

Much attention has been given to the celebrations of the Nazi regime and the plethora of nationalist and party celebrations that aimed to contribute to the appearance of unity (Lidtke, 1982) such as the adapted National Labour Day (1 May), Day of the Reich (30 January) in honour of the takeover in 1933, Day of the Party (24 February), Memorial Day of the Putsch of 1923 (9 November) and the NSDAP annual party rallies *Parteitage* (in August/September).

A devastated Germany did not recognize any official celebrations after the Second World War and the day that first provided national attention in the post-war Federal Republic of Germany (FRG) was the commemoration of the people's uprising in East Berlin in the former German Democratic Republic (GDR) in 1953. Hattenauer writes:

The citizens of the Federal Republic of Germany would probably have been without a national day for a long time, had not the workers' uprising on 17 June in 1953, taken place in the competing DDR [Deutsche Demokratische Republik] [...] While Soviet tanks were still on the streets of East Berlin, the German Parliament in BRD [Bundesrepublik Deutschland] convened and commemorated the dead, who had died in the struggle for freedom and national unity. (1990, pp. 168–9)

The uprising in East Germany in 1953 started as a protest against the high productivity norms imposed by the Soviet regime (Kappler and Reichart, 1996, p. 38). As a protest, the flag with the communist symbols was lowered at the Brandenburg Gate (Brandenburger Tor, Unter den Linden) under fire from the Soviet tanks. Besides the 25 000 East Germans who were arrested, condemned to harsh sentences of imprisonment or high fines, a minimum of 125 people were executed, among these 41 Soviet soldiers who had refused to obey orders and shoot at the Germans. The '17 June Committee' was established in West Germany with the aim of protecting the memory of this event. It is still active in organizing national commemorations and participates in the march through the Brandenburg Gate in honour of the people who died there. The 50th anniversary of the uprising in East Berlin was celebrated at the Brandenburg Gate in 2003. An opinion poll in 1984 concluded that over 80 per cent of West Germans accepted 17 June as the national holiday (Hattenauer, 1990, p. 174).

With the reunification of West and East Germany in 1990, Unification Day (*Tag der Deutschen Einheit* on 3 October) was officially adopted. In 1990 hundreds of thousands of people came together from both sides of the Brandenburg Gate and 71 per cent of the population claimed to celebrate unification. Church bells rang all over Germany and the flag for a united Germany was raised as a mark of unification (CNN, 1990). The 20th anniversary of the fall of the wall on 9 November 2009 was also a high profile event with a speech delivered by US Secretary of State Hillary Clinton and a broadcast message from US President Barack Obama at the Brandenburg Gate (CNN, 2009). However, Unification Day, despite these two extraordinary events, has primarily remained an elite event and mass participation is not evident. Instead, the main ceremony of the day is arranged by a different federal state annually and marks unification rather than celebrating a *national* day. The nature of the German televised coverage is characterized by ceremonies of a 'sit-down' character (Simon, 2008). The Unification ceremony is part of a larger educational framework of debates and documentaries but also dramas with the theme of reunification. In 2009 the Unification concert had been arranged in Saarland and it was the European anthem that concluded the televised ceremony instead of the German anthem (*Tag der Deutschen Einheit*, 2009). Thus, the emphasis is on civic elements and the constitutional basis of Unification Day and German symbolism (flag and anthem) is used sparingly.

In short, there has never been a national day in Germany around which the different social, political and cultural groups have been able to unite. Celebrations in the past were identifiable mostly or partly by 'others' and by the reviving of anti-French, anti-Semitic or anti-Communist feelings. Furthermore, when Nazi Germany, its leaders and their actions, were condemned after the Second World War, the moral basis of the nation was challenged. When nations are under scrutiny, the moral (re-)making attempted through national celebrations turn into a highly complex issue. The lack of national festivities in recent times is indicative of contradictory feelings towards nationality, and celebrations have turned towards the regions – *Länder* – and to some extent towards Europe, both foci providing new channels of acquiring a new neutral past and a re-invented history.

Successful national day designs

Most national days attract participation and engage people in one way or another. In this section we draw on the case studies, the celebrations in Europe as a whole and in particular the unrivalled celebrations on Constitution Day in Norway, to outline significant elements of successful national days structure and design. Having explored a number of cases in this book, a few criteria stand out as significant for participation and for engaging the public. As a rule, successful national days are attributed to celebrations becoming part of a living history that justifies the cause of the present, especially in the formative years. However, national day design and ceremonial choreography is also relevant in order to sustain an image of unity or commonality through which the nation traditionally is expressed.

Participation as key

Research conducted for the British Social Attitudes survey (Heath et al., 2007) found that whereas religious identity has declined most in Britain, religious communities remain strongest in terms of normative reference groups associated with a distinctive set of values. Participation in religious services was therefore understood as key for this sense of belonging to develop. So whereas religious identity is in decline it has retained a normative base. In terms of the much discussed British identity, however, it constitutes the weakest example as a normative reference group. It is less clear which attitudes and values are associated with a supra-national British identity and a sense of belonging does not seem to have any marked effect on social attitudes. Heath et al. (2007, p. 28, emphasis added) write:

> While we regularly interact with our fellow-citizens in our daily lives, there is very little which brings us together specifically as British citizens. Indeed, while Britain does commemorate the fallen on Remembrance Sunday, it is relatively unusual in not having any great public days of national celebration, such as Bastille Day in France, Independence Day in Greece, Constitution Day in Norway, Liberation Day in Bulgaria, or 4th July in the USA. *Imagination cannot, it seems, entirely make up for the lack of any real community relations.*

A sense of belonging or cohesion does not refer to an absence of conflict or a national idyll. On the contrary, Simmel (1964) drew attention to the role of external war and conflict as a form of sociation that helps make boundaries more distinct and draws people together. In Britain during the First World War expressions of unity could be found in the war effort and conflict with the external world did create a strong national bond. The First World War has been said to have virtually saved England from a civil war (Nairn, 1977) but domestic disunity was channelled through strikes and demonstrations for peace. In other words, despite internal conflict, an overall sense of unity based on opposition against external aggression was possible. However, wars and conflicts may simultaneously foster and undermine cohesion (A.D. Smith, 1981). In Russia during the First World War internal conflicts predominated over external ones as expressed through the fall of Tsarist Russia and the rise of Bolshevism.

Uniting (founding) myths

The differences with regards to the popularity of national days in Norway, Sweden and Denmark suggest that historical prerequisites are crucial. Appealing and uniting narratives – sometimes founding myths – are clearly important in the formative years as they help establish ceremonial content and direction. Foundation myths are likely to emerge in a crisis as they provide a framework for reinterpretation and compensation of the past. A golden age and the construction of links between founding fathers and members of the nation also highlight that 'historiography cannot, as a matter of fact, be easily separated from myths and myth building' (Stråth, 2000, p. 25) (A.D. Smith, 1986, 2003). The past provides justification for the present as most national days provide access to such significant events. The latter is in particular an issue with the many newly established Independence Days in Europe. Independence Days in Finland and Iceland – from Russia and Denmark respectively – are also based on such claims of nationhood (Thorsen, 2000). The Norwegian, Finnish and Icelandic national days are celebrated in different ways but receive more attention than their Danish and Swedish counterparts. The Danes and the Swedes honour their corresponding foundations connected with their constitutional reform but these have never appealed to the imagination of the people to the same degree. One explanation is linked to a higher degree of identification with the state in Sweden and Denmark, countries that occupied positions as great powers up until 1800 (Aagedal, 2002; Stråth, 2000), and nationhood was not mobilized in order to justify these states. It may not come as a surprise that the 1890s marks the beginning of the first 'flag-waving-celebration' in Stockholm with the Day of the Swedish Flag (1893) (Elgenius, 2011). The timing and organization must be seen as a reaction of hurt national pride as the celebrations of Constitution Day in Norway (against the union) reached mass-participating levels. The introduction of the national day in Sweden can also be interpreted as a remedy for internal disunity. Additionally it came to highlight the Swedish constitutional reform of 1809, significantly earlier, we note, than the Norwegian Constitution of 1814 and the Danish constitutional reform of 1849. The Swedish national day has been argued to be part of a package forging a common sense of nationhood (Rodell, 2009) and, seemingly, a not altogether successful one. Whereas the first official celebrations took place in 1916, the national day was only officially adopted in 1983 and did not become a public holiday before 2005, which suggests some ambivalence towards such a Day.

The differences with regards to the popularity and character of national days in Norway, Sweden, Denmark, Finland and Iceland suggest that historical prerequisites are important and that appealing uniting and national myths provide part of the explanation towards the success of national days. Few historical events seem to match the signing of a constitution that is no longer threatened in one of the wealthiest nations of the world, something that may suggest that historical complexities are not the only important factor for popular ceremonies. However, this Day played a significant role in the notion of linear development – birth, growth, decline and rebirth – and linked the Norwegians to 'all free peoples and to those who expected similar freedom'. In the formative years, the Norwegian case demonstrates that a unifying narrative is crucial. In this context the forming of the constitution coincided with the founding of the nation and has aptly been described as the history of a national cathedral (Thorsen, 2000).

Rivalry, days and contra days

The raising of boundaries against others facilitates ceremonial enthusiasm in the formative years and symbolic construction and embellishment generally increases in times when boundaries are undermined, blurred or weakened (Alba, 2005; A. Cohen, 1995). The development of national days has clearly provided a platform for the expression of rivalry with others as with national revival after the First and the Second World Wars characterized by 'great victory parades' led by military commanders. Moreover, national day rivalry and internal disunity between the classes and between the right and the left have also been factored into national days as has been described in France, Britain, and Norway but also in Germany. For example, Bastille Day in France was characterized by internal disunity along ideological lines and during 1906–14 the left regarded Bastille Day as the day for the bourgeoisie but rivalling political fractions united against the outbreak of fascist sympathies in France, 1935–36, and used Bastille Day as a means to revive their ideological basis. Lloyd George and his government in Britain were also keen to revive their ideological basis when planning the peace celebrations in July 1919 and noted that it 'was desperately considering any proposal to dampen revolutionary ardour'. Thus, demobilized soldiers were asked to march through towns and cities and during the 'period of difficulty in industrial centres [...] public opinion should be stirred up to the highest pitch' (Homberger, 1976, pp. 1429–30). Previous orders restricting any kind of amusements were also withdrawn. In order to encourage 'flag waving' Austen Chamberlain suggested that 'every brass band in the country should be let loose as often as possible' and 'everything possible should be done to work up a high patriotic feeling from the results of victory' (Homberger, 1976, pp. 1429–30). Thus, the patriotism, present in abundance in the streets was encouraged and coexisted with deep political discontent.

The popularity of Constitution Day in Norway follows the development of other postcolonial societies in which independence was achieved relatively late and nationhood perceived as vulnerable (T.H. Eriksen, 2005). However, the success of the independence movement is also explained by the existence of a Norwegian bourgeoisie and urban intelligentsia, found not only in Sweden. They had the foremost place in the national movement that was joined to wider issues of democratization. The latter became part of the nexus of symbolism associated with Constitution Day. Norway had maintained the Constitution of 1814 because of the social composition of the Parliament (Storting); its members were not from the landed aristocracy but from the bureaucracy merged with the politically engaged bourgeoisie. Urban representation in the Storting (1815–27) was 48 per cent officials to 45 per cent merchants, (1830–42) 60 per cent officials to 34 per cent merchants, and (1845–57) 50 per cent officials to 32 per cent merchants. The influence of the peasantry also increased with rural representation for the same periods: (1815–27) 45 per cent peasants and 47 per cent officials, (1830–45) 59 per cent peasants and 31 per cent officials, and (1845–57) 63 per cent peasants and 29 per cent officials (Hroch, 1985, p. 36). The rural public was also engaged with the publication of popular books and periodicals (*Nationalbladet* and subsequently *Statsborgeren*) that advocated democratization of Norway's institutions. In this context, the Norwegian flag appeared in Constitution Day parades and was transformed into a powerful political symbol of democracy and rights first associated with the politics of the liberals and the socialists and articulated against their more union-friendly opponents and the ruling classes. The Norwegian flag and national day thus emerged as mass-symbols associated with the struggle for equality in a wider perspective contributing to their original appeal.

Returning to rivalry between different nationalisms and the outstanding claims to nationhood in the context of Scandinavia it is clear that Norway was not the only country affected, as illustrated by the dates of adoption and counter-adoption of flags, anthems and national days in Table 5.6.

The symbolic pattern of Scandinavia appears with territorial symbolism linked to the growing states of Denmark and Sweden with constant warfare between these two arch enemies. The first likely use of the Swedish flag is linked to the many wars with Denmark and adopts a similar symbolic code of the cross with different colours. The flags of Norway, Finland and Iceland appeared as symbols claiming nationhood for states-to-be. The introduction of the flags and national days in Scandinavia demonstrates considerable competition between rival nationalisms, characterized by Denmark and Sweden wanting to dominate the other countries. The differences between the date of

170 *Symbols of Nations and Nationalism*

Table 5.6 Scandinavian rivalry and claims to nationhood

Country	Flag	Anthem	National day
Denmark	1340	1835	1849
Sweden	1523	1844	1893 (1983)
Norway	1821 (1905)	1864	1827 (1905)
Finland	1862–63 (1917)	1867	1840 (1917)
Iceland	1918 (1945)	1944	1911 (1945)
Faroe Islands	1948	1948	1948

Note: Dates in parentheses demonstrate official recognition of national symbol if later than original introduction.

introduction and official dates of establishment in Norway (1905), Finland (1917) and Iceland (1945) are considerable and signs of achieved independence. Thus, the production of rival ethno-national symbols drew distinct markers against Denmark and Sweden and authenticated the existence of new states as the history of the nation was brought into the present. In Norway the bourgeoisie was in charge of producing such a package of expressions of peasant culture (customs, folk costumes, music and food) that was to be identified as typically Norwegian.

Ceremonial design and choreography

Whereas the historical origins are especially important in the formative years of national days, their continued appeal relies on the suitability of national day design and ceremonial choreography. A couple of matters stand out as significant for the design of celebrations, namely, elite sponsorship, the style and nature of the celebration and the inclusion of increasingly diverse national groups.

Sponsorship

Declaring the national day a public holiday is a prerequisite if it is to become part of public and private calendars alike (Elgenius, 2009e). The majority of national days in Europe are public holidays and citizens exempted from work. Public holidays are a costly affair, which speaks of the significance attached to them. The recently recognized national day (1983) and established public holiday (2005) in Sweden therefore replaced a religious holiday and expressions of Swedishness were encouraged without incurring extra costs (Elgenius, 2005a). The Swedish national day was for a long time a low profile event but increased awareness of its existence was granted with this central change. Just to get an idea of the price tags involved we note that, when it was announced that

St Andrew's Day in Scotland was to become a public holiday and exempt from work, the conservative opposition complained it would cost in the region of £180m (McCrone, 2009). St Andrew's Day was made a national day in 2007 but not a public holiday as the private sector did not approve (Scottish Parliamentary Corporate Body, 2005). Similarly, when the Confederation of British Industry discussed the future existence of a British Day, it argued that it ought to be introduced on an existing bank holiday because 'an extra bank holiday would cost the economy up to 6bn' (McCrone, 2009, p. 35). Such considerations did not prevent the declaring of a public holiday for the day of the Royal Wedding between Prince William and Catherine Middleton in April 2011.

It is thus noteworthy that the national days of Europe are costly annual affairs but nevertheless public holidays and demonstrate considerable financial commitment on behalf of elites, in itself an interesting route to explore. State and elite sponsorship of national days is intimately related to controlling images of the past that help justify social structures through ritual performances (Connerton, 1989) and the integration of national days into narratives and sites of memory. Constitution Day in Norway has throughout history enjoyed the support of various elite structures and has never been fundamentally challenged. As a national day it has also been successfully exported to the relatively small Norwegian communities around the world. For the centennial celebrations of Independence in 2005, the Norwegian Ministry of Foreign Affairs planned an ambitious programme of concerts, festivals, exhibitions and seminars world-wide. This highlights the fact that Constitution Day has remained a high profile political event thought significant for community regeneration. This is facilitated by the incorporation of Constitution Day into the curricula of primary and secondary schools, the extensive involvement of teachers and schools in the organization of children's processions and their interpretation of national identity and its relationship to Constitution Day. Furthermore, the encouraged relationship between children, the national day and the nation provides a route to early socialization into nationhood, children at an early stage becoming part of the public sphere as *Norwegians*.

Another aspect of elite sponsorship and contributions to sustaining national days is the support given to official and dominant narratives. The representation of historical themes through mass-media and television coverage is a major force in the narration of public historical culture (Simon, 2008) and the presentation of national day design. The contributions of television coverage are multi-dimensional: it contributes to the diffusion and recognition of underlying national narratives, to the presentation of a shared experience through simultaneous performance (Elgenius, 2005b), to the development of national day design with the increased sophistication of televised coverage. Clearly, mass-medial loyalty can change over time and with political circumstances (Dayan and Katz, 1992; Sanson, 1976) but loyalty to an overall ceremonial message undermines potential criticism. The televised coverage of the military parade on Bastille Day, Remembrance Sunday or Constitution Day maintains a loyal portrayal of the main message behind these ceremonies as discussed earlier.

Styles and signs of commonality

Feelings of membership are at their highest intensity when awareness of boundaries is heightened and the use of symbols reinforces the appearance of commonality in the context of national days. Belonging is thus visualized by signs of commonality that emphasize a common heritage. Whereas the display of the different national flags representing England, Wales and Scotland would emphasize difference and even division, the non-national poppy does the opposite and has become one of the few British symbols. The Ethnic Minority Election Survey, British Election Survey (2010) had even considered listing 'wearing the Poppy' as a measure of identification with Britain. Interestingly, the *non-denominational* poppy in England has become contested as a *denominational* symbol in Northern Ireland.

The success of Constitution Day in Norway over time is attributed to a unique ceremonial design with the children's parades, which has made a significant impact and ensured encompassing inter-generational participation of siblings, parents, aunts, uncles and grandparents. Overall, civilian and children's parades are seemingly more successful than any other form of parades and generate less public criticism and draw the different parts of the adult society together.

> The celebrations are well attended, and Norwegians presentations of self seldom fail to stress their unique character. While other states demonstrate their independence by sending tanks and soldiers to the streets, Norwegian celebrates their freedom by peaceful parades of children. They also thereby indicate the harmlessness of their own brand of nationalism, or so the say. (Blehr, 1999b, p. 175)

Similarly, waving the Norwegian flag, wearing the red ribbon (hung on the left side of the chest over the heart) and the regional costumes (*bunad*) help transform the reality of diversity into an appearance of similarity. This has made Eriksen (1997) argue that Norway is one of the most nationalist countries in Europe in which cultural homogenization and legitimation of the state has been facilitated through invented national symbols. By definition, regional costumes vary in style but since they are considerably different from contemporary fashions they contribute in their difference to a similarity of style. In effect, Constitution Day brings everybody in Norway back to pre-industrial times, as seen in the dress code, and citizens dress as if they have just arrived from the countryside. As noted, the cost of wearing such an outfit just once a year varies from £1500 (1800€) to £5000 (6000€) (Nielsen in Aagedal, 2002). This unique use of folk costumes on 17 May has lead Eriksen (2005) to depict Norwegian identity as essentially a rural identity and Kramer (1984) to describe it in terms of 'a lineage-based tribal community' in which rural origins are displayed. Displaying regional diversity as part of the national community has also made it possible to embrace a national identity that does not exclude regional loyalties. The regional costumes may be different in terms of decoration but their overall mode of expression is identical and points to a shared *national* ceremonial style. These costumes were designed by nationalists as part of the nationalization process early in the twentieth century. Depicted as typically Norwegian, the folk costumes have also been argued to have originated from the mountain valleys of southern Norway (T.H. Eriksen, 2002) as they intended to establish and visualize the unique heritage of Norwegian culture, in turn contributing to the justification for the independent Norwegian state.

The politics of inclusion

Little is known of the appeal of and the participation in national ceremonies especially in relation to gender, age, class or ethnicity. As noted by Gillis, the working class, ethnic minorities and women 'gained admission to national memories at an even slower pace than they were admitted to national representative and educational institutions' (Gillis, 1994, p. 10). For these reasons, marginalized groups and communities can use ceremonies of the dominant culture to subvert, co-opt or reject social structures (Etzioni, 2004), which constitutes one reason as to why their inclusion is understood as a prerequisite in nation-building terms. Generally speaking, men participate to a higher degree than women in formal ceremonies, as seen clearly with the military parades. However, the original success of Bastille Day was always described as a change away from ceremonial exclusion as citizens from the working

174 *Symbols of Nations and Nationalism*

classes now were invited into the national performances imagined as class*less*.

> From 1880s on, the majority of the French [...] threw themselves wholeheartedly into the day's activities, so that July 14 became a symbol, if not *the* symbol, of republican strength at the village level [...] French people of modest station no longer felt excluded from, and reduced to the role of mere spectators at, the nation's official celebrations as had been the case under the constitutional monarchy and the Empire. Now they were invited to become full-fledged participants [...] The national holiday was everybody's holiday, an occasion for families, children, and the elderly. For one day the strict social hierarchy was abolished. (Amalvi, 1996, p. 135)

Having said this, the official Bastille Day ceremony today has remained a primarily male and military event. In protest against the male notions of nationhood being prioritized, Monique Wittig and Christine Delphi in company with other French feminists, laid a wreath for the Unknown Soldier's wife on the tomb of the Unknown Soldier at the Arc de Triomphe in Paris in the 1990s. Accused of dishonouring and violating the memory of the soldier, the women were arrested and held at the nearest police station. In recent years Paris has also seen violent protests just on Bastille Day and car-burnings in run-down suburban areas have become expected occurrences. In 2009, police reported that 240 people were arrested and that the figure had doubled from the previous year (DeutscheWelle, 2009). Military ceremonies face additional challenges in order to appeal to a diversity of opinions. However, from a ceremonial point of view, landmark changes have taken place in recent years as seen in unprecedented reconciliation strategies – with reference to the international community at least. The German Chancellor was invited as guest of honour in 1994 and German troops were included in the military parade, a highly controversial decision at the time. In 2009, the German president Horst Koehler was also invited as guest of honour together with 13 of the former sub-Saharan colonies 50 years after becoming independent (in 2010). Similarly, Victory Day in Russia in 2010 marked the 65th anniversary of the end of fascism. For the first time, allied troops (from France, Britain and the United States) were invited. Significantly, Polish troops also participated and the guest of honour for this high profile event was the German Chancellor, Angela Merkel (RussiaToday, 2010a, 2010b). Such reinvention of ceremonial form in line with visible reconciliation strategies is thus found also with other military celebrations.

The design of Remembrance Sunday has also been modernized in recent years in order to combat its appearance of being an exclusive occasion. Representations at the Cenotaph in London include today not only Christian Clergy of the Anglican Church but also representatives of other faith communities whose members lost lives in the wars. Members of the Commonwealth have been invited for some time. However, the losses among Britain's former allies or enemies does not factor into these ceremonies. An initiative to formally acknowledge women in war led to the construction of the monument to Women in the Second World War (in bronze) unveiled by the queen in 2005 alongside the ceremonial route of the (off-white) Cenotaph. The politics of recognition is thus related to the possession of great patience or, in this particular context, 60 years after the end of the Second World War, *one year after*, we may add, a monument to the animals that died alongside the British, Commonwealth and Allied Forces was unveiled in 2004 (Park Lane, London).

Inclusion discussed with reference to Constitution Day in Norway must be explored from a number of angles. First, girls and women were invited to participate in the parades at a comparatively early stage towards the end of the nineteenth century by the nation builders on the left, with emerging ideals of democratization and inclusion. In short, widespread participation would only ever be guaranteed with a focus on the children of the community, especially in times of internal division. The high degree of participation is facilitated by this design that involves the school children in Norway, which secures encompassing participation in terms of numbers. With the above in mind, it is clear that elites have acted as important sponsors of this event. However, they are not the only directors of Constitution Day. The many school teachers involved in the organization of the event have played a crucial role in Norwegian ceremonial history and in the interpretation of Norwegian identity and its intricate relationship to Constitution Day. Today, the rhetoric of inclusion has brought Constitution Day back to the political-moral arena and has resurfaced with the encouraged participation of Norway's immigrants. For reference, there are 423 000 immigrants in Norway (10.6 per cent) and 86 000 Norwegian-born persons born to immigrant parents (Statistics Norway, 2009).

The debate about inclusion and multiculturalism in the context of Constitution Day illuminates the significance of the adoption of national symbols as signs of membership and commonality. The expressions of Norwegian identity in the ceremonial sphere have traditionally relied on the flag, the *bunad* (regional costume) and the participation in the children's parade on 17 May. The inclusion of children with immigrant background in the latter would therefore inevitably come to be discussed with reference to the adoption of these symbols.

First, the question of whether it would be possible to concede to the display of flags other than the Norwegian one in the parades was debated publicly in 2005 and again in 2008. The flag debate flared up prior to the annual 17 May celebrations in 2005 when members of the Sami community wanted to use the Sami flags (Eriksen and Jenkins, 2007) in order to raise awareness of their communities as part of but different from mainstream Norwegian society. A similar debate came to the fore in 2008 when in consequence the question was asked whether flags representing Norway's immigrant communities would be allowed in the parades. The 17 May Committee and the formal organizers of the Oslo parades responded in no uncertain terms: 'the 17 May Committee is in complete agreement that we should only display Norwegian flags on this only day that is the Norwegian national day' (Barstad and Buan, 2008; Ryste, 2008). Today Sami flags and UN flags are the only two other flags allowed in the parades. That such guidelines exist is in itself illuminating of this discussion.

Secondly, discussions about the possibility of developing *bunad*-related symbolism were first heard officially in 2010 as it was suggested that perhaps a *multicultural-bunad anno 2010* – ought to be produced in view of the increasing diversity in contemporary Norway. Such a costume could, it was suggested, highlight ethnic origins other than Norwegian ones through colours and patterns inspired by, for example, Vietnam, Morocco, India and Chile and come with a detachable *hijab*. Contrary this suggestion, it was also argued that immigrants instead ought to be encouraged to adopt one of the existing costumes and display regional affiliations in Norway (Hovland and Maaland, 2010). Historically, the Norwegian flag, the national day and the regional costumes developed in the context of raising boundaries against the neighbouring kingdom, and it appears little has changed. Thus, against the stated intentions of the innocence of the children's parades, the celebrations have 'come to support a narrowly defined Norwegian normality' (Blehr, 1999b, p. 175) and unintentionally has ascribed to diaspora and ethno-cultural communities a controversial character with little ceremonial flexibility as celebrations are expected to be embraced in its traditional form. As noted by Eriksen (2008), if people are to identify with a Norwegian national identity in the course of this century 'this cannot be based on perceptions that there is one or few ways only of expressing belonging to this country.' Although, 17 May is said to have been transformed into a cosmopolitan ritual of inclusion with the participation of different ethnic communities, this particular debate resembles a take-it-or-leave-it situation and is seemingly protecting an image of sameness perceived as compromised by the use of 'deviant' symbols. The latter contributes to one explanation of their prohibition. The rules set out for membership in this ceremonial context is thus more sharply defined than first meets the eye. Having said this, the debate on inclusion and multiculturalism with reference to the national day in Norway is in the public domain, which is relatively unusual in a European perspective where many issues relating to inclusion remain outstanding.

Towards a typology of successful national day design

In Table 5.7 we see a number of conditions linked to successful national days and national day design as suggested with reference to discussed cases, their origins and characters. A founding myth can be significant in the establishment of a successful national day and indicates that ceremonies are not easily invented or exported to other nations without a suitable and unifying narrative (may this be the founding myth or not). A unifying myth is fundamental – in the case of modern Norway coinciding with its historical genesis – and explaining how well it may perform its Durkheimian functions. However, a founding narrative would not adequately explain the sustained appeal of national days over time. Regardless of their origins which may be aided by the founding and uniting narratives and struggles for independence in the past, national day design must transform over time in order to remain appealing and inclusive by modern standards. The inclusion of traditionally marginalized groups such as the working classes, women and ethnic communities has become part of the rhetoric of change in ceremonial contexts and to various degrees in the cases above. Many national days were designed with a defensive position against 'others' in mind, which facilitates the drawing of boundaries but cannot easily be sustained over time. Therefore, in terms of inclusion, successful ceremonies manage to include those that used to be perceived as former 'enemies'. Depending on ceremonial design the scope for re-invention varies. However, re-invention of national day design and ceremonial narratives help explain how celebrations of a constitution that by no means are threatened today, have remained significant over generations. Furthermore, successful national day designs will with time help drain the original meaning of the national day (such as the fight for independence in Norway, the revolution in France or the celebrations of victory in

Table 5.7 Successful national days: Norway, France and Britain

Criteria	Constitution Day	Bastille Day	Remembrance Sunday
Date of first celebration	1827	1880	1919
Formative years			
Symbol of independence	✓	–	–
Nationhood perceived as vulnerable	✓	–	–
Founding myth	✓	✓	–
Uniting narrative	✓	✓	✓
Elite involvement/support	✓	✓	✓
Positioned against 'others'	✓	✓	✓
Political and moral arena/debate	✓	✓	✓
National day design			
Public holiday	✓	✓	–
Televised coverage	✓	✓	✓
Inter-generational participation	✓	✓	–
Mass-event	✓	✓	–
Civilian parades	✓	–	✓
Integration of official/private events	✓	–	–
Celebratory	✓	✓	–
Commemorative	✓	✓	✓
Symbols of commonality	✓	✓	✓
Non-religious focus	✓	✓	–
Display of regional diversity	✓	–	–
Inclusive by design	✓	–	–
Reconciliatory	✓	✓	–
Reinvention of ceremonial style	✓	✓	–
Transformation and modernization	✓	✓	✓
Drained of original meaning	✓	✓	✓
Sacred status	✓	✓	✓

Britain) in such a way that transformation of ceremonial style becomes possible and facilitates the re-invention of national holidays of modern nations. Simultaneously, national days that achieve a sacred status are not easily criticized (nor changed) and demonstrate that the national day has been placed in a category above the ordinary as a symbol of the nation and ultimately confirm to us the appeal of nationhood.

The future of national day design and the politics of recognition

Ceremonial community-building projects are thus employed in a Durkheimian vein to celebrate, recognize, promote, (re)negotiate, (re)create and (re)enforce identities in ways that have been described in this book. Participation in the same ceremonies are thus understood as a function of creating a commonality and strengthening communities (Elgenius, 2008). This trend is particularly visible in multi-ethnic states where national days have been placed on the political agenda as part of the politics of recognition and inclusion but also regret, apology and reconciliation. Previously marginalized communities have been recognized on days such as Martin Luther Day in the United States or Aboriginal Day in Australia. These initiatives illuminate ongoing nation-building strategies but also conflicts associated with mainstream national days in countries with aboriginal populations, whose experiences and contributions traditionally remained unrecognized (Elgenius, 1993). Australia Day, for example, marks a colonial event and thus cause to divisive interpretations. It marks the landing of the first fleet in Sydney Cove in 1788 (and establishment of the penal colony) and has traditionally been associated with celebrations of the politically domineering population of British ancestry. The association of Australian Aboriginal Sovereign Nations wanted the day acknowledged as Aboriginal Sovereignty Day. Invasion Day and Survival Day were also heard as protests as the Aborigines Progressive Association called for a day of mourning as early as 1938 (Inglis, 1967). We note that Aboriginal Australians were not deemed citizens of Australia until 1967. (Similarly, for Maori activists, Waitangi Day in New Zealand (1934) commemorating the ceding of land and signing of the treaty of Waitangi (1840) between the Maori chiefs and the British crown, is a Day of broken promises over tribal autonomy.) On Australia Day, organized forms of protests commenced with the Aboriginal Tent Embassy erected outside Parliament House in Canberra in 1972, which by 1992 was a permanent feature for the first Survival Day Concert. However, it was not until the bicentenary of Australia Day in 1988 that active participation of the indigenous Australians and non-British immigrants was sought by governments and community groups. However, contemporary Australia Day is said to have become a reflection of the multi-ethnic and 'plural character of modern Australia, the complex and contested nature of Australian culture and identity' (Pearson and O'Neill, 2009, p. 73). In this context it is noted that in 2008 the life expectancy gap between Aboriginal and non-Aboriginal Australians was 17 years.

The Olympics in Sydney (2000) brought an infusion of enthusiasm for Australia Day and the National Australia Day Council measured participation at 53 per cent in 2007, when 14 000 people also became Australian citizens in citizenship ceremonies and an estimated 78.3 per cent of Australians claimed Australia Day a significant event. It has been argued that 'Australia is not a nation of spontaneous flag-wavers – it is a nation of organized flag-wavers' (Pearson and O'Neill, 2009, p. 86). In terms of Australia Day's deliberate design and syncretic origin it would be hard not to agree with this statement. The creation of a public culture based on national values and a historical tradition has been part of the revamping and reinvention of this day. From a political perspective nationalism and patriotism associated with Australia Day have been identified as useful tools: 'to be politically effective, to be successful advocates for change and reform, you have to engage the minds of other citizens. At its most powerful, politics is a drama in which citizens are characters [...] So when it comes to crafting a story for citizens, it is a national story that carries the most weight [...] To deny patriotism, then, is a sure path to political impotence' (Soutphommasane, 2009, p. 30).

The above serves as a background for understanding related ceremonial initiatives in Britain. The British Citizenship Review (Rimmer, 2008) suggested that Britain was in need of a national day and proposed that a British National Day (National Citizenship Day) be introduced as a permanent feature of the public calendar. The Home Office had in fact introduced a Citizens' Day as a low-key initiative in 2005, with the intention of breaking down barriers and offering an opportunity for people from all backgrounds to come together, in a first phase in ethnically-divided parts of Britain. Gordon Brown went further suggesting that Remembrance Sunday would make a suitable Britain Day. Closely related are the citizenship ceremonies in place since 2004 marking the new status for new citizens. Through these citizenship has became part of a process that is earned, learned and celebrated.

In contrast to the model used by most nations when establishing their national days, it was suggested that for Britain it may be 'advantageous to have a day without historical significance' in order 'to forge a new modern citizenship identity and to encourage the celebration' (Rimmer, 2008, p. 96). The reason for such an unorthodox suggestion was surely the associations of British history being considered as 'too divisive and contradictory' (McCrone, 2009, p. 27) in terms of its colonial history, internally and externally. Moreover, Britain has been described as being challenged from within and from without and research demonstrates that ethnic and Diaspora communities live parallel lives. Moreover, groups classified as 'white British' are more likely to identify with Britain as opposed to other ethnic groups that are less likely to do so. Alongside a steady decline of British identity (Britishness) a shy growth of English identity (Englishness) has been observed in the past decade (following the earlier reassertion of Scottish and Welsh identities) (Heath, 2006; Heath et al., 2007) (see Table 5.8). British identity is by nature found more civic and inclusive whereas Englishness has been connected to ethnic conceptions of belonging and to 'whiteness' (Hewitt, 2005). Thus, the trend with reference to preferred identity developing over time was found to be a cause for concern.

A number of scholars (Hall, 1992; Held, 1989) suggested that the glue that used to hold Britain together is losing power, and others that the boundaries are characterized by fuzziness and fuzzy frontiers that take place at the ambiguous edges of identity where nationhood turns into 'other-hood' (R. Cohen, 1995). Moreover, the decline of traditional national identities has been claimed to have left individuals

Table 5.8 Is Britain a failed nation?

	1979	1992	1997	1999	2001	2003	2005	2006
England								
English	n/a	32	33	44	43	39	40	47
British	n/a	63	56	44	45	48	48	39
Other	n/a	5	11	12	12	13	12	14
Scotland								
Scottish	56	72	73	77	77	72	79	78
British	38	25	20	17	16	20	14	14
Other	6	3	7	6	7	8	7	8
Wales								
Welsh	58	n/a	63	57	57	60	n/a	n/a
British	34	n/a	26	30	31	27	n/a	n/a
Other	8	n/a	11	13	12	13	n/a	n/a

Note: Figures are percentages.
Source: Figures are adapted from Heath et al. (2007, p. 11).

free to choose from a much wider range of newer identities (Dogan, 1994; Heath et al., 2007; Savage et al., 2005). Britain is claimed to be particularly sensitive to such changes with the breakdown of the Empire, the decline in salience of religion and the loss of a clear 'other' since the Second World War (Colley, 1992). There are also inevitable implications as older generations with a stronger British national identity die out (Tilley and Heath, 2007). The question was thus asked whether Britain was becoming too diverse to identify with in order to sustain mutual obligations that sustain the welfare state (Goodhart, 2004).

A Britain Day has been discussed, debated and promoted in terms of a nation-building device that could help reinforce a civic British identity. Having said this, the citizenship debate has – in contrast to its stated intentions – been nationalized with the intentions to celebrate British values, history, heritage and achievements. Bringing diverse groups together at such celebrations could, it was argued, 'prevent communities from becoming more divided' (Kelly and Byrne, 2007). Inspired by the Australian experience (the re-invention of a divisive colonial event, the encouraged participation of ethnic communities, the marking of entry of new citizens, the introduction of high-profile citizenship ceremonies and the heightened enthusiasm infused with the Olympic Games) it was thus unsurprisingly argued that 'as China begins the hand-over of the Olympic flame to Britain, there is a unique chance to seize the moment and lay the foundations for the annual national celebration of our own' (Kelly and Byrne, 2007, p. 19). Simultaneously, part of the package of invented traditions, a new Armed Forces Day was also planned (first celebrated in 2009) as a complement to Remembrance Sunday with the intention of fostering inter-generational links, between veterans and citizens, veterans and children, and encouraging and demonstrating support for the troops. Such celebrations would nurture the connections between the past, present and future and foster younger generations into a political culture accepting war and sacrifice.

The first issues regarding the celebration of when and what was followed by the question of how such a celebration would be designed. It was agreed at an early stage that Britain Day would have to cater for all tastes, groups and ages through a number of celebrations over a few days. In fact such a celebration took place at the Golden Jubilee of Queen Elizabeth II, celebrating her fifty years' reign in 2002. With a variety of ceremonial activities – carefully planned – including a display of royal tradition (a Royal Jubilee procession) a religious service (in St Paul's) the emphasis on diversity (Commonwealth Parade) and youth (carnival parade), as well as military engagement (a fly-past), it was designed to appeal to the whole generational spectrum of tastes (classical and pop concerts at Buckingham Palace, fireworks and Party in the Park). The Golden Jubilee offered, in other words, a variety of events – a combination of tradition and diversity, old and new – in order to appeal to all groups. More than a million people lined the streets of London to watch the Jubilee parade and to watch the Queen's golden state coach make its way to St Paul's Cathedral for the televised service of thanksgiving. Police estimated that more than a million people gathered in parks around Buckingham Palace to watch the fireworks and the pop concert with Sir Paul McCartney. The concert was seen by 12.3 million Britons and more than 200 million viewers world-wide. As a comparison, less than half a million gathered outside Buckingham Palace for the wedding of the Prince of Wales in 1981, an event watched by an estimated 36 million Britons and 700 million people world-wide (BBC, 4 June 2002; Studd, 7 June 2006). Moreover, the Golden Jubilee coincided with the FIFA World Cup in 2002, which reinforced the celebrations with football fans and the nationalism associated with such a sporting event. With national fervour at its peak a much criticized monarchy was successfully re-invented. The numbers gathering were among the largest London has ever seen and beats records set by royal weddings and the Silver Jubilee in 1977 (Studd, 7 June 2006) (see Illustrations 5.3 and 5.4). Similar numbers (about one million) turned out to see the Royal Wedding Parade in 2011.

Illustration 5.3 The Golden Jubilee: pomp and circumstance
The Golden Jubilee Parade in 2002 on the Mall leading to Buckingham Palace, London. Photography courtesy of Unusual Rigging Ltd (2002).

184

Illustration 5.4 The multi-dimensional future of national day design
The Carnival and Commonwealth Parade at the Golden Jubilee 2002. In view Buckingham Palace, London. Photography by the Press Association (2002).

With the experience of the Golden Jubilee in mind, it is also noted that an extra bank holiday has already been instated to celebrate the Queen's Diamond Jubilee in 2012 a celebration that will coincide with the Olympic Games held in London. A similar formula of ceremonial diversity is likely to be part of the Queen's Diamond celebrations now fused with ceremonial citizenship elements of Australia Day. It is not an overstatement to say that the ceremonial and symbolic forms of nations continue to inspire nation builders as their potential for community building is acknowledged. Ceremonies and national days continue, in other words, to be understood as contributing to nation building – whether invented or not – through the participation in celebrations. Governments continue to operate from a set of Durkheimian assumptions to encourage celebrations, participation and cohesion and to mobilize support for existing socio-political structures. Similar measures were also adopted by the elites of the European Union as it looked to the nation for inspiration and adopted a flag, an anthem and Europe Day. National day celebrations may appear as symbols of consensus and unity – enforced by national day design – but they do not necessarily inspire the participation of the citizens over time and cohesion and solidarity need not follow, as comparative research demonstrates. A unifying narrative (sometimes the historical genesis) is especially significant in the establishment of national days as is the nature of the national day design. Without a suitable narrative such initiatives remain short-lived.

6
The Symbolic Regimes and Nation Building

The aim of *Symbols of Nations and Nationalism* has been to shed light on the role of national symbols and ceremonies as markers of nation building and to highlight ways in which these express complex meanings and act as unifying or divisive forces. This study has explored the mechanisms by which national symbols and ceremonies operate and how they turn into powerful political instruments by symbolizing unity and commonality without compromising private associations of nationhood. It is the self-referential qualities of national symbolism and ceremonials that keep the imagined boundaries illuminated and raise awareness of membership. In exploring these and related questions it is possible to contribute to the explanation as to how it is possible that a piece of cloth (flag) can provoke such powerful emotions and why historic events honouring, at times, a distant past (national day) have such continued significance. The process of nation building has been traced alongside the ongoing adoption and production of national flags and national days and some attention given to national anthems as part of this founding community-oriented nexus or package. As the information about dates of introduction, adoption and establishment are systematized different *symbolic regimes* and nation-building narratives appear. We explore the basis of these in this final chapter.

Building and celebrating nationhood

The national flag and the national day constitute two main images of nationhood through which nations become visible. The flag is the first national symbol to emerge whereas national days constitute younger strata of nations and highlight the fact that nations are layered and their formations ongoing. National flags and national days are used to present, represent, create, re-create, justify, glorify and model nations. They provide short-cuts to the nation and furnish, in their form, a symbolic and ceremonial structure similar to religious communities.

The European national flags express different national narratives some of which survived from pre-modern times whereas others were formed in the age of modern or post-imperial nations. As a general rule, most flags have originated in wars and conflicts, with independence and new state-formations. During struggles for recognition and independence, the boundary-raising quality of flags has been used to sharpen blurred boundaries. With the emergence of modern nations, national flags started to give form to more complex notions of *sameness* and *oneness* placing the aspirations and claims to inherited lands onto the international area among those of other nations. Flags continue to constitute a prerequisite for national representation and public ceremonies in national and international contexts. This relationship between the flag and the nation is protected by law to prevent it from desecration and the nation from violation. Thus, an insult to the flag assumes a transcendent meaning as an insult to the nation. However, the regulatory framework surrounding national flags also turn them into powerful double-edged counter instruments and political tools for governments and citizens alike. Flags are burned, defaced, hung upside down, symbols are cut out or added in order to protest against national authorities.

National flags constitute short cuts to nation building being intimately linked to the expression of national history in graphic form and, by establishing links to the past, the existence of the nation justifies the state in the present. Flags became attached to territories in the pre-modern era and signify early territorial loyalties, although different to understanding of modern nations these flags provide in form a successful code copied to other nations with the emergence of modern nationalism. First, the earliest flags are symbols of warfare (of which some appeared as cross flags or as naval flags) as in the cases of Denmark, Sweden, England, Switzerland, the Netherlands and Russia. Secondly, the flags of revolutions (and transformations) are those of France, Italy, Germany, Portugal, Spain, and the former Communist countries (variations on the Red Flag for the latter). Thirdly, the flags of independence include those of the Netherlands, Belgium, Greece, Hungary, Finland, Bulgaria, Norway, Ireland, Poland, Lithuania, Estonia, Latvia, Iceland, Croatia, Slovenia, Ukraine and Belarus. Fourthly, several flags appear as flags of state-reconstitution with the formations of unions and with the dissolution of the empires, as with the United Kingdom (the Union

Jack), Romania, Finland, Austria, the Federal Republic of Yugoslavia, Czechoslovakia, Germany, Russia, the Czech Republic, Slovakia, Bosnia-Herzegovina and Kosovo. The pre-modern (cross) flags that survived over time stand in contrast to the modern (tricolours) and the majority of the post-imperial (heraldic or post-historical flags) that have been adopted, established, re-adopted and re-established, modified, prohibited and altered. As seen in the development of flag-symbolism, it follows that the major changes of nations are connected to revolutions (France), formation of unions (Switzerland, Britain), transformations from monarchies to republics (Netherlands, France, Italy, Russia) and vice versa (France 1814, Italy 1861), the Soviet Union domination (of the Baltic States and Central and Eastern Europe) and anti-communist transformations (with removal of communist symbols) and fascist (Italy and Germany and their satellite states during the Second World War) and anti-fascist transformations (with the re-adoption of national flags).

The national days of Europe have also been adapted with political change in a similar pattern to the flags, as existing religious festivities were appropriated, transformed or combined with new celebrations into national holidays. The majority of national days appear in such ways suggesting a new tradition had been invented. Most European national days are celebrated in honour of founding moments: political events (independence, republics, union, sovereignty, constitution and liberation) and national personifications (saints, monarchs, heroes with reference to a golden age). Occupying forces during, for example, the Second World War, outlawed existing national days and introduced a cycle of commemorations honouring the particularities of their ideologies. The many changes recorded with regards to national days have also taken place when the associations between these and nations were contested, challenged and renegotiated. The symbolic battles over what may seem superficial details have further established national flags and national days as significant national symbols that are anything but decorative fragments of nations. Instead, they are at the forefront of battles for nation and statehood. Thus the national day transpires as a proxy for a number of related issues with regards to membership and territory. The clearest example is the absence of a national day in Bosnia-Herzegovina. In view of the complicated process of agreeing on a flag (1992–98) and the many years (1999–2009) it took to find suitable words for the national anthem, it was inevitable that it would be even more complicated to agree on a narrative for celebrations. Bosnia-Herzegovina is the only country in Europe that does not currently have a national day, something which highlights its divisive propensities and internal disunity in the country.

Symbols and ceremonials are at the core of the formative process as seen in the three case studies exploring different paths to nationhood through the formations of their flags and ceremonies. The formation of the Union in 1801 was reflected in the combination of the retained pre-modern cross flags in England, Scotland and Ireland (excluding Wales) corresponding to more or less celebrated Saint Days. Although modern Britain does not have such an overall celebratory national day, Remembrance Sunday constitutes the only but unrecognized national day for a supra-national state. It is a misconception that national days must be celebratory but recent ceremonial plans for Britain suggest that a package of celebrations has been initiated to celebrate Britishness. As a contrast, France, rich in medieval royal and religious symbolism made a clear break with the past by adopting the Tricolour and later with the adoption of Bastille Day reflecting the ideals of the Republic. The ideals of liberty, brotherhood and equality did not stand unchallenged in the decades following the Revolution and it took a century before the various political groupings could unite behind the celebrations of Bastille Day. The Norwegian case is particularly appropriate in this context as it demonstrates how the movement for independence used the newly established symbols of the flag in the celebrations of the constitution as part of the fight for recognition, before sovereignty had been attained. Early on, Constitution Day became an effective forum – a national workshop and moral arena – debating, expressing and negotiating identity also within Norway – but it was to take 77 years before the Norwegian flag was formally recognized also in Sweden.

Moral communities

National ceremonies in their forms furnish structures similar to that of religious ceremonies, which has led several scholars to suggest that the popularity of national ceremonies reflects the desire for immortality through posterity after the waning of religious beliefs in modern society. In any case, ceremonies facilitate by context the process whereby nations are transformed into the sacred sphere where they cannot be criticized without consequences. National life constitutes by form an annual repetition of ceremonial structures that ultimately justify the existence of nations and states. The ritual contexts in which national symbols appear follow in its forms a religious structure. There are many examples of how symbols of nations are worshipped and treated as if they were sacred. For example, the flag's non-negotiable status on official flag days, as in protection by law and regulations when used in mourning, on tombs of the Unknown Soldier, at funerals when flown at half-mast. The breaking of flag etiquette clarifies the significance of the emotional investment in these practices. In a similar fashion, national days remember the war dead or celebrate moral victories that contribute to the forming of moral communities. It is in particular through definition of sacrifical boundaries and the sacrifices worth remembering (and by default the exclusion of other sacrifices) that nations appear as moral communities. The general decline of organized Christianity in Europe (in terms of decreased appeal of its institutions, beliefs and practices) (Bruce, 2002; Davie, 1994) suggests that there was space for a new form of (territorial) symbolism. The cross flags in Britain, Scandinavia and Switzerland, originally religious symbolism, survived nationalized into modern times as did the celebrations of national saints (St Patrick, St Stephen and St Andrew) that emerged early on. Whereas some surviving religious festivities were nationalized (Ireland, Hungary and Scotland) others were combined with celebrations of secular heroes and golden ages (Spain and Greece). Religious and national ceremonials are also fused through context (Remembrance days in Britain and Belgium) and through the remembering the nation's great or fallen that constitute an integral part of national day designs.

Successful flag-symbolism: flags and counter-flags

Flags indicate by their existence some measure of success for politicized identities and raised awareness of groups that consider themselves nations. The symbolic codes used by European nations reject to a degree preceding symbolism in such fashion that the modern, revolutionary and republican tricolours (type 2) broke with the tradition and symbolism of the pre-modern (religious and monarchial) cross flags (type 1), whereas the recently emerging post-historical, counter-nationalist flags (type 4) by necessity have had to move away from the traditional nationalism claimed by the post-imperial heraldic flags (type 3).

The influence of flag-symbolism as means of communicating aspirations relating to nationhood is also demonstrated by the fact that it may become divisive for territories in which 'history' remains undefined or contested. The recently emerging flag-type – post-historical and counter-nationalist by nature – has therefore emerged along non-hereditary lines and been claimed as flags of the future. Historical references, heraldic devices and colours were avoided completely in the imposed flags of Bosnia-Herzegovina (1998) and Kosovo (2008). Clearly the divisive agents of nationalism and ethnicity were main considerations in the move beyond historical signs and highlight the complexities of understanding nationhood in terms of oneness. These are considerations also contributing to the design of the European Union Flag (1985) that has avoided historical and potentially divisive symbolism representing a union of rival memories. Naturally, the symbolic representation of Bosnia-Herzegovina and Kosovo also express dependence on the European Union for military security and economic survival. Comparatively, the former British dominions also reproduced variations of British flags (Australia, New Zealand, British Columbia, etc.) as did the former flags of the former Soviet Socialist Republics such as the flags of Soviet Estonia, Soviet Latvia or Soviet Lithuania, etc. Flags of dominions or protectorates are derivative and express dependence on the Centre. Furthermore, the continued reproduction of flags in non-national contexts tells us something about the effective use of flag-related symbolism in the politicization of identities. Thus, the production of new flag-codes is ongoing. The Greenland (1985) and Sami (1986) flags, with clear intentions of breaking with the Scandinavian cross tradition, have in a way been introduced as non-colonial flags claiming uniqueness and distinctiveness by the adoption of timeless references to nature. Appearing as a tribute to the influence of flag-symbolism is the adoption of the Rainbow flag (1978) and the annual celebrations of the diversity of lifestyle choices with Gay Pride festivals. These flags (and corresponding celebrations) highlight the fragmentation of national identities but also notions of sameness transcending national territories.

Successful national day design

National day symbolism continues to be perceived as an integral part of nation building and has also become part of the politics of recognition, regret and apology, acknowledging the diversity of multi-ethnic nations challenging notions of a collective memory and sameness. The trend of modernizing national day designs in order to produce inclusive ceremonials reveals ongoing concern for nation builders who hope to renew or contribute to community-building. National ceremonies and national days certainly do not necessarily create solidarity, unity and cohesion, as argued by Durkheim (1976) who maintained that societies become united through rituals bringing about feelings of exaltation and enthusiasm carried over into daily life. In this way consensus or conformity about social taboos and values come into existence. There are many issues to address here and include the following.

First, it does not seem feasible to assess adequately to what extent ceremonial enthusiasm is carried over into daily life, nor to what degree it is able to influence communities afterwards. Second, nations include highly-fragmented populations in terms of class, religion, ethnicity, region and gender and very little is known of how national ceremonies are perceived by various groups. Third, symbols and ceremonies cannot manage to produce cohesion or togetherness on their own and without popular support will have little effect. The symbolic measures taken by the European Union with the EU flag, anthem and Europe Day are illustrative examples here. Germany's Unification Day is not the only example of an unsuccessful national day (the long-term influence of recent initiatives and anniversaries yet to be assessed) but the nations that do not have a popular national day have, as a rule, another national event in which people participate (Poland, Croatia, Russia). Some of the national days without visible popular support have been introduced relatively recently in the post-imperial age and stand in contrast to many of the 'pre-modern' national days transformed into national holidays (Ireland and Hungary) or 'modern' celebrations (France, Norway, Greece and the Netherlands). In short, considerable ceremonial activity is seen among European nations and most nations have a popular national day. Fourth, ceremonial triumph is also attributed to national day design in a majority of cases linked to uniting myths and golden ages. In successful cases these have transformed over time and ceremonial choreography has been reinvented to inspire intra-generational participation. The inclusion of local, regional and national symbolic markers and initiatives are of importance in this process. Moreover, elite sponsorship has remained a significant factor for sustained ceremonies over time.

National symbols and ceremonies are imbued with meanings and thus contested and negotiated. They do not by default produce (an image of) unity or cohesion and can instead highlight, advertise and enforce divisions. Whereas historical complexities have been crucial in explaining the success of national days in Europe, national day design and choreography are also understood as crucial for their survival over time. Thus, the exportability of successful national days has limitations in that it will depend on the success in finding a unifying narrative and a suitable national day design. This has become increasingly difficult in multi-national and multi-ethnic states. Suitable narratives and ceremonial designs are fundamental in the establishing of national celebrations and stand in direct relation to the success of the national day and the extent to which they may perform the assumed Durkheimian functions. In view of a European comparison the findings suggest that the formation of popular national days combine a number of ceremonial components leading to participation that, in turn, can contribute to community building. Whereas historical complexities are crucial in the formative years they do not explain the sustained significance of national days over time (see Table 5.7).

(1) First, national days are more likely to be successful and popular in cases where nationhood has been perceived as threatened and where celebrations became symbols of independence before statehood had been achieved. (2) The national days therefore developed distinctly and in relation to visible 'others' and helped raise boundaries and has as a rule (3) linked the nation to golden ages, myths of rebirth. (4) Many national days also became appealing when related to processes of democratization and inclusion whether in France and in Norway towards the end of the nineteenth century or in more recent times in the former Soviet Socialist Republics. These national days drew on participation of a large part of the population and (5) managed to become a platform for the negotiation of internal conflicts. They hereby gain increased meaning as a political-moral arena. (6) The nature of national day design and the mobilization of inter-generational participation are also crucial. This has become transparent with the inclusion of children's parades and the cooperation of all primary and secondary schools in the unique case of the Norwegian Constitution Day. The organization of these joyful parades has also secured the participation of parents, grandparents, aunts, uncles, siblings and cousins. (7) The incorporation of the national day into the educational curricula promotes a link between nationalism, nationhood and childhood and allows children to assume nationality and citizenship early on. (8) Furthermore, ceremonial success is facilitated by the integration of other living symbols such as national flags, anthems, national food, national colours, folk costumes or signs of remembrance. These visualize commonality and raise awareness of membership. (9) Particular reference to the display of local or regional symbols such as clothing and food, as part of national day design, allows for diversity to be celebrated and is thus an embrace of both regional and national loyalties. (10) Similarly, a non-religious framework in ethnically diverse nations in Europe does not exclude non-Christians. (11) This

194 *Symbols of Nations and Nationalism*

leads us to other dimensions of national day design and ceremonial success, namely the transformation of the overall ceremonial message over time and (12) the re-invention of ceremonial design. These two criteria are prerequisites if ceremonies are to benefit from being perceived as meaningful, inclusive or reconciliatory. (13) Moreover, elite sponsorship over time and the declaration of national days as public holidays are crucial contributions for the transformation of national days into community days and the integration or joining of public ceremonies and private festivities. The adaption of national day ceremonies for televised coverage is also part of this nexus and for the perceptions of simultaneous or shared celebration or commemoration. Likewise, the official narration of national days and televised coverage providing a loyal portrayal to ceremonial messages over time contribute to understandings of shared history. (14) Although historical prerequisites are of upmost importance in the formative years, a true sign of successful national day design is the draining of original meaning, as with the revolutionary origin of Bastille Day, the defensive and guarded celebrations of the Norwegian constitution or the Victory Parade transformed into Remembrance Sunday. (15) A number of factors thus contribute to explaining why many national days have achieved a sacred status and cannot easily be criticized or changed. (16) The latter is ultimately related to the appeal of nationhood that provides a foundation for the survival of national celebrations over time.

The findings support overall that the historical genesis is significant in the formative years of national days and that successful ceremonies are not easily exported to other nations unless a suitable narrative can be found. A unifying narrative is fundamental and sometimes coincides with the historical genesis or founding myth. However, to this must be added the importance of the design of the national day and the re-invention of the historical complexities and ceremonial forms that also contribute to the appeal of national days and, in turn, the extent to which they may perform their Durkheimian functions. Moreover, we have noted that ceremonial design operates as a *proxy* for related debates on citizenship and membership as traditionally marginalized groups have gained access to national ceremonies at an even later pace than to other social institutions.

Symbolic regimes and layered nations

Nations cannot be dated in a precise manner but by identifying the adoption of flags, anthems and national days as they are introduced alongside nation building we find they have something to say also about the complexity of this process. Three periods stand out as pivots for categorization of the European symbolic regimes. The first symbolic regime appears during the age of pre-modern nations and its associated symbolism; the second marks the beginning of the age of modern nations and modern symbolism (1789–1913); whereas the symbolic regime that transcends after the First World War adopts a character linked to the age of post-imperial nations. The flags and national days respond to the narratives that emerge from these periods.

Table 6.1 lists the European nations in accordance with the appearance of the first symbol of the nation, the national flag. The early use of some of these have something to say about emerging territorial relationships and pre-modern loyalties – at least among the elites. Symbols adopted before 1789 are not national in the sense of the modern nation, but their existence illuminates territorial patterns that survived into modern times. National anthems and national days appear as younger strata of nationhood and mainly in the age of nationalism. In a majority of cases these three symbolic variables appear in the order of flag, anthem (as melody and/or lyrics) and national day. The final column of the table identifies the symbolic regimes during which symbolic measures have been introduced and indicates thus the complexity of the symbolic creation and nation making. The nation-building process may be further illuminated by the dating of other national symbols such as national monuments, public places, ceremonial routes, national museums and their collections, operas, dictionaries or stamps, to give some examples (see Aronsson and Elgenius 2011). National initiatives such as these contribute to illuminate that which is imagined as community.

With reference to symbolic content above, four flag types are linked to the three regimes: the cross flags of pre-modern origins, the modern tricolours and the post-imperial heraldic and post-historical flags. Naturally, meanings change over time and the cross flags that once constituted highly significant symbolism of religious affiliations today ironically represent some of the most secular nations in Europe. The symbol of the cross, however, being no less controversial today, at the time emerged as a symbols of defiance against papacy, the cross flags surviving primarily in Protestant states with secular monarchs. The tricolours, in contrast, form a new code of republican symbolism, many of which developed in places where previously a variety of cross flags had been flown. The post-imperial flags assert claims of the independent nations after the First World War by the means of heraldic colours and devices, such as on the flags of Austria, Poland, the Czech Republic, Slovakia, Wales, Ukraine, Croatia, Serbia, Slovenia,

196

Table 6.1 The symbolic regimes of Europe

Country	National flag	National anthem	National day	Symbolic regime
Denmark	1340	1835	1849	Pre-modern – Modern
Switzerland	1480 (1848)	1841	1891	Pre-modern – Modern
Sweden	1523	1844	1893	Pre-modern – Modern
Britain	1606–1801	1745	1919	Pre-modern – Modern – Post-imperial
England	1348	1745	(14th)	
Scotland	1385	1965/1974	(14th) 2007	
Wales	1950s	1858	(18th) 2000	
Netherlands	1630–60	1815	1891	Pre-modern – Modern
Russia	1705/1991	2000	2004	Pre-modern
				Post-imperial
Spain	1785	1770	1613/1892	Pre-modern
Catalonia	1932	1889, 1993	(1930s) 1970s	Modern
Basque Country	1895, 1936	1905/1983	(1930s) 1970s	Post-imperial
France	1789	1793	1790/1880	Modern
Norway	1821	1864	1827/1905	Modern
Belgium	1831	1860	1890	Modern
Greece	1833	1865	1838	Modern
Italy	1848	1946	1946	Modern – Post-imperial
Germany	1848	1848, 1990	1990	Modern – Post-imperial
Hungary	1848	1844	(11th) 1764	Modern – Pre-modern
Finland	1863–63	1867	1917	Modern – Post-imperial

Romania	1867	1989	Modern – Post-imperial
Bulgaria	1878–79	1964	Modern – Post-imperial
Portugal	1910	1910	Modern – Post-imperial
Ireland	1916	1926	Post-imperial
Austria	1918	1946	Post-imperial
Poland	1918	1926	Post-imperial – Modern
Lithuania	1918	1919	Post-imperial
Estonia	1918	1920	Post-imperial
Latvia	1918	1920	Post-imperial
Iceland	1918	1944	Post-imperial
Czech Republic	1920	1918/1993	Post-imperial
Faroe Islands	1948	1948	Post-imperial
Croatia	1990	1991	Post-imperial
Moldova	1990	1994	Post-imperial
Slovenia	1991	1989	Post-imperial
Slovakia	1992	1993	Post-imperial
Ukraine	1992	1917	Post-imperial
Albania	1992	1912	Post-imperial
Belarus	1995	1955, 2002	Post-imperial
Macedonia	1995	1945/1991	Post-imperial
BiH	1998	1999, 2009	Post-imperial
Serbia	2004, 2006	2004	Post-imperial
Montenegro	2004, 2007	2004	Post-imperial
Kosovo	2008	2008	Post-imperial

		1989	
		1878	
		1880/1933	
		(11th) 1922–31	
		1955	
		1791	
		1918	
		1918	
		1918	
		1945	
		1919	
		1948	
		2003	
		1992–92	
		1991	
		1992	
		1991	
		1991–92	
		1944-45	
		1992	
		In process	
		1992, 2004, 2007	
		2004, 2007	
		2008	

Albania and Macedonia. An illuminating example, the Slovakian flag displays a coat of arms originating in the ninth century. The shy emergence of the recent category of flags are best described as non-hereditary, post-historical and counter-nationalist, with regard to their avoidance of divisive historical references. National days fall into two categories: those honouring national personifications and golden ages are primarily religious holidays that have been nationalized or transformed into national holidays, whereas the national days originating in 'modern' or 'post-imperial' times honour political events such as independence. The national days in Europe are as a rule public holidays with few exceptions. Furthermore, the majority are civilian but the military plays a central part in some celebrations as does the church. The general trend, however, suggests that significance of the military parades and church ceremonials in these celebrations are on the decrease.

By adding to the approximate dates of national flags, those of national anthems and national days, various layers of nations are uncovered. As a general rule, national flags appear before anthems and national days and anthems in between the two. The flag constitutes an older stratum of the nation, whereas the national day appears in the nineteenth and twentieth centuries. The exceptions are the national days with a religious past that have been nationalized or those existing in an earlier period of state formations. Here the aim is to demonstrate that not only are nations layered, but their creation is a continuous process traced alongside a continuum of symbolic expression. Britain and Russia have pre-modern flags but post-imperial national days. The Netherlands displays a pre-modern flag and celebrates a modern national day, whereas Italy and Germany have modern flags and post-imperial national days. Poland's symbols, owing to political ruptures, comprise a post-imperial flag but a modern national day, whereas Portugal's flag is modern and the national day dated to a pre-modern origin although first celebrated nationally in post-imperial times. Ireland's flag is post-imperial and the national day has pre-modern origins as a saint's day but retained a national focus after independence. The considerable complexity with regard to nation building is also expressed in that flags and national days are introduced centuries apart.

Keeping in mind the debates on whether nations are pre-modern or modern, discovered or invented, nation building is highly complicated and cannot be reduced to neat conceptualizations in this regard. Whereas flags are usually older than national days, the latter appear closer to the period of the mass-production of invented traditions (1870–1914). It is striking that the majority of national days appear from the mid-nineteenth century onwards, in the age of nationalism when the national communities began to celebrate their ideals and distinctiveness as religious communities of the past. Out of the 42 national days accounted for, 11 are older than 1870 (few with a national focus), six appear during 1870–1914 and 25 are introduced after 1914, which supports the argument that a new tradition had been invented. With national anthems the pattern is equally clear as only two anthems were in use before the French Revolution, 12 between the latter and the First World War and 21 were introduced after this. Generally speaking, national anthems and national days provide further layers around nations, adding to the national fervour during the periods of political instability in the decades before and after the First World War. The invention of tradition is an appropriate term for the age of mass-politics but less applicable to the development of traditions and symbols in earlier periods. The ethno-symbolist perspectives here provide an alternative in exploring the emergence of pre-modern flags and festivities. However, the early cross flags did not constitute national flags at the time of their introduction and the first celebrations had a religious focus as they speak of early territorial associations and loyalties. Their early existence indicates that pre-modern loyalties existed although modern nations (in the modern sense) did not. Moreover, some flags and national days may have existed early but attained a nationalist focus much later on. The patterns of the symbolism and ceremonial forms demonstrate that the nations in Western and northern Europe, as a whole, adopted their national symbols and ceremonies earlier compared with the nations of Central and Eastern Europe. No consistent pattern as such is found as regards the nations in southern Europe. The development of symbolic regimes has been identified in order to explore underlying symbolic narratives. In other words, this book has sought to draw attention to the complexity of the nation-building process, which by necessity requires an encompassing theoretical framework. With the evidence presented here, the process of nation building speaks of (re)creation, (re)construction and (re)invention.

It has been argued that national holidays have lost their meaning in today's world but this is not consistent with the findings of this study. Instead, national days serve as convenient means of analysing the building and re-building of nations as they continue to be created, re-created, contested and re-contested according to their meanings, celebrations or commemorations. National days may constitute unifying elements and have therefore continued to engage nation builders who perceived them as community-building devices and occasions. However, national days can make people aware of membership but they do not necessarily create cohesion. Imbued with meaning, national days will by default be contested and negotiated and can, on the contrary, highlight and reinforce divisions in ways similar to the use of national flags in conflicts described previously. Some ceremonies do not even create consensus as regards to what is commemorated, others are drained of historical meanings whereas yet others thrive on foundation myths. Few national days remain unnoticed. As a rule, the nations of Europe have one day in which the imaginations of one national community are displayed by the participation of its members, something which highlights their syncretic and partly invented character.

In conclusion, nations clearly cannot be dated in a precise manner since they come into being by stages but their formations are marked by the adoption of national symbols, such as the national flag and the national day. The complexity of the nation-building process can therefore be traced alongside the establishment of national flags and national days as they are adopted, altered, modified, abolished and re-established to reflect significant events in the (re)making of nations. As this information is systematized, three distinct symbolic regimes emerge alongside pre-modern, modern and post-imperial narratives. These patterns may, in turn, be linked to symbolic types and ceremonial styles and the socio-political context in which they emerge. Whereas some nations are represented by pre-modern religious or monarchical imagery others reproduce symbolic codes of the modern and republican age. Post-imperial narratives, in turn, point as rule towards an ancient past prior to more recent state formations. *Symbols of Nations and Nationalism* has aimed to draw attention to the complexity of the layered and ongoing process of the building of nations.

Bibliography

Aagedal, O. (2002). Nasjonal symbolbruk in Skandinavia [The Use of National Symbols in Scandinavia]. Paper presented at the Racisme og ekstremtoleranse [Racism and extreme tolerance] at Det Norske Diakonhjemmet.

Abd Rabbo, A. (Photograph). (2008). Jets Fly Over Paris on Bastille Day 14 July. Paris: Balkis press.

Abd Rabbo, A. (Photograph). (2008). Presidential Podium, Place de la Concorde, Bastille Day 14 July Paris: Balkis Press.

Adnkronos International (30 November 2009). Italy: Right-wing Minister Wants 'Cross' on Flag, from http://www.adnkronos.com/AKI/English/Religion/?id=3.0.4053943099

Adriansen, I. (2003). *National Symboler i Det Danske Rige 1830–2000*. Købehavns Universitet: Museum Tusculanums Forlag.

Agulhon, M. (1998). Paris: A Traversal from East to West. In Nora (Ed.), *Realms of Memory: The Construction of the French Past* (Vol. 3, pp. 522–53). Symbols, NY: Columbia University Press.

Alba, R. (2005). Bright vs. Blurred Boundaries: Second-generation Assimilation and Exclusion in France, Germany, and the United States. *Ethnic and Racial Studies*, 28(1).

Alter, P. (1994). *Nationalism* (2nd ed.). London: Edward Arnold.

Alvarez Junco, J. (2001). *Mater Dolorosa: La idea de España en el Siglo XIX*. Taurus Ediciones.

Amalvi, C. (1996). Bastille Day: From Dies Irae to Holiday. In Nora (Ed.), *Realms of Memory: The Construction of the French Past* (Vol. 3, pp. 117–62). Symbols, NY: Columbia University Press.

Anderson, B. (1991). *Imagined Communities: Reflections on the Origin and Spread of Nationalism* (2nd rev. ed.). London: Verso.

Andreouli, E. and Stockdale, J.E. (2009). Earned Citizenship: Assumptions and Implications. *Journal of Immigration Asylum and Nationality Law*, 23(2), 164–80.

Anholt, S. (2007). *Competitive Identity: The New Brand Management for Nations, Cities and Regions*. New York: Palgrave Macmillan.

Ansari, H. (2009). *Proving Loyalty? Muslims and Britain's Armed Forces*: Muslim Council of Britain / Professor Humayun Ansari, OBE, Director, Centre for Minority Studies, Royal Holloway, University of London.

Armstrong, J. (1982). *Nations before Nationalism*. Chapel Hill: University of North Carolina Press.

Aronczyk, M. (2009). Research in Brief. How to Do Things with Brands: Uses of National Identity. *Canadian Journal of Communication*, 34, 291–6.

Aronczyk, M. (2011). *Branding the Nation: Mediating Space, Value and Identity in Global Culture*. Oxford: Oxford University Press.

Aronsson, P., and Elgenius, G. (2011). National Museums in Europe: A comparative study of the politics of recognition and representation. Paper presented at the EUNAMUS Conference, University of Bologna, March. Article in progress.

Arvidsson, C. and Blomqvist, L. (eds). (1987). *Symbols of Power: The Esthetics of Political Legitimation in the Soviet Union and Eastern Europe*. Stockholm: Almqvist and Wiksell International.

Bagge, S. (1995a). The Middle Ages. In W.H. Hubbard, J.E. Myhre, T. Norby and S. Sogner (eds), *Making a Historical Culture. Historiography in Norway* (pp. 111–31): Scandinavian University Press.

Bagge, S. (1995b). Nationalism in Norway in the Middle Ages. *Scandinavian Journal of History*, 20(1), 1–18.

Balkan Insight (23 February 2009). Bosnia Anthem Gets Lyrics after 10 Years. Retrieved July 2010, from http://www.balkaninsight.com/en/main/news/16893/

Barrachina, M.A. (2000). 12 de octubre: Fiesta de la raza, Día de la Hispanidad, Día del Pilar, Fiesta Nacional. *Bulletin d'histoire contemporaine de l'Espagne*, 30, 119–34.

Barstad, S. and Buan, V. (2008). 17 mai-komiteen står på sitt. Retrieved 30 April 2008, from http://www.aftenposten.no/nyheter/iriks/article2388763.ece

Barth, F. (ed.). (1969). *Ethnic Groups and Boundaries*. London: George Allen & Unwin.

Barton, A. (2005). Scandinavianism, Fennomania, and the Crimean War. *Journal of Baltic Studies*, 36(2), 131–56. Retrieved from http://www.informaworld.com/smpp/content~content=a770915582~db=all~tab=content~order=page

Basque Country (2010). Retrieved 10 August 2010, from http://www.fotw.net/flags/es-pv.html

Baumgarten, M.P. (1984). Social Control from Below. In D. Black (ed.), *Toward a General Theory of Social Control* (Vol. 1, pp. 305–45). New York: Academic Press.

BBC (4 June 2002). The Jubilee Procession, from http://news.bbc.co.uk/1/hi/uk/2024634.stm

BBC (4 November 2009). Jail Threat for Urinating Student, from http://news.bbc.co.uk/1/hi/england/south_yorkshire/8342191.stm

BBC (9 July 2005). Memorial to War Women Unveiled, from http://news.bbc.co.uk/1/hi/england/london/4667705.stm

BBC (11 June 2008). Kosovo MPs Choose National Anthem. Retrieved July 2010, from http://news.bbc.co.uk/1/hi/7447583.stm

BBC (22 November 2005). Ukraine Marks Orange Revolution 2005, from http://news.bbc.co.uk/1/hi/world/europe/4459224.stm

BBC (2004a). Montenegro Picks National Symbols, from http://news.bbc.co.uk/1/hi/world/europe/3889355.stm

BBC (2004b). Serbia Changes National Symbols, from http://news.bbc.co.uk/1/hi/world/europe/3573958.stm

BBC (2005). Swedes Mark Tsunami Anniversary, from http://news.bbc.co.uk/1/hi/world/europe/4560468.stm

BBC (July 23 1998). UK Flags at Half-mast for Diana, from http://news.bbc.co.uk/1/hi/uk/138174.stm

BBCNEWS (11 November 2000). An inclusive Remembrance Sunday? Retrieved 6 September 2010, from http://news.bbc.co.uk/1/hi/uk/1017067.stm

BBCNews (2009). Nation unites to remember fallen (8 November 2009). Retrieved from http://news.bbc.co.uk/1/hi/uk/8348225.stm

Beaufort-Spontin, P. (2004). Unpublished correspondence. London: Austrian Cultural Forum.

Beck, U. and Beck-Gernsheim, E. (2002). *Individualization: Institutionalized Individualism and its Social and Political Consequences*. London: Sage.
Belgian Information Service (2005). Unpublished correspondence. New York: Foreign Agents Section, Department of Justice.
Bhabha, E. (ed.). (1990). *Nation and Narrative*. London: Routledge.
Bichler, C. (2004). Interview and Unpublished correspondence. London: Austrian Embassy.
Billig, M. (1995). *Banal Nationalism*. London: Sage Publications.
Blehr, B. (1999a). On Ritual Effectiveness: The Case of Constitution Day. *Ethnologia Scandinavica*, 29, 28–43.
Blehr, B. (1999b). Sacred Unity, Sacred Similarity: Norwegian Constitution Day Parades. *Ethnology*, 38(2), 175–89.
Breuilly, J. (1993). *Nationalism and the State* (2nd ed.). Manchester: Manchester University Press.
Bristow, J.M. and Reed, L.W. (eds). (1993). *National Anthems of the World*. London: Cassell / Avon: Bath Press.
Bruce, S. (2002). *God is Dead: Secularization in the West*. Cambridge: Blackwell.
CatalanAssociationVexillologia (1995). Catalonia. Retrieved 15 August 2010, from Catalan Association Vexillologia http://personal.telefonica.terra.es/web/vexicat/catalunya.htm
CatalanAssociationVexillologia (15 August 2010). Catalonia, from http://personal.telefonica.terra.es/web/vexicat/catalunya.htm
Catalonia (2010). Retrieved 10 August 2010, from http://www.fotw.net/flags/es-ct.html
Cenarro Lagunas, A. (1997). La reina de la Hispanidad: Fascismo y Nacionalcatolicismo en Zaragoza 1939–1945. *Revista de historia Jerónimo Zurita*, 72, 91–102.
Cerulo, K. (1995). *Identity Designs: The Sights and Sounds of a Nation*. New Brunswick, New Jersey: Rutgers University Press.
Clayton, A. (1995). *The Moscow Victory Parade*: C86, Conflict Studies, Conflict Studies Research Centre.
CNN (1990). German Reunification, from http://www.youtube.com/watch?v=RVE6sjS2jGo&feature=related
CNN (2009). President Obama and Hillary Clinton on the 20th Anniversary of the Fall of the Berlin Wall, from http://www.youtube.com/watch?v=1SN0Thj___U
Cohen, A. (1995). *The Symbolic Construction of Community*. London: Routledge.
Cohen, R. (1995). Fuzzy Frontiers of Identity: The British Case. *Social Identities*, 1(62), 35–62.
Colley, L. (1992). *Britons: A Forged Nation 1707–1837*. Yale University Press.
Colrat, J.-C. (2010). A Study of Jeanne d'Arc's Standard. Original title 'Les Compagnons d'Arms de Jeanne d'Arc'. Retrieved 22 January 2010, from http://www.stjoan-center.com/j-cc/
Confino, A. (1997). *The Nation as a Local Metaphor: Württemberg, Imperial Germany, and National Memory 1917–1918*. Chapel Hill and London: University of North Carolina Press.
Connerton, P. (1989). *How Societies Remember*. Cambridge: Cambridge University Press.

Connor, W. (1992). The Nation and its Myth. *International Journal of Comparative Sociology*, 33(1–2), 48–57.
Connor, W. (1994). *Ethnonationalism: The Quest for Understanding*. Princeton, New Jersey: Princeton University Press.
Constitutional Commission of the Republic of Kosovo (2008). *Constitution of the Republic of Kosovo*. Retrieved from http://www.kushtetutakosoves. info/repository/docs/Constitution.of.the.Republic.of.Kosovo.pdf
Costa, A. (2004). Portuguese Heritage Society of California. Retrieved 22 November 2004, from www.diadeportugal.com
Crampton, W. (1989). *The Complete Guide to Flags: Identifying and Understanding the Flags of the World*. London: Kingfisher Books.
Crampton, W. (1992). *The World of Flags: A Pictorial History* (2nd ed.). London: Studio Editions Ltd.
Cravo, A. (2000). Dia de Portugal. *Luso-Americano*, Newark, NJ.
Czech Republic Official Website (2004). The State Symbols of the Czech Republic. Retrieved 8 November 2004, from www.Czech.cz
Daily Mail (20 November 2009). Herman Van Rompuy is the 'Shrewd Master of the Shabby Compromise', from http://www.dailymail.co.uk/news/article-1229670/Herman-Van-Rompuy-shrewd-master-shabby-compromise.html
Davie, G. (1994). *Religion in Britain Since 1945: Believing without Belonging*. Cambridge: Blackwell.
Dayan, D. and Katz, E. (1992). *Media Events: The Live Broadcasting of History*. Cambridge, MA: Harvard University Press.
DeutscheWelle (2009). German president attends Bastille Day celebrations for first time. *Deutsche Welle* from http://www.dw-world.de/dw/article/0,,4486955, 00.html
Devereux, E. (1992). *Book of World Flags*. London: New Burlington Books.
Devoldere, S. (2005). Interview. Flanders House, Embassy of Belgium.
Dillistone, W.F. (1986). *The Power of Symbols in Religion and Culture*. New York: Crossroad.
Dimbleby, D. (Commentator) (8 November 2009). Remembrance Sunday at the Cenotaph: BBC.
Dimbleby, D. (Commentator) (10 November 2001). Remembrance Sunday at the Cenotaph: BBC.
Dimrilieri, N.V. (2005). Flemish Representation. Interview with Embassy Representative. London: Flanders House, Embassy of Belgium.
Dogan, M. (1994). The Decline of Nationalisms within Western Europe. *Comparative Politics*, 26, 281–305.
Doordarshan News (DD News) (2009). France honours India in Bastille Day military parade, from http://www.youtube.com/watch?v=2PSLK2TNHfU&feature=related
Durkheim, E. (1976). *The Elementary Forms of the Religious Life* (2nd ed.). London: George Allen & Unwin.
Economist (1997). Flagging Progress. *The Economist*, 6 September, 52.
Elgenius, G. (1993). *A Minority's Struggle for Cultural Survival – The Mohawk Indians of Akwesasne*. Växjö Högskola today Linneus University, Växjö.
Elgenius, G. (2005a). Expressions of Nationhood: National Symbols & Ceremonies in Contemporary Europe. London School of Economics & Political Science, University of London, London.

Elgenius, G. (2005b). National Days & Nation-building: A Contemporary Survey. In Eriksonas and Müller (eds), *Statehood beyond Ethnicity*. Brussels: Peter Lang Publishers, Presses Interuniversitaires Européennes.
Elgenius, G. (2007a). The Appeal of Nationhood: Celebrating and Commemorating the Nation. In Sturm and Young (eds), *Nationalism in a Global Era: The Persistence of Nations*. London: Routledge.
Elgenius, G. (2007b). National Expressions and Diversity in Europe. *International Journal for Diversity in Organisations, Communities and Nations*, 6.
Elgenius, G. (2007c). Origin of European National Flags. In T.H. Eriksen and R.P. Jenkins (eds), *Flag, Nation and Symbolism in Europe and America*. Oxford: Routledge.
Elgenius, G. (2008). Promoting Britishness: Citizenship and Nation-building. Paper presented at the Britishness versus Englishness: Ethnicity under Scrutiny, AHRC/ERSC Conference St Catharine's College, University of Oxford, July. Article in progress.
Elgenius, G. (Photograph). (2009a). Fields of Remembrance at Westminster Abbey, London.
Elgenius, G. (Photograph). (2009b). Marching Past the Cenotaph. Cenotaph Ceremony, Remembrance Sunday.
Elgenius, G. (Photograph). (2009c). Monument to Women of the Second World War, Ceremonial Route of Remembrance, London.
Elgenius, G. (Photograph). (2009d). Nationalism, Christianity and Sacrifice, Cenotaph Ceremony, Remembrance Sunday.
Elgenius, G. (2009e). Successful Nation-Building and Ceremonial Triumph: Constitution Day in Norway. In McCrone and McPherson (eds), *National Days: Constructing and Mobilizing National Identity*. Basingstoke: Palgrave Macmillan.
Elgenius, G. (Photograph). (2010a). Ceremonial Focus and the Royal Castle, Constitution Day Parade in Oslo, Karl Johan's Avenue, 17 May 2010.
Elgenius, G. (Photograph). (2010b). Children's Parade on Avenue Karl Johan, Constitution Day in Oslo, Norway, 2010.
Elgenius, G. (2011). The Politics of Recognition: Symbols, Nation-building and Rival Nationalisms. *Journal of Nations and Nationalism*, Issue 17.2. April, Wiley-Blackwell.
Embassy of Belgium (2004). Unpublished correspondence. London.
Embassy of France Official Website (2010). La Marseillaise. Aux Armes, Citoyens! Retrieved 14 August 2010, from http://www.info-france-usa.org/spip.php?article617
Embassy of the Republic of Macedonia (2005). Retrieved 4 April 2005, from info@macedonianembassy.org.uk
Embassy of the Republic of Poland (2004). Personal Correspondence. London.
Embassy of the Russian Federation (2004). Personal Correspondence. London.
Encyclopaedia Britannica (2004). Flag, from http://members.eb.com/bol/topic?eu=35082&sctn=4
ENDirect (2009). La Légion Étrangère – Défilé 14 juillet 2009 from http://www.youtube.com/watch?v=5KOD7NboKPI&feature=related
ENDirect (2010a). France 14th July 2010 – Défilé for the 'Fête nationale' in Paris – The Bastille's Day – Part 3/4 from http://www.youtube.com/watch?v=ephed2gIQ90

ENDirect (2010b). France 14th July 2010 – Défilé for the 'Fête nationale' in Paris – The Bastille's Day – Part 4/4 from http://www.youtube.com/watch?v=v46iXc LSA_Q&p=47A3DC98281B26D1&index=2&playnext=2
Engene, J. (1997a). First Flag of Independence 1814. Retrieved 10 September 2001, from http://www.crwflags.com/fotw/flags/no-hrank.html#1814
Engene, J. (1997b). Norway Historic Flags: National War Ensign, Union Flags 1844. Retrieved 10 September 2001, from http://www.crwflags.com/fotw/flags/no-hrank.html
Engene, J. (2000a). Kingdom of Norway. Retrieved 12 September 2001, from http://www.crwflags.com/fotw/flags/no.html
Engene, J. (2000b). Norwegian Royal Standard. Retrieved 11 September 2001, from http://www.crwflags.com/fotw/flags/no-royal.html,2003
English Heritage (14 April 2008). English Heritage launch St George's Day campaign. Retrieved 3 September 2010, from http://www.easier.com/56643-english-heritage-launch-st-george-s-day-campaign.html
Eriksen, A. (2007). The Domestication of a National Symbol. The Private Use of Flags in Norway. In E. Jenkins (ed.), *Flag, Nation and Symbolism in Europe and America* (pp. 157–70). London: Routledge.
Eriksen, T.H. (2002). *Ethnicity and Nationalism: Anthropological Perspectives* (2nd ed.). London: Pluto Press.
Eriksen, T.H. (2005). Keeping the Recipe: Norwegian Folk Costumes and Cultural Capital. *Focaal*, 44, 20–34.
Eriksen, T.H. (2008). *Et mer fleksibelt fellesskap: Nasjonsbygging mot 2014. Anbefalinger og rapport fra Mangfoldsåret 2008*. Kultur- og Kirkedepartmentet. Culture and Church Department, Oslo, Norway.
Eriksen, T.H. and Jenkins, R. (eds) (2007). *Flag, Nation and Symbolism in Europe and America*. London: Routledge.
España, Kingdom of Spain, Reino de España (2010). Retrieved 10 August 2010, from http://www.fotw.net/flags/es.html
Etzioni, A. (2004). Holidays and Rituals: Neglected Seedbeds of Virtue. In A. Etzioni and J. Blom (eds), *We Are What We Celebrate: Understanding Holidays and Rituals*. New York and London: New York University Press.
European Flag. History of the Flag (2010). Retrieved 22 January 2010, from http://europa.eu/abc/symbols/emblem/index_en.htm
European Values Study Group and World Values Survey Association (2006). *European and World Values Surveys Four-wave Integrated Data File*.
Evans-Pritchard, E. (1965). *Theories of Primitive Religion*. Oxford: Oxford University Press.
Federal Ministry for Education and Cultural Affairs (1990). 26 October. Zur Geschichte des Österreichischen Nationalfeiertags *Austria: Facts and Figures* (pp. 40–1). Vienna: Federal Press Service.
Field, M. (2010). Interview with Member of the Executive Board of MINAB, Mosque and Imams National Advisory Board on the MCB report on 'Remembering the Brave. The Muslim Contribution to Britain's Armed Forces'.
Firth, R. (1973). *Symbols Public and Private* (2nd ed.). London: George Allen & Unwin Ltd.
Flag of the United States of America Website (2005). The Pledge of Allegiance (2005). Retrieved 15 August 2010 from http://www.usflag.org

Flagmaster (1995a). The Balkan Question Resolved? Macedonian Flag Issue Settled. *The Flag Institute Bulletin, Chester Flag Institute* (81), 1–2.

Flagmaster (1995b). Greece and Macedonia. *The Flag Institute Bulletin, Chester Flag Institute* (81), 2–3.

Flagmaster (1995c). Macedonia. Star of Vergina to go. *The Flag Institute Bulletin, Chester Flag Institute* (80), 8–9.

Florence, M. and Jealous, V. (2003). *Vietnam* (7th ed.). Victoria, Australia: Lonely Planet Publications.

FOTW (1991a). Belarus – Flag Legislation. Retrieved 3 June 2004, from http://www.crwflags.com/fotw/flags/by_law.html#2004

FOTW (1991b). White and Red Flag in Belarus. Retrieved 10 August 2004, from http://www.crwflags.com/fotw/flags/by_1991.html#tri

FOTW (1998a). Flagging Progress: Bosnia-Herzegovina Flag Change, from http://www.crwflags.com/fotw/flags/ba-fc98.html

FOTW (1998b). Official Flag Days in Belgium. Retrieved 7 November, 2004, from http://www.crwflags.com/fotw/flags/be-days.html

FOTW (1999). Etymology of Vexillological Terminology, from http://fotw.digibel.be/flags/flagetym.html,1999

FOTW (2002). Lithuania in the Soviet Union (early flags). Retrieved 25 November 2004, from http://www.crwflags.com/fotw/flags/su-lt_h.html

FOTW (2003a). The Prinsevlag of the Netherlands. Retrieved 18 July 2004, from http://www.crwflags.com/fotw/flags/nl_prvlg.html

FOTW (2003b). Spain, Historical Flags 1931–39. Retrieved 8 September 2003, from http://www.crwflags.com/fotw/flags/es1931.html

FOTW (2003c). Spain, Historical Flags 1945–77. Retrieved 9 September 2003, from http://www.crwflags.com/fotw/flags/es1945.html

FOTW (2003d). Spain, Medieval Heraldry in Modern Form. Retrieved 8 August 2004, from http://www.crwflags.com

FOTW (2003e). Spain: Historical flags 1936–38. Flags of the Rebel or National Forces. Retrieved 8 August 2004, from http://www.crwflags.com/fotw/flags/es1936.html

FOTW (2003f). Spain: Historical flags 1938–45. Retrieved 8 September 2003, from http://www.crwflags.com/fotw/flags/es1938.html

FOTW (2004a). Bosnia and Herzegovina – Flag Legislation. The Flag Law 2004. The Flag Law 1998. From http://www.crwflags.com/FOTW/flags/ba-law.html

FOTW (2004b). Denmark. Retrieved 29 September 2004, from http://www.crwflags.com/fotw/flags/dk.html

FOTW (2004c). Northern Ireland. Retrieved 5 June 2003, from http://www.crwflags.com/fotw/flags/gb-ulste.html#redhand

FOTW (2004d). Official Flag Days in Latvia. Retrieved 26 December 2004, from http://www.crwflags.com/fotw/flags/lv.html#days

FOTW (2005a). Banner of Joan of Arc (Jeanne d'Arc). Retrieved 22 January 2010, from http://www.crwflags.com/FOTW/flags/fr_hyw.html#joan

FOTW (2005b). Kingdom of the Netherlands: Official Flag Days. Retrieved 27 July 2004, from http://www.crwflags.com/fotw/flags/nl.html#days

FOTW (2007). Crusader Cross Flags 1188, from http://www.crwflags.com/fotw/flags/rel-c188.html

FOTW (2009a). Bosnia and Herzegovina: Flags Proposed upon Independence'. From http://www.crwflags.com/fotw/flags/ba-prop.html

208 Bibliography

FOTW (2009b). Controversy with Greece: the Greek Point of View. From http://www.crwflags.com/fotw/flags/mk-1992.html#gre

FOTW (2009c). France: Flags used in the Bastille Day parade. From http://www.crwflags.com/FOTW/flags/fr%5E1407.html

FOTW (2009d). Gay Pride / Rainbow Flag. Retrieved 22 January 2010, from http://www.crwflags.com/fotw/Flags/qq-rb.html

FOTW (2009e). Heraldry and the Origin of the Bosnian Fleur-de-lis. Retrieved 10 January 2009, from http://www.crwflags.com/fotw/flags/ba-1992.html

FOTW (2009f). History of the Gay Pride / Rainbow Flag. Retrieved 22 January 2010, from http://www.crwflags.com/fotw/flags/qq-rb_h.html

FOTW (2009g). Macedonia: The 1997 Flag Law, from http://www.crwflags.com/fotw/flags/mk.html

FOTW (2009h). Serbia: State Flag and National (Civil) Flag Retrieved January 2010, from http://www.crwflags.com/fotw/Flags/rs.html

FOTW (2009i). St Davids Flag (Wales): Dewi Sant. Retrieved 21 January 2010, from http://www.fotw.net/flags/gb-w-std.html

FOTW (Flags of the World) (2010). Kosovo before the declaration of independence. Kosovo under United Nations administration. Dardania (flag of uncertain status). Retrieved 17 August 2010, from http://www.crwflags.com/fotw/flags/rs-koso1.html#dar

FOTW (2010a). Flag of Sami People, from http://www.crwflags.com/fotw/flags/xn_sami.html

FOTW (2010b). Flags of the World Website, from http://www.crwflags.com/fotw/flags/

FOTW (2010c). Kalaallit Nunaat, Grønland. Greenland (Denmark). Retrieved 1 June 2010, from http://www.crwflags.com/fotw/flags/gl.html

FOTW (2010d). Republic of Srpska (Bosnia and Herzegovina) Republika Srpska, Republic of Serbska, Serb Republic. From http://www.crwflags.com/FOTW/flags/ba_serbs.html

FOTW (2010e). Socialist and Communist Parties 1931–39 (Spain). Retrieved 9 September 2010, from http://www.crwflags.com/fotw/flags/es%7Dsc931.html

FOTW (2010f). Soviet Union. Retrieved 9 September 2010, from http://flagspot.net/flags/su.html

FOTW (2010g). Switzerland, from http://www.crwflags.com/fotw/flags/ch.html

France 24 (12 July 2009). Indian Army to be Guest of Honour on Bastille Day. From http://www.france24.com/en/20090712-indian-army-be-guests-honour-bastille-day-france-july-14

Freeman, P. (2004). *St Patrick of Ireland: A Biography*. New York: Simon and Schuster.

French Embassy Official Website (2000). From http://www.info-france-usa.org/atoz/marianne.asp

French Foreign Legion: What is the Foreign Legion (2010). Retrieved 14 August 2010, from http://www.ambafrance-us.org/spip.php?article533

Frous, D. (2004). Personal Correspondence. London: Embassy of the Czech Republic, Information Office.

Gateway to Scotland Website (2004). Gateway to Scotland. Retrieved 22 April 2004, from http://www.geo.ed.ac.uk/home/scotland/scotland.html

Gatty (2009). United Kingdom: Use and Status of the Flag. From http://www.crwflags.com/fotw/flags/gb-use.html

Geisler, M. (ed.). (2007). *The Calendar Conundrum: National Days as Unstable Signifiers*. Basingstoke: Palgrave Macmillan.
Gellner, E. (1993). *Nations and Nationalism*. Oxford: Blackwell.
Giddens, A. (1991). *Modernity and Self-Identity: Self and Society in the Late Modern Age*. Cambridge: Polity Press in association with Blackwell.
Gilliat-Ray, S. (1999). Civic religion in England: Traditions and transformations. *Journal of Contemporary Religion*, 14(2), 233–44.
Gillis, J. (ed.). (1994). *Commemorations: The Politics of National Identity*. New Jersey: Princeton University Press.
Girardet, R. (1998). The Three Colors: Neither White nor Red. In Nora (ed.), *Realms of Memory: The Construction of the French Past* (Vol. 3: Symbols, pp. 3–26). NY: Columbia University Press.
Goldstein, R.J. (2000). *Flag Burning and Free Speech: The Case of Texas v. Johnson*. Lawrence, Kansas: University of Kansas Press.
Goodhart, D. (2004). Too Diverse? *Prospect* (February).
Government Publications (1989). *Admiralty Flag Book BR20, Ministry of Defense, Director General of Supplies and Transport (Navy), D/ST31/364/12 (1989)*. London: HMSO.
Green, C. (2010). Representation of Faith Communities by the Cenotaph on Remembrance Sunday in London. (DCMS) Public Engagement & Recognition Unit, Department for Culture, Media & Sport.
Greenfeld, L. (1992). *Nationalism: Five Roads to Modernity*. Princeton, NJ: Harvard University Press.
Grimnes, O.K. (2007). Nationalism and Unionism in Nineteenth-century Norwegian Flags. In E. Jenkins (ed.), *Flag, Nation and Symbolism in Europe and America* (pp. 146–56). London: Routledge.
Guerra, A. (1999). Correspondence: National Day and Symbols. Embassy of Portugal, Box 10194, 10055 Stockholm.
Guibernau, M. (1996). *Nationalisms: The Nation-State and Nationalism in the Twentieth Century*. Cambridge: Polity Press.
Gusfield, J.R. and Michalowicz, J. (1984). Secular Symbolism: Studies of Ritual, Ceremony, and the Symbolic Order in Modern Life. *Annual Review of Sociology*, 10, 417–35.
Gutiérrez, N. (November 2004). Unpublished correspondence. Spanish Embassy, Cultural Office/Press Office in London.
Hall, S. (1992). The question of cultural identity. In S. Hall, D. Held and T. McGrew (eds), *Modernity and its Futures*. Cambridge: Polity Press.
Hang, X. (2003). *Encyclopedia of National Anthems*. Scarecrow Press.
Hansen, J. and Hundevadt, K. (11 March 2008). Cartoon Crisis – How it Unfolded. Retrieved December 2009, from http://jp.dk/udland/article1292543.ece
Hattenauer, H. (1990). *Geschichte der deutschen Nationalsymbole: Zeichen und Bedeutung* (Part of *Geschichte und Staat, Band 285*). München: Orlag Verlag.
Heath, A. (2006). *British Identity*. Cabinet Office Report.
Heath, A., Martin, J. and Elgenius, G. (2007). Who Do We Think We Are? The Decline of Traditional Social Identities. In A. Park, J. Curtice, K. Thomson, M. Phillips and M. Johnson (eds), *British Social Attitudes: The 23rd Report – Perspectives on a Changing Society*. London: Sage for the National Centre for Social Research (NatCen).

Heimer, Ž. (1996a). Latvia in the Soviet Union. Retrieved 23 December 2002, from http://www.crwflags.com/fotw/flags/su-lv.html

Heimer, Ž. (1996b). Lithuania in the Soviet Union. Retrieved 21 March 2005, from http://www.crwflags.com/fotw/flags/su-lt.html

Heimer, Ž. (2004). European Union. Retrieved 1 May 2004, from http://www.fotw.net/flags/eu-eun.html#com

Held, D. (1989). The Decline of the Nation State. In S. Hall and M. Jacques (eds), *New Times: The Changing Face of Politics in the 1990s*. London: Lawrence & Wishart.

Hewitt, R. (2005). *White Backlash and the Politics of Multiculturalism*. Cambridge: Cambridge University Press.

History of Switzerland (2004). History of the Swiss Flag. Retrieved May 2010, from http://history-switzerland.geschichte-schweiz.ch/history-flag-switzerland.html

Hobsbawm, E. (1992). *Nations and Nationalism since 1780 – Programme, Myth, Reality* (2nd ed.). NY: Cambridge University Press.

Hobsbawm, E. and Ranger, T. (1992). *The Invention of Tradition*. Cambridge University Press (Canto).

Homberger, E. (1976). The Story of the Cenotaph. *Times Literary Supplement*, 1429–30.

Hopkin, A. (1989). *The Living Legend of St Patrick*. London: Grafton Books.

Hovland, K. and Maaland, B. (2010). Foreslår blandingsbunad. Urnorsk plagg adoptert av innvandrere. Retrieved 20 June 2010, from http://www.vg.no/rampelys/artikkel.php?artid=10006450

Howse, C. (30 October 2009). Poppy Appeal: Pinning Down Poppy Etiquette. From http://www.telegraph.co.uk/news/6461635/Poppy-Appeal-pinning-down-poppy-etiquette.html

Hroch, M. (1985). *Social preconditions of national revival in Europe: A comparative analysis of the social composition of patriotic groups among the smaller European nations*. Cambridge: Cambridge University Press.

Hroch, M. (1995). National Self-Determination from a Historical Perspective, *Periwal, Notions of Nationalism* (pp. 65–82). London: Central European University Press.

Hroch, M. (1996). From National Movement to the Fully-Formed Nation: The Nation-Building Process in Europe. In E. Suny (ed.), *Becoming National* (pp. 60–78). Oxford: Oxford University Press.

Hulme, E. (1915). *Flags of the World: Their History, Blazonry, and Associations, From the Banner of the Crusader to the Burgee of the Yachtsman*. London: Frederick Warne & Co.

Humlebaek, C. (2003). La Cuestión de la Fiesta Nacional Durante la época Socialista. *Spagna Contemporanea*, 23, 77–88.

Humlebaek, C. (2004). La Nación Española Conmemorada: La Fiesta Nacional en España Después de Franco. *Iberoamericana: Ensayos sobre Letras, Historia y Sociedad*, 13, 87–100.

Hutchinson, J. (1994). *Modern Nationalism*. London: Fontana Press.

Hutchinson, J. (2009). Warfare and the Sacralisation of Nations: The Meanings, Rituals and Politics of National Remembrance. *Millennium*, 38(2), 401–17.

Hutchinson, J. and Smith, A.D. (eds). (1994). *Nationalism*. Oxford: Oxford University Press.

iCasualties.org. Operation Enduring Freedom. Casulties by nationality and year. Retrieved 22 September 2010, from http://icasualties.org/oef/Nationality.aspx?hndQry=UK

Ignatieff, M. (1976). Soviet War Memorials. *History Workshop Journal*, Oxford University Press, 1, 157–63.

Ignatieff, M. (1993). *Blood and Belonging: Journeys into the New Nationalisms*. London: Vintage.

Inglis, K. (1967). Australia Day. *Historical Studies*, 13(49), 20–141.

Inglis, K. (1993). Entombing Unknown Soldiers: From London and Paris to Baghdad. *History and Memory*, 5(2), 7–31.

ISSP (2003). National Identity II. From International Social Survey Programme.

Joan of Arc Museum (2010). Joan of Arc's Banners. Retrieved 22 January 2010, from http://pagesperso-orange.fr/musee.jeannedarc/banner.htm

Joshi, M. (14 July 2009). Indian Armed Forces Contingent Leads Bastille Day Parade in Paris. From http://www.topnews.in/indian-armed-forces-contingent-leads-bastille-day-parade-paris-2189024

Judah, T. (2008). *Kosovo. What Everyone Needs to Know*. Oxford: Oxford University Press.

Kapferer, B. (1988). *Legends of People, Myths of State: Violence, Intolerance and Political Culture in Sri Lanka and Australia*. Washington DC/ London: Smithsonian Institute Press.

Kaplan, Y. (2010). Unpublished interview and correspondence with reference to inter-faith aspects of Muslim representation on Remembrance Sunday. (Interfaith Adviser, University of Westminster and Muslim Chaplain to UCL.) University of London.

Kappler, A. and Reichart, S. (1996). *Facts about Germany*. Frankfurt am Main: Societäts-Verlag.

Karjalainen, S. (1997). *FINFO, No 20*. Helsinki: Ministry of Foreign Affairs, Department for Press and Culture.

Karjalainen, S. (2004). *Traditional Festivities*: University of Helsinki, Ministry for Foreign Affairs of Finland, Department for Communication and Culture/Unit for Promotion and Publications.

Kelly, R. and Byrne, L. (2007). A Common Place. *Freethinking* (June). Retrieved from http://www.ivydene2.co.uk/liambyrne/resources/common_place.pdf

Ker-Lindsay, J. (2009). *Kosovo: The Path to Contested Statehood in the Balkans*. London: I.B.Taurus.

Kertzer, D. (1989). *Ritual, Politics, and Power*. Yale University Press.

King, A. (1998). *Memorials of the Great War in Britain: The Symbolism of Politics of Remembrance*. Oxford: Berg.

Kingstone, S. (2007). Franco Bill Divides Spain. Retrieved 3 February, 2011, from http://news.bbc.co.uk/1/hi/world/europe/7103867.stm

Knell, S., Aronsson, P., Amundsen, A.B., Barnes, A.J., Burch, S., Carter, J., Gosselin, V., Hughes, S.A. and Kirwan, A. (2011) *National Museums: New Studies from Around the World*. London and New York: Routledge.

Knight, S. (2005). Millions across Europe stop to observe Armistice Day. *The Times. The Sunday Times*. Retrieved 3 September 2010, from http://www.timesonline.co.uk/tol/news/uk/article589211.ece

Kolstø, P. (2006). National Symbols as Signs of Unity and Division. *Ethnic and Racial Studies*, 29(4), 676–701.

Kramer, J. (1984). Norsk identitet – et produkt av underutvikling og stammetilhørighet [Norwegian identity – a product of underdevelopment and tribal belonging]. In A.M. Klausen (ed.), *Den Norske Væremåten* [The Norwegian way of Being] (pp. 88–97). Oslo: Cappelen.

Krasniqi, A. (2010). Interview on Symbols of Kosovo. First Secretary of the Embassy of the Republic of Kosovo.

Leiren, T. (2005). 1905 – Norway's Defining Moment. Norwegian-American Foundation. *Norway.com* Retrieved 30 November, 2010, from http://noram.norway.com/publish.asp?id=218&mid=59

Leonard, H. (1996). *National Anthems from Around the World*. Hal Leonard Corporation.

Levi-Strauss, C. (1962). *La Pensee Sauvage*. Paris: Plon.

Lichfield, J. (2005). Tide of Grief Sweeps through Sweden, from http://www.nzherald.co.nz/tsunami-in-asia/news/article.cfm?c_id=500851&objectid=9005678&pnum=1

Lidtke (1982). Songs and Nazis: Political Music and Social Change in Twentieth-Century Germany. In S. Lackner (ed.), *Essays on Culture and Society in Modern Germany*. Texas University Press.

Lindblad, H. (2010, 30 July). Skända flaggan? Totalitär tendens när Frankrikge fridlyser trikoloren. *Dagens nyheter* [*Daily News*], Stockholm.

Llobera, J. (1998). Historical and Comparative Research. In C. Seale (ed.), *Researching Society and Culture* (pp. 72–81). London: Sage Publications.

Löfgren, O. (2007). A Flag for all Occasions? The Swedish Experience. In Eriksen and Jenkins (eds), (pp. 136–45). London: Routledge.

Lukes, S. (1975). Political ritual and social integration. *Sociology*, 9, 289–308.

Lunden, K. (1995). Was there a Norwegian National Identity in the Middle Ages? *Scandinavian Journal of History*, 20(1), 19–33.

MacAskill, E., Laville, S., and Harding, L. (4 February 2006). Cartoon Controversy Spreads throughout Muslim World. Retrieved December 2009, from http://www.guardian.co.uk/world/2006/feb/04/muhammadcartoons.pressandpublishing

Madriaga, M. (2007). Star-Spangled Banner and 'Whiteness' in American National Identity. In Eriksen and Jenkins (eds), (pp. 53–67).

Magnergård, O. (2003). Frågor och svar om nationaldagen. *Stiftelsen Sveriges Nationaldag*. Retrieved 16 January 2003, from http://www.nationaldagen.a.se

Marvin, C., and Ingle, D.W. (1999). *Blood Sacrifice and the Nation: Totem Rituals and the American Flag*: Cambridge: Cambridge University Press.

Massot (24 de mayo de 2000). Riquer: La leyenda de las cuatro barras nació en 1555, a partir de una crónica castellana *La Vanguardia*, p. 39, from http://hemeroteca.lavanguardia.es/preview/2008/04/30/pagina-39/34054746/pdf.html

MCB (2009). *Remembering the Brave. The Muslim contribution to Britain's Armed Forces. A Special Report by the Muslim Council of Britain*: Muslim Council of Britain (MCB).

McCormack, B. (2000). *Perceptions of St Patrick in Eighteenth-Century Ireland*. Cornwall: Four Courts Press.

McCrone, D. (2009). Scotland Days. Evolving Nation and Icons. In D. McCrone and G. McPherson (eds). Basingstoke: Palgrave Macmillan.

McCrone, D. and McPherson, G. (eds). (2009). *National Days: Constructing and Mobilising National Identity*. Basingstoke: Palgrave Macmillan.
Metro (5th November, 2009). Student who Urinated on Poppies is Facing Jail, from http://www.metro.co.uk/news/762831-student-who-urinated-on-poppies-is-facing-jail
Meyeux, E. (2005). Unpublished interview and correspondence. Embassy of Belgium in London.
Miller, D. (1995). *On Nationality*. Oxford: Oxford University Press.
Ministère de la Défense de France (1992). Marches et Chants de la Légion Etrangère, from http://www.defense.gouv.fr/histoire/musique_militaire/index.html
Ministère de la Défense de France (2002a). *14 Juillet 2002: Bicentenaire de la Legion d'Honneur*. Paris: Délégation à l'information et à la communication de la Défense.
Ministère de la Défense de France (2002b). *Programme Public: Bicentenaire de la Legion d'Honneur*. Paris: Délégation à l'information et à la communication de la Défense.
Ministerio de Asuntos Exteriores (1987). *Establecimiento del Doco de Octubre como Dia de la Fiesta Nacional de España: Circular Numero 3.103*. Madrid: Ministerio De Asuntos Exteriores.
Ministry of Foreign Affairs (1992). *National Days of the Republic of Hungary*. Budapest: Ministry of Foreign Affairs Printing Shop.
Ministry of Foreign Affairs (1996). *Hungary's National Days*. Budapest: Ministry of Foreign Affairs Printing Shop.
Morgan, T. (1993). *Saints: A Visual Almanac of the Virtuous, Pure, Praiseworthy, and Good*. San Francisco: Chronicle Books.
Moriarty, C. (1991). Christian Iconography and First World War Memorials. *Imperial War Museum Review* (6), 63–75.
Mosse, G. (1975). *The Nationalization of the Masses: Political Symbolism and Mass Movements in Germany from the Napoleonic Wars through the Third Reich*. New York: Howard Fertig.
Mosse, G. (1990). *Fallen Soldiers: Reshaping the Memory of the World Wars*. Oxford: Oxford University Press.
Mosse, G. (1993a). *Confronting the Nation: Jewish and Western Nationalism*. Hanover/London: Brandeis University Press, University Press of New England.
Mosse, G. (1993b). National Anthems: The Nation Militant. In G. Mosse (ed.), *Confronting the Nation: Jewish and Western Nationalism* (pp. 13–26). London: Brandeis University Press.
Muro, D. and Quiroga, A. (2004). Building the Spanish Nation: The Centre–Periphery Dialectic. *Studies in Ethnicity and Nationalism*, 4(2).
Myhre, J.E. (2006, 6–7 April). The Problems of Decline and Continuity: The Middle Ages in Norwegian Historiography. Paper presented at the European Science Foundation (EST) Conference – Representation of the Past: The Writing of National Histories in Europe in the Nineteenth and Twentieth Centuries, Oxford, United Kingdom.
Mykland, K. (1996). The 17th of May: A Historical Date and a Day of National Celebrations. Retrieved 2 March 2004, from http://odin.dep.no/odin/engelsk/norway/history/032005-990492/index-dok000-b-n-a.html

Nagle, J. (2005). Everybody is Irish on St. Paddy's: Ambivalence and Alterity at London's St. Patrick's Day 2002, *Identities*, 12(4), 563–83.
Nagle, J., and Clancy, M.-A. (2011). *Shared Society or Benign Apartheid*. Basingstoke: Palgrave Macmillan.
Nairn, T. (1977). *The Break-up of Britain: Crisis and Neo-Nationalism*. London: New Left Review Editions.
National Anthems Website (2010). List by Region. Retrieved 22 September 2010, from http://www.national-anthems.org/ref-world.htm#nnn
National Inventory of War Memorials (1997). *Conservation of War Memorials*. London: Imperial War Museum.
Nelson, P. (2007a). Norway: Flag Proposals. Retrieved 8 November 2007, from http://www.crwflags.com/fotw/flags/no-flprp.html#1815
Nelson, P. (2007b). Norway: State Arms. Retrieved 11 September 2004, from http://www.crwflags.com/fotw/flags/no).html
Netherlands Government National Archief (2004). Unpublished correspondence. The Hague.
Nettle, P. (1967). *National Anthems*. New York: Frederick Ungar Publishing Co.
Neuman, A. (2004). Unpublished correspondence. London: Swedish Embassy.
Nevéus, C. (1993). Svenska Flaggan: Historik och utveckling i praxis och lagstiftning, *From Campaigns to National Festivals*. Stockholm: Nordic Association.
Nevéus, C. (1996). Interaction in Heraldry between Norway and Sweden. Paper presented at the Genealogica et Heraldica. The 22nd international congress of Genealogical and Heraldic sciences. University of Ottawa (Proceedings published by University of Ottawa Press in 1998).
Newsline Radio Free Europe (1997). Lukashenka Opponents Stage Flag Protest 1(165), Part II, 21. Retrieved from www.rferl.org
Nilsson, T. (2004). Svensk-norska unionen 1814–1905: Erövring, harmoni och skilsmässa. Retrieved 11 September 2007, from http://www.regeringen.se/content/1/c6/03/81/15/b5af0801.pdf
Nora, P. (ed.). (1998). *Realms of Memory: The Construction of the French Past. Vol.3, Symbols*. NY: Colombia University Press.
Notholt, S. (1995). Denmark: History of the Flag, from http://fotw.digibel.be/flags/dk.html#hist
Notholt, S. (1996). United Kingdom History of the Flag. Retrieved 4 May 2003, from http://fotw.digibel.be/flags/gb.html#hist
NRK1 (2008). Royal and National Anthems of Norway, Royal Palace, May 17th from http://www.youtube.com/watch?v= 9g8a21gKYY4&feature= related.
NRK1 (2002–10, 17 May). TV Broadcast of 17 May and the parade at Karl Johan's Gate in Oslo. Annual broadcasts 2002–10.
Numerical representation of the Kosovo Assembly (2010). Retrieved 17 August 2010, from http://www.assembly-kosova.org/?krye=grup&lang=en
Nundy, J. (13 July 1994). Bonn's Troops Drum up Storm for Bastille Day. From http://www.independent.co.uk/news/world/europe/bonns-troops-drum-up-storm-for-bastille-day-1413477.html
Office of the High Representative in Bosnia and Herzegovina (OHR) (1999). New Flag of Bosnia in Herzegovina. Retrieved 15 February 2000, from http://www.ohr.int/flags.htm

Office of the High Representatives (1998). The Law on the Flag of Bosnia and Herzegovina, Adopted by the Office of the High Representatives, Sarajevo. Retrieved 3 March 2000, from http://fotw.digibel.be/flags/ba-law.html

Official French Website in the United States (2010). Republic Symbols: Bastille Day 14 July Retrieved 9 July, 18 August, 2004, 2010, from http://www.info-france-usa.org/atoz/14july.asp and http://www.franceway.com/w3/Facts&Figures/politics/republiquesymbols.html

Olsson, H. (2002, 6 June). Nationaldagen. *Dagens Nyheter [Daily News]*, Stockholm, p. 7.

Organization for Security and Co-operation in Europe (2009). *Kosovo non-majority communities within the primary and secondary educational systems*. Department of Human Rights and Communities. Retrieved from http://www.internal-displacement.org/8025708F004CE90B/(httpCountrySummaries)/9EF427B6237964B3C12576B2005CC29C?OpenDocument&count=10000.

Origins of the Aragonese-Catalan Flag (Spain) Senyera (2010). Retrieved 14 August 2010, from http://www.fotw.net/flags/es-ct_ar.html

Orridge, A. (1981). Varieties of Nationalism. In Tivey (ed.), *The Nation-State: The Formation of Modern Politics* (pp. 39–58). Oxford: Martin Robertson.

Ortner, S. (1967). On Key-Symbols. *American Anthropolgist*, 75, 1338–46.

Ory, P. (1980). 'La République en fête: Les 14 Juillet.' *Annales historiques de la Révolution Francaise* (52), 443–61.

Oslo Kommune (2010). Program for Dagen (Constitution Day Programme). Oslo: Municipality of Oslo, Norway.

Østergård, U. (1997). Geopolitics of Nordic Identity from Composite States to Nation-states. Retrieved 1 November 2007, from http://www.ciaonet.org/wps/osu01/

Østerud, Ø. (1987). *Det moderne statssystem og andre politisk-historiske studier*. Oslo: Gyldendal Norsk Forlag.

Östros, T. (2004). Nationaldagen den 6 juni som allmän helgdag, SOU, Regeringens proposition (Vol. 5, 23).

Osvalds, E. (1996). Tre dagar i Ungerns Tusenåriga historia. *Populär Historia* (2), 26–30.

Overy, R. (1997). *Why the Allies Won*. London: W.W. Norton & Co.

Ozouf, M. (1988). *Festivals and the French Revolution*, [Original title: La fête révolutionaire, 1789–1799]. Cambridge, MA: Harvard University Press.

Ozouf, M. and Furet, F. (eds). (1989). *The French Revolution and the Creation of Modern Political Culture, Vol. 3, The Transformation of Political Culture 1789–1848* (Vol. 3). Oxford: Pergamon Press.

Parliament of the Czech Republic (1992). The Act of the Czech National Council on the State Symbols of the Czech Republic.

Pearson, W. and O'Neill, G. (2009). Australia Day: A Day for All Australians? In McCrone and McPherson (eds), *National Days: Constructing and Mobilising National Identity* (pp. 73–88). Basingstoke: Palgrave Macmillan.

Pedersen, R.N. (1992). *One Europe 100 Nations*. Avon: Channel View Books.

Pellinen, P. (2004). Personal Correspondence. London: Press and Cultural Section, Embassy of Finland.

Penketh, A. (2008, 22 August). Syria Seeks Weapons Deal with Russia Amid 'Cold War' Ripples. From http://www.independent.co.uk/news/world/politics/syria-seeks-weapons-deal-with-russia-amid-cold-war-ripples-905449.html

Plamenatz, J. (1976). Two Types of Nationalism. In E. Kamenka (ed.), *Nationalism: The Nature and Evolution of an Idea* (pp. 22–37). London: Edward Arnold.
Podeh, E. (2010). From Indifference to Obsession: The Role of National State Celebrations in Iraq, 1921–2003. *British Journal of Middle Eastern Studies*, 37(2), 179–206.
Poels, J. (1998). Bosnia and Herzegovina: A New 'Neutral' Flag. Retrieved 15 February 2000, from http://www.flaginst.demon.co.uk/fibosnia.htm
Polish Cultural Institute (1974). *Poland: A Handbook*. Warsaw: Interpress Publishers.
Polish Government Official Website (2004). Fighting for Independence. Retrieved 7 January 2005, from http://www.poland.gov.pl/
Poulter, J. (2009). Remembering the Nation: Remembrance Days and the Nation in Ireland. In McCrone and McPherson (eds), *National Days: Constructing and Mobilising National Identity* (pp. 57–72). Basingstoke: Palgrave Macmillan.
Preble, H. (1980). *The Symbols, Standards, Flags, and Banners of Ancient and Modern Nations*. Winchester, Mass: The Flag Research Centre.
Press Association (Photograph) (2002). The Carnival and Commonwealth Parades at the Golden Jubilee. In view The Mall and Buckingham Palace. London: Press Association.
Quilley, J. (2000, 11 November). *Remembrance and Reconciliation: Reflection and Hope*. Paper presented at the 'Peace is Growing' Northern Friends Peace Board.
RandomHistory (2010). History vs. Legend. The Story of Saint Patrick's Day. Retrieved 19 September 2010, from http://www.randomhistory.com/history-of-st-patricks-day.html
Reich Law Gazette (1935, 15 September). Nuremberg Laws: Reichsbürgergesetz, Gesetz zum Schutze des deutschen Blutes und der deutschen Ehre Part 1. Retrieved 25 September 2005, from http://learning.dada.at/res/pdf/B006BT02E.PDF
Reicher, S., Hopkins, N. and Harrison, K. (2009). Identity matters: On the importance of Scottish identity for Scottish society. In F. Bechhofer and D. McCrone (eds), *National Identity, Nationalism and Constitutional Change* (pp. 17–40). Basingstoke: Palgrave Macmillan.
Renan, E. (1939). What is a Nation? In A. Zimmern (ed.), *Modern Political Doctrines*: Oxford University Press.
Republic of Kosovo Assembly (2008). *Kosovo Declaration of Independence*. Retrieved 17 August 2010 from http://www.assembly-kosova.org/common/docs/Dek_Pav_e.pdf.
Republic Symbols: Bastille Day 14 July (2010). Retrieved 9 July, 18 August 2004, 2010, from http://www.info-france-usa.org/atoz/14july.asp / http://www.franceway.com/w3/Facts&Figures/politics/republiquesymbols.html
Reynolds, S. (1997). *Kingdoms and Communities in Western Europe 900–1300* (2nd ed.). Oxford: Clarendon Press.
Ria-Novosti (2004a, 24 November). An Odd Choice of Holidays: Deputies Play with the Calendar. Russian News and Information Agency.
Ria-Novosti (2004b, 25 November). Russians against Eliminating Constitution Day. Russian News and Information Agency.
Rimmer, M. (2008). *The Future of Citizenship Ceremonies. Lord Goldsmith's Citizenship Review*. London: Ministry of Justice.
Riquer, M. (2001). *Legendes historiques catalanes*. Barcelona: Quaderns Crema.

Robinson, H. (2010). Remembering War in the Midst of Conflict: First World War Commemorations in the Norethern Irish Troubles. *Twentieth Century British History*, 21(1), 80–101.
Rodell, M. (2009). Mediating the Nation: Celebrating 6th June in Sweden. In D. McCrone and G. McPherson (eds), *National Days: Constructing and Mobilizing National Identity*. Basingstoke: Palgrave Macmillan.
Roede, L. (2002). Iceland: Flag Days. Retrieved 20 April 2005, from http://www.crwflags.com/fotw/flags/is-days.html
Ross, J. (1999a, 25 March). Greece Celebrates Independence. *Athens News*, 3.
Ross, J. (1999b, 25 March). On Freedom and Greece. *Athens News*.
Royal British Legion (Official Website) (2004). Poppy Appeal: History of the Poppy. Retrieved 8 October 2004, from http://www.britishlegion.org.uk/who/poppy_history.asp
Royal British Legion (Official Website) (2010). Field of Remembrance. From http://www.poppy.org.uk/remembrance/field-of-remembrance
Royal Danish Embassy (2004). Personal Correspondence. London: Press and Information Office.
Royal Netherlands Embassy (2004). Personal Correspondence. London: Press and Cultural Department.
RussiaToday (2010a). Military Parade in Moscow on Victory Day 2010. 65th anniversary. Part 1.
RussiaToday (2010b). Military Parade in Moscow on Victory Parade 2010, 65th Anniversary, Part 2.
Ryste, C. (2008). To av tre vil bare tillate norske flagg i 17. mai-toget. Retrieved 30 April 2008, from http://www.aftenposten.no/nyheter/iriks/article2383278.ece
Sanson, R. (1976). *Les 14 Juillet (1789–1975). Fête et conscience nationale*. Paris: Flammarion.
Santarsieri, M. (2004). Unpublished interview and correspondence. Hungarian Cultural Centre in London.
Santschi, C. (1991). *La mémoire des Suisses: Histoire des fêtes nationales du XIIIe au XXe siècle, Schweizer Nationalfeste im Spiegel der Geschichte*. Zürich: Chronos Verlag.
Savage, M., Bagnall, G. and Longhurst, B. (2005). *Globalization and Belonging*. London: Sage.
Schneiter, U. (2004). Unpublished correspondence. Embassy of Switzerland, Department of Information and Media in London.
Schöpflin, G. (1997). Functions of Myth and a Taxonomy of Myths. In Hosking and Schöplin (eds), *Myths and Nationhood* (pp. 19–35). London: Hurst & Company in association with the School of Slavonic and East European Studies, University of London.
Schöpflin, G. (2000). *Nations, Identity, Power: The New Politics of Europe*. London: Hurst Publishers Ltd.
Schulze, H. (2002). Unpublished interview with the Director of GHIL. German Historical Institute in London.
Scott, F.D. (1988). *Sweden, the Nation's History*. Southern Illinois University Press.
Scottish Parliamentary Corporate Body (2005). St Andrew's Day Bank Holiday (Scotland) Bill. Policy Memorandum. St Andrew's Day Bank Holiday (Scotland) Bill (SP Bill 41) as introduced in the Scottish Parliament on 19 May 2005.

Seip, A-L. (1995). Nation-building within the Union: Politics, Class and Culture in the Norwegian Nation-State in the Nineteenth Century. *Scandinavian Journal of History*, 20(1), 35–50.
Seip, J. (1974). *Utsikt over Norges historie 1*. Oslo: Universitetsforlaget.
Sensen, M. (1997). Post-War Germany 1945–49: Abolition of the Swastika. Retrieved 24 September 2005, from http://www.crwflags.com/fotw/flags/de-1945.html
Serrano, C. (1999). *El Nacimiento de Carmen: Símbolos, Mitos, Nación*: Taurus Ediciones.
Seton-Watson, H. (1977). *Nations and States: An Enquiry into the Origins of Nations and the Political Nationalism*. London: Methuen.
Shachar, N. (2010, 30 July). Striden om Spaniens symboler går vidare. *Dagens nyheter [Daily News]*, Stockholm.
Shils, E. and Young, M. (1953). The Meaning of the Coronation. *Sociological Review*, 1, 62–81.
Shipman, T. (2009). Revealed: How One War Memorial is Desecrated in Britain Every Week. *Daily Mail*. Retrieved 25 August 2010, from http://www.dailymail.co.uk/news/article-1225880/Revealed-How-war-memorial-desecrated-Britain-week.html
Shore, C. (1993). Inventing the 'People's Europe': Critical Perspectives on European Community Cultural Policy. *Man*, 28(4).
Shore, C. (2000). *Building Europe: The Cultural Politics of European Integration*. London: Routledge.
Simmel, G. (1964). *Conflict and the Web of Group-Affiliations*. London: Macmillan.
Simon, V.C. (2008). Nations on screen: live broadcasting of Bastille Day and Reunification Day. *European Review of History: Revue europeenne d'histoire*, 15(6), 615–28.
Site officiel du Parlement de la Communauté Française (2004). Fête de la Communauté française – le 27 septembre Les origines de la Fête du 27 septembre. Retrieved 7 September 2004, from http://www.pcf.be/ROOT/fete_27_septembre/fete_generalites.html
Skey, M. (2009). 'We Wanna Show 'em Who We Are': National Events in England. In McCrone and McPherson (eds), *National Days: Constructing and Mobilising National Identity* (pp. 41–56). Basingstoke: Palgrave Macmillan.
Smith, A.D. (1981). War & Ethnicity: The Role of Warfare in the Formation, Self-images and Cohesion of Ethnic Communities. *Ethnic & Racial Studies*, 375–97.
Smith, A.D. (1986). *Ethnic Origins of Nations*. London: Blackwell.
Smith, A.D. (1987). *Patriotism and Neo-Classicism: The 'Historical Revival' in French and English Painting and Sculpture, 1746–1800*. University of London.
Smith, A.D. (1988). Myth of the 'Modern Nation' and the Myths of Nations. *Ethnic and Racial Studies*, 11(1), 1–26.
Smith, A.D. (1989). Suffering Hero: Belisarius and Oedipus in Late Eighteenth-Century French and British Art. *Journal of the Royal Society of Arts*, 137, 634–40.
Smith, A.D. (1995). Formation of National Identity. In H. Harris (ed.), *Identity (Essays Based on Herbert Spencer Lectures)* (pp. 129–54). Oxford: Clarendon Press.
Smith, A.D. (1996). *Commemorating the Dead, Inspiring the Living: Maps, Memories and Moralities in the Recreation of National Identities*. Paper presented at the Euroconference on Collective Identity and Symbolic Reconstruction, Foundation Nationale des Sciences Politiques, Paris.

Smith, A.D. (1998). *Nationalism & Modernism*. London: Routledge.
Smith, A.D. (2001). *Nationalism: Theory, Ideology, History*. London: Polity Press.
Smith, A.D. (2003). *Chosen Peoples: Sacred Sources of National Identity*. Oxford: Oxford University Press.
Smith, W. (1969). *Prolegomena to the Study of Political Symbols*. Boston University (University Microfilms International), Boston.
Smith, W. (1975a). *Flags Throughout the World and Across the Ages*. London: McGraw-Hill Book Company.
Smith, W. (1975b). France: From the Oriflamme to the Tricolour. *Flags Throughout the World and Across the Ages* (pp. 130–9). London: McGraw-Hill Book Company.
Smith, W. (1975c). Kingdom of Norway. *Flags Throughout the World and Across the Ages* (p. 269). London: McGraw-Hill Book Company.
Smith, W. (1975d). Netherlands: 'Oranje boven' ('Orange on top'). *Flags Throughout the World and Across the Ages* (pp. 156–63). London: McGraw-Hill Book Company.
Smith, W. (1975e). Spain: Medieval Heraldry in Modern Form. In W. Smith (ed.), *Flags Throughout the World and Across the Ages* (pp. 124–9). London: McGraw-Hill Book Company.
Smith, W. (1975f). United Kingdom: The Noble Lineage of the Union Jack. In W. Smith (ed.), *Flags Throughout the World and Across the Ages* (pp. 180–9). London: McGraw-Hill Book Company.
Smith, W. (2004a). Flag of France. Retrieved 16 August 2004, from http://www.britannica.com/eb/article?eu=96076
Smith, W. (2004b). Flag of Spain. Retrieved August 16 2004, from http://www.britannica.com/eb/article?eu=96174
Smith, W. (2004c). Flag of Switzerland. Retrieved 16 August 2004, from http://www.britannica.com/eb/article?eu=96180
Smith, W. (2004d). Flag of the United Kingdom. Retrieved 16 August 2004, from http://www.britannica.com/eb/article?eu=76215
Sørensen, Ø. (2004). 1905 – A Peaceful Separation. Retrieved 10 January 2005, from http://www.emb-norway.ca/history/after1814/1905/separation.htm
Soutphommasane, T. (2009). *Reclaiming Patriotism. Nation-building for Australian Progessives*. Cambridge: Cambridge University Press.
Sperber, D. (1974). *Rethinking Symbolism*. Cambridge: Cambridge University Press.
Spreckelsen, T. (2010). Relative Importance of National Identity in Comparison to Other Social Identities. Unpublished paper. Nuffield College, University of Oxford.
Stanner, W. (1963). *On Aboriginal Religion* (Vol. 11). Oxford: Oxford University Press.
Statistics Norway (2009). Immigration and Immigrants. From http://www.ssb.no/english/subjects/00/00/10/innvandring_en/
Steine, B. (2003). The Military in 1905. Retrieved 9 November 2004, from www.2005.norway.info/background/military/MarianneFosland
StGeorgesDay.com (2010). StGeorge's.com. A Site for England. Retrieved 3 September 2010, from http://www.stgeorgesday.com/home
Stilling, R. (1995). Wales: Ddraig Goch (Red Dragon). Retrieved 27 November 2004, from http://fotw.digibel.be/flags/gb-wales.html

Stråth, B. (2005). *Union och demokrati. De Förenade rikena Sverige–Norge 1814–1905 [Union and Democracy. The United Kingdoms Sweden–Norway 1814–1905].* Nora: Nya Doxa.
Stråth, B. (ed.). (2000). *Myth and Memory in the Construction of Community. Historical Patterns in Europe and Beyond.* Peter Lang.
Studd, H. (2006, 7 June). Record Crowds Keep the Peace. *The Times.*
Tag der Deutschen Einheit (2009). Tag der Deutschen Einheit 2009 [Konzert]. From http://www.youtube.com/watch?v=Si6HlCdaTI8&feature=related
Tajfel, H. and Turner, J. (2004). An Integrative Theory of Intergroup Conflict. In M.J. Hatch and M. Schultz (eds), *Organizational Identity: A Reader* (pp. 56–65). Oxford: Oxford University Press.
Telegraph.co.uk (2010). St George's Day celebrations across England. Celebrations to mark St George's Day will take place across the country today. Retrieved from http://www.telegraph.co.uk/news/uknews/7622404/St-Georges-Day-celebrations-across-England.html
Tenora, J. (Unknown). *Time to Cut the Umbilicus Between Heraldry and Vexillology.* Portsmouth: Bruce Nicholls.
The Guardian (2009). Swiss Voters Back Minarets Ban. From http://www.guardian.co.uk/world/2009/nov/29/swiss-minarets-ban-referendum
Therborn, G. (1995). *European Modernity and Beyond: The Trajectory of European Societies, 1945–2000.* London: Sage Publications.
Therborn, G. (2002). Monumental Europe: The National Years. On the Iconography of European Capital Cites. *Housing Theory and Society*, 19, 26–47.
Therborn, G. (2006). Eastern Drama: Eastern European Capital Cities in the 20th Century. *International Review of Sociology*, 2.
Therborn, G. (2007). Capital Cities and their Contested Role in the Life of Nations. *New Left Review* 46, 69–88.
Thorsen, A. (2000). Foundation Myths at Work: National Day Celebrations in France, Germany and Norway in a Comparative Perspective. In B. Stråth (ed.), *Myth and Memory in the Construction of Community*: Peter Lang.
Tilley, J. and Heath, A. (2007). The Decline of British National Pride. *British Journal of Sociology*, 58(4), 661–78.
Tilly, C. (ed.). (1975). *The Formation of National States in Western Europe.* London: Princeton University Press.
Tivey, L. (ed.). (1981). *The Nation-State: The Formation of Modern Politics.* Oxford: Martin Robertson.
Tønnesson, S. (2009). The Class Route to Nationhood: China, Vietnam, Norway, Cyprus – and France. *Nations and Nationalism*, 15(3), 375–95.
Trevor-Roper, H. (1992). Invention of Tradition: The Highland Tradition of Scotland. In Hobsbawm and Ranger (eds), *Invention of Tradition* (pp. 15–41). Cambridge University Press.
Turajlac, J. (2010). Interview on National Symbols of Bosnia-Herzegovina. Cultural and Political Secretary. Embassy of Bosnia-Herzegovina.
Turner, V. (1967). *Forest of Symbols.* Ithaca: Cornell University Press.
Turner, V. (1969). *The Ritual Process.* London: Routledge & Kegan Paul.
TV5 Monde (Juli 2007). Die Fremdenlegion in Paris am 14. From http://www.youtube.com/watch?v=QWXYMYgAMq0&feature=PlayList&p=7EA96A1EDE7535A4&index=28&playnext=10&playnext_from=PL

Unusual Rigging Ltd (Photograph) (2002). The Golden Jubilee Celebration in London, The Mall in London. London: Unusual Rigging Ltd.
United States of America Flag Site (2005). Proper Disposal of the American Flag. Retrieved 7 April 2005, from http://www.usa-flag-site.org/faq/disposal.shtml
US Defense Department (Uniformed Services) (2010). Flag Folding Ceremony. From http://www.usa-patriotism.com/reference/flag_folding.htm
Uzelac, G. (forthcoming). Authenticating the Nation: The Case of Armistice Day. Submitted journal article (details to be confirmed).
Uzelac, G. (2010). National Ceremonies: The Pursuit of Authenticity. *Ethnic and Racial Studies*, 33(10), 1718–36.
Vedung, E. (2001). Why the secession of Norway in 1905 did not lead to war. In M. Ruiz and De Pazzis di Corrales (eds), *When the Light Came from the North: Sweden, Norway and Modernist Catalunya. Spain and Sweden: Encounters Throughout History* (pp. 145–70). Madrid: Fundación Berndt Wistedt.
Velde, F. (1995). Bosnian fleur-de-lys. Retrieved 2 March 2005, from http://fotw.digibel.be/flags/ba_heral.html
Vernet i Llobet, J. (2003). Símbolos y fiestas nacionales en España. *Teoría y realidad constitucional*, 12, 99–122.
Virtual Vienna (2004). Austrian National Day (Nationalfreiertag) 26 October. Retrieved 1 November 2004, from www.virtualvienna.net/community/modules.php?name=News&file=article&sid=103
Vovelle, M. (1998). La Marseillaise: War or Peace. In Nora (ed.), *Realms of Memory: The Construction of the French Past*. (Vol. 3: Symbols, pp. 28–74). NY: Columbia University Press.
Walzer, M. (1967). The Facsimile Fallacy. *American Review of Canadian Studies*, 12(2), 82–6.
Website of the Office of High Representative (1999). Decision Imposing the Law on the National Anthem of BiH. Retrieved July 2010, from http://www.ohr.int/decisions/statemattersdec/default.asp?content_id=354
Week's Newsflash (2004). July 14th Military Parade Avenue des Champs-Elysées, Paris. Retrieved 9 September 2004, from http://www.paris-touristoffice.com/va/events/14juillet.html
Weitman, R.S. (1973). National Flags: A Sociological Overview. *Semiotica*, 8(4), 328–69.
Westendorp Commission (1998). The 1998 Flag Change, Proposals from the Westerndorp Commission. Retrieved 15 February 2000, from http:fotw.digibel.be/flags/ba-fc98.html
Wilkinson, A. (1978, second edition 1996). *The Church of England and the First World War*. Canterbury: SCM – Canterbury Press
Winter, J. (1995). *Sites of Memory, Sites of Mourning: The Great War in European Cultural History*. Cambridge: Cambridge University Press.
Woodcock, T. and Robinson, J. (eds). (1990). *The Oxford Guide to Heraldry*. Oxford: Oxford University Press.
World Values Survey (WVS) (2005). World Values Survey 2005 Official Data File v.20090901, 2009. Publication from World Values Survey Association www.worldvaluessurvey.org
Wray, J. (2008, July 14). France Paris Bastille Day Military Parade. From http://www.monstersandcritics.com/news/europe/features/article_1416895.php/In_photos_France_Paris_Bastille_Day_Military_Parade#ixzz0d6Yliovz

Wright-Mills, C. (1963). *Power, Politics and People: The Collected Essays of C. Wright Mills*. London: Oxford University Press.
Zahorski, A. (1991). *Constitution of May 3rd: Document of Independence on the Bicentennial of Adoption* (Government Document No. 3: Ministry of Foreign Affairs in Poland.
Zimmer, O. (1999). Forging the Swiss Nation, 1760–1939: Popular Memory, Patriotic Invention, and Competing Conceptions of Nationhood. London School of Economics & Political Science, University of London, London.
Znamierowski, A. (2004). *World Encyclopedia of Flags: The Definitive Guide to International Flags, Banners, Standards and Ensigns*. Hermes House Anness Publishing.

Index

*References to tables, figures and illustrations are in **bold**.*

aesthetics of politics, 17
Afghanistan War, 85, 129–31, 156–60
Agulhon, Maurice, 149
Alba, Richard, 16, 168
Albania
    Albanian anthem, **142**
    Albanian flag, 53–5, 75–8, **88**, 198
    Independence Day, 101–2, **135–6**
Amalvi, Christian, 105, 111, 152, 174
American Revolution, 36
Anderson, Benedict, 7, 19–20, 155
Andrew, St
    St Andrew's Day, **97**, 123, 171
    St Andrew's Flag, 32, 38, 41
Armistice Day, *see under country entries*
Armstrong, John, 16–8, 75
Australia
    Aboriginal Day, 21, 179–80
    Australia Day, *also* Invasion Day *and* Survival Day 21, 179–80, 185
    Australian flag, 41, 79, 191
Austria
    Austrian anthem, **142**
    Austrian flag, 33, 53–5, **62**, 75, **88**, 89
    National Day, *also* Day of the Austrian Flag and Sovereignty *and* Constitution Day *and* Republic Day, **102–3**, 138–9, 161, 188, 195

Bagge, Sverre, 113–14
banal nationalism, 27–8, 79–80
Basque Country
    Basque flag, *also* Ikurriña, **69–71**
    Basque National Day, *also* Aberri Eguna, 71–2
    Basque nationalism, 70

Bastille Day, 12, 23–5, **99**, 104–12, 132, 138, 141–4, 152, 166–8, 174, **178**, 189, 194
Beck, Ulrich, 25
Beck-Gernsheim, Elisabeth, 25
Belarus
    Belarusian anthem, **142**
    Belarusian flag, 54–5, **65–6**, **88**–9
    Independence Liberation Day, 101–2, **135–6**, 139
Belgium
    Armistice Day, 152–3, 160–1, 190
    Belgian anthem, **142**
    Belgian flag, 33, **53**, **88**–9
    Flanders Crusader Flag, 32
    Flanders Day, 101, 153, 161
    Independence Day, **99–101**, **135–9**,
    Walloon Day, *also* Fête de la Communauté Française, 153, 161
Billig, Michael, 28, 79–81, 91
Bjørnson, Bjørnstjerne, 120, 145
Blehr, Barbro, 112, 118–22, 172, 176
Boer War, 154
Bosnia-Herzegovina (BiH),
    Bosnia-Herzegovina anthem, **142**, 145–6
    Bosnia-Herzegovina Day, **102–4**, 188
    Bosnia-Herzegovina flag, 10, 55–6, 67, **72–9**, **88–90**, 188–9, 191
boundaries
    authentication of, 1–3, 57, 71, 78, 121, 131–2
    creation of, 7, 13–19, 51, 79–80, 83, 166–8, 177–9, 186–93
Breuilly, John, 8, 17

224 *Index*

Britain (United Kingdom)
  Armed Forces Day, *also* Veterans
    Day, 159, 182
  Armistice Day, 122–7, 154
  British anthem, *also* God Save the
    Queen, 128, **142**–4
  British flag, *see under* Union Jack
  Britain Day, 13, 180–3
  British Legion, *see under* Royal
    British Legion
  Britishness, 12–13, 122, 156–8, 181
  Citizens' Day, 12, 181
  Citizenship Review 2008, 12, 180–1
  England, *see under main entry*
  Golden Jubilee of Queen Elizabeth
    II, 182–5
  National Citizenship Day, 12, 181
  Northern Ireland, *see under main*
    entry
  Poppy Day, *see under* Poppy
  Remembrance Sunday, *see under*
    main entry
  Scotland, *see under main entry*
  St Andrew's Day, *see under* Scotland
  St Andrew's Flag, *see under* Scotland
  St George's Day, *see under* England
  St George's flag, *see under* England
  St Patrick's Day, *see under* Ireland
    and Northern Ireland
  St Patrick's flag, *see under* Ireland *and*
    Northern Ireland
  Union Jack, *see under main entry*
  Wales, *see under main entry*
British Election Survey (BES), 172
British Social Attitudes (BSA) surveys,
  165
Brown, Gordon, 12, 94, 159, 180
Bruce, Steve, 190
Bulgaria
  Bulgarian anthem, **142**
  Bulgarian flag, 40, **53**–4, **60**–1, **88**–9,
    187
  Liberation Day, 12, **99**–100, **135**–9,
    166
Byrne, Liam, 182

Canada
  Aboriginal Day, 21
capital cities, 2, 13, 63, 146–7

Catalonia
  Catalonia Day, 71–2
  Catalonian flag, *also Senyera*, 63,
    69–71
  Catalonian nationalism, *also*
    Renaixença, 70–1
Catholic, *also* Catholicism, 31, 68, 87,
  127, 152, 157, 162–3
Cenotaph, London, *see under*
  Ceremonial routes
Cenotaph Ceremony, 125–9, 153–60
Ceremonial routes
  in London, 21, 94, 124–29, 140,
    147–50, 153–60, 175
  in Paris, 106–9, 147–9, 153–6, 174
  in Oslo, 119–22, 147–50
  theoretical aspects, 95, 146–50
ceremonies
  ceremonial choreography, 3, 95,
    115, 137–41, 170–3, 192
  ceremonial design, 115–19, 158,
    179, 192–4
  ceremonial foci, 134–7
  ceremonial routes, *see under main*
    entry
  ceremonial statistics, 5, 94–96, 131
  ceremonial style, 17, 115, 138,
    172–9, 200
  citizenship ceremonies, 4, 13
  national ceremonies, theoretical
    aspects, 1–11, 12–25, 79–82,
    189–194
  Remembrance ceremonies, *see under*
    main entry
Cerulo, Karen, 9, 14, 63, 80, 82, 86,
  92, 143
Christian Fredrik, Prince, 46, 113
Christianity, *also* Christian faith,
  29–32, 51, 76–7, 84–5, 105, 128,
  151–7, 175, 190–3
citizenship
  Citizens' Day, *see under* Britain
  citizenship ceremonies, *see under*
    ceremonies
  Citizenship Review 2008, *see under*
    Britain
  theoretical aspects, 12–13, 181, 194
civic nationalism, 3, 82, 155, 165,
  181–2

Index 225

class, social, 26, 33, 48, 116–18, 146, 163, 168–9, 174–7, 192
Cohen, Anthony, 15–16, 168
Cohen, Robin, 181
cohesion, 12–13, 23, 166, 185, 191–2, 199
colonialism, *also* colonies, 21–2, 36, 105, 110, 169, 175, 179–82
colours, symbolism of, 30–7, 40–7, 51–5, 89–92, 193, 195
Columbus, Christopher, 79, 98, **135**–7
Colley, Linda, 16, 182, 193
Commonwealth flags, 41
Connerton, Paul, 171
Constantine, Emperor, 29–30, 34
Constitution Day, *see under country entries*
Croatia
 Croatian anthem, **142**
 Croatian flag, 53–5, **72**–5, **88**–9, 187
 Statehood Day, **102**, **135**–6, **138**, 140, 160–1, 192
cross flags
 as national symbols, 24–5, 30–35, **39**, 49–**51**, 86–9, 187–90, 195–9
 Crusader Cross, 30–2
 Scandinavian Cross, 46–50
 Cross of St Andrew, 31–2, 38
 Cross of St Denis, 31–5, **42**
 Cross of St George, 31–3, 38–41
 Cross of St Patrick, 32, 38–41
 war flags, **35**
Culloden, Battle of, 64
cultural copyright, 8, 16, 75
curricula, educational, 172, 193
Czech Republic, *also* Czechoslovakia
 Czech anthem, **142**
 Czech flag, 54–**5**, 75, **88**–9
 Day of Nationalization, 103
 National *or* Statehood Day, **102**–3, **135**–**6**, 139, 188
 Victory Day, 103

Dardanian flag, 78
Davie, Grace, 190
Dayton Agreement, 73

democracy
 democratic community, 28, 51, 59, 76–7, 104, 113–18, 152–3, 169, 175, 193
 democratization, 23, 69, 120, 193
Denmark
 Constitution Day, 95, **99**–100, **135**–**6**, **138**–9, 160–1, 166–8, **170**
 Danish anthem, **142**, **170**
 Danish flag, *also Dannebrogen*, 32, 35, 46, 49, 51–**2**, **62**, 79–81, **88**–9, **170**, 187
desecration of national symbols, 25, 63–6, 92, 160, 187
diaspora groups, 3, 95, 177, 181
Durkheim, Emile, 12–14, 28, 58, 82–3, 91, 151, 177–9, 185, 191–4

Eastern Europe, 11, 20, 56, 89, 101, 188, 199
educational institutions, 31, 78, 140, 146, 165, 174, 193
Elgenius, Gabriella, 8, 13, 28, 47, 52–4, 62, 113, 122, 167, 170–2, 179, 195
elites
 elites and social order, 17, 27, 32–3, 63, 76, 94, 138, 165
 elites sponsorship, 8, 17–18, 21, 88, 91–4, 134–40, 170–2, 175–**8**, 192–5
England, *see also* Britain
 English anthem, *also God Save the Queen*, 128, **142**–4
 Englishness, 181
 St George's Day, **97**, 123
 St George's flag, 31–5, 38–40, 50–**2**
equality, 51, 92, 115–16, 151–2, 169, 189
Eriksen, Anne, 120
Eriksen, Thomas Hylland, 81, 115, 121–2, 169, 173, 176–7
Estonia
 Estonian anthem, **142**
 Estonian flag, 55–6, 60–1, 78, **88**–90, 187, 191
 Independence Day, 101–2, **135**–6, **138**–9
Ethnic Minority Election Survey, 172

ethnicity
  ethno-national symbols, 16, 72, 78, 121, 170, 174, 181–2, 191, 199–200
  multi-ethnic flags, 78
  multi-ethnic nations or societies, *see under main entry*
European Union
  Europe Day, 77, 161, 185, 192
  European Constitution, 77
  European Union anthem, *also Ode to Joy*, 77, 146, 165, 192
  European Union flag, 76–7, 88, 192
  Europeanization, 10, 76
European Values Study Group, 26, 81

Fallen, remembrance *or* cult of the, 9, 12–13, 19–21, 94, 104–7, 122–5, 129–30, **135**, 149, 152–60, 190
Faroe Islands
  Faroe Islands anthem, **142**, **170**
  Faroe Islands flag, 46, 49, **55**, **88**, **170**
  St Olav Day, **102**, **135–8**, **170**
Finland
  Finish anthem, **142**, 147, **170**
  Finish flag, 32, 49–50, **53**, 62–3, **88**–90, 169–**70**, 188
  Independence Day, 101–2, **135**–9, 167–**8**, **170**
First World War, 8, 23–4, 51, 109, 122–4, 132, 134, 153, 166
  First World War Pardon Association, 157
Firth, Raymond, 58, 61, 63–5, 82, 87
flag-folding ceremony in the United States, 84–5
flags (general)
  burning of, *see under* desecration
  counter-nationalist flags, *see under* post-historical flags
  cross flags, *see under main entry*
  Crusader flags, *see under* cross flags
  desecration, *see under main entry*
  early modern flags, 32–6
  laws *and* etiquette, 3, 21, 25, **62**–6, 70, 75, 82, 92, 187, 190
  flag of Charlemagne, 31, 41–2
  Heraldic flags, *see under main entry*

merchant flags, 36, 62, 127
Middle Ages, flags and banners in the, 30–2
national flags, *see under main entry*
naval flags, 36–7, 41–3, **62**, 68, 89, 187
post-historical flags, *see under main entry*
saltire flags, 32, 38–41, 46–7, **52**, **69**–71
tricolour flags, *see under main entry*
vexillology, *see under main entry*
waved and unwaved flags, 79–81
founding myths, *see under* myths of origin
France
  Arc de Triomphe, Paris, *see under* ceremonial routes
  Armistice Day, 105–6
  Bastille Day, *also* Fête Nationale *and* 14 Juillet *and* Fête de la Fédération, 12, 23–5, **99**, 104–12, 132, 138, 144, 152, 166–8, 173–4, **178**, 189, 194
  First Republic, 99, 105
  Foreign Legion, 108–9
  French anthem, *also La Marseillaise*, 142–**4**, **151**
  French tricolour flag, 25, 36–8, **41**–**7**, 50–1, 65, 109–10, 144, 151
  Grand Axe, Paris, *see under* ceremonial routes
  Marianne, symbol of, **45**
  Third Republic, 18, 41, 105
  Victory Day, 105
Franco, Francisco, 62, 67–71, 75, 98, 137
freedom, as political value, 51, 79, 115, 118, 143–5, 164
French Revolution, 7, 23–4, 37, 51, 59, 152

Gellner, Ernest, 7
gender, 26, 174, 177, 192
Germany
  German anthem, *also Deutschlandlied*, **142**–5
  German tricolour flag, 37, **53**, 62, **88**–9, 187, 198

German Unification, *also* Reunification, 164–5
Nazi symbols, 21–2, 63–4, 101–3, 144–5, 163
Nuremberg Flag Law, *also* Reich Flag Law, 64
Second German Empire, 18, 162
Sedan Day, *also Sedan Tag*, 162–3
Unification Day, *also Tag der Deutschen Einheit*, 23, **102**, **135**–9, 161–5, 192
Weimar Republic, 37, 163
Gillis, John R., 156, 173
God Save the Queen, 128, **142**–4
Golden Age, myth of the, 11, 13, 18, 55, 67, 74–5, 91, 131, **135**, 145–6, 166–7, 188–93, 193, 198
Goodhart, David, 182
Greece
 Greek anthem, **142**
 Greek flag, 10, 32, 52–3, **62**, 75, **88**–90, 187
 Independence Day, *also* Feast of Annunciation, 12, 96, **99**–101, **135**–40, 166, 192
Greenland, 92, 191
Grimnes, Ole Kristian, 47–50, 114–16
Grunnlovsdagen, 112, 115
Guest of Honour, 108–11, 175
Guibernau, Montserrat, 8
Gustav Vasa, King of Sweden, **99**–100, 137

Hattenauer, Hans, 162–4
heraldic flags, 5, 24, 28, 32–5, 41–2, 53–6, 71, 82, **88**–9, 188–91, 195
Heath, Anthony, 12, 26, 122–3, 156–8, 165–6, 181–2
Hewitt, Roger, 181
Hobsbawm, Eric, 7, 17, 58, 113, 134
Holy Roman Empire, 31–37, 42, 51, 55
Hroch, Miroslav, 8, 169
Hugo, Victor, 152
Hungary
 Hungarian anthem, **142**
 Hungarian flag, 33, 37, **53**–4, **62**, **88**–9, 187
 St Stephen's Day, 97–8, **135**–8, 190–2

Iceland
 Icelandic anthem, **142**, **170**
 Icelandic flag, 46, 49–50, **55**, 63, **88**–9, 169–70, 187
 Independence Day, 101–2, **135**–8, 167–8, **170**
iconography, 22, 146, 151, 154
Ignatieff, Michael, 61, 72, 139
imagined communities, 2, 7, 15, 19, 63, 88, 137, 155, 195
inclusion, politics of, 4, 59, 79, 115, 119–23, 134, 171, 173–9, 192–3
independence, as political value, 2–4, 8, 24, 28, 36, 45–8, 51–2, 58, 61, 79, 88–91, 99–102, 113–14, 131–2, 134–5, 167–9, 177–9, 187–8, 193, 195
Independence Day, *see under country entries*
Ingle, David, 16, 19, 83
Inglis, Ken, 105–6, 124–6, 129–30, 153, 179
International Social Survey Programme (ISSP), 25–6
invented traditions, 5, 17, 20, 71, 105–10, 121, 131, 133–4, 165, 173, 177, 182–5, 188, 192, 198–200
Iraq
 Iraq War, 22, 66, 130–1, 156–60
 Iraqi National Day, 22
Ireland, *also* Republic of Ireland
 Irish anthem, **142**
 Irish diaspora, 96
 Irish tricolour flag, 37, **55**, 63, 77, **88**–90, 187, 198
 Northern Ireland, *see under main entry*
 St Patrick's Day, 96–7, **135**–8, 140, 190–2, 198
 St Patrick's Flag, 32, 38–9, 41
Islam, 30
Italy
 Italian anthem, **142**
 Italian flag, 24, **32**, 37, **53**, **62**, **88**–9, 187, 198
 Republic Day, **102**, **135**–8, 188

Kapferer, Bruce, 8, 149
Karl Johan's Avenue, Oslo, *see under* ceremonial routes
Kelly, Ruth, 182
King, Alex, 125, 154
Kolstø, Pål, 49, 72–3, 79–80, 118
Kosovo
  Independence Day, 101–2, **135**–6
  Kosovo anthem, **142**, 145–6
  Kosovo flag, **55**–6, 76–9, **88**–90, 188, 191
Kramer, Julian, 173

Labour Day, *also* 1 May *and* Workers' Day, 49, 101–3, 118, 163
Latvia
  Latvian anthem, **142**
  Latvian flag, 40, **55**–6, **60**–1, 75, 78, 85–9, 187, 191
  National Day, 85, **102**, **135**–9
Left, political, 8, 49, 69, 168, 175
Levi-Strauss, Claude, 58, 82
Liberation Day, *also* Victory day, *see under country entries*
Lithuania,
  Independence Day, 101–2, **135**–40
  Lithuanian anthem, **142**
  Lithuanian flag, **55**–6, **60**–2, 79, **88**–9, 187, 191
Löfgren, Orvar, 80
Lukes, Steven, 14

Macedonia (FYROM), Former Yugoslav Republic of,
  Independence Day, 101–2, **135**–8
  Macedonian anthem, **142**
  Macedonian flag, 54–**5**, 75–**6**, **88**, 198
McCrone, David, 5, 71, 123, 171, 181
Madriaga, Manuel, 66, 84
Marvin, Carolyn, 16, 19, 83
mass-media, 119, 158, 172
membership in the national community, 2–4, 7–9, 15–16, 23, 79–81, 95, 104–5, 111, 115, 121, 141, 150–3, 158, 172, 176–7, 188, 193–4, 200
memorials, 2, 13, 84, 149–54

military celebrations *or* parades, 110–12, 139, 172–5, **178**, 198
Miller, David, 7, 9
Mohammed flag, 30–1
Moldova,
  Independence Day, **102**
  Moldovan anthem, **142**
  Moldovan flag, **55**, **60**, 75, **88**
Monnet, Jean, 77
Montenegro
  Independence Day, **102**–3, **135**–6
  Montenegro anthem, **142**
  Montenegro flag, **55**, 73–5, **88**
monuments, national, 2, 18–20, 63, 146–50, 160, 195
moral community, 19–21, 83, 150–6, 189–93
Moriarty, Catherine, 20, 124, 154
Mosse, George, 17, 124–6, 141, 151–3, 162–3
multi-ethnic *and* multi-national nations or societies, 4, 7, 10, 19, 67, 77–8, 84, 88, 121–2, 133, 156–8, 175, 179–82, 191–3
multi-faith nations or societies, 156–8, 162
music, 95, 141–5
Muslim, 30, 127, 157–8
  Muslim Council of Britain, 158
Mykland, Knut, 46, 49, 114–20
myths of origin, *also* founding *or* uniting myths, 3, 11, 16–18, 51, 55, 74, 94–5, 131, 151, 166–8, 177–8, 192–4, 200

Nairn, Tom, 23, 166
Napoleonic Wars, 36–7, 44–6, 106, 112, 117, 141, 149
nation, *also* nation-state
  nation building, *also* nation making, 1, 4–6, 17–19, 23–25, 38, 61, 83–6, 91, 104, 131, 179, 185–200
  nation branding, 8
  national identity, theoretical aspects, 9, 15, 91
    theoretical aspects, 2–5, 7–10, 14–15

national anthems
  appearance of, **196–7**
  national anthems in Europe, 142
  theoretical aspects, 141–6, 198
national day design, 3, 10–11, 23–4,
  95–6, 104, 110, 119, 133–85,
  190–4
national days
  appearance of, 134–7, **196–7**
  ceremonial routes, *see under main
    entry*
  Constitution Days, *see under country
    entries*
  future of, 179–85
  Guest of Honour, *see under main
    entry*
  Independence Day, *see under country
    entries*
  modern national days, 99–101
  national day design, *see under main
    entry*
  post-imperial national days, 101–4
  pre-modern days, 96–8
  saint days, *see under main entry*
  success *or* failure of, 10, 23–4,
    160–7, 177–9, 191–4
national flags
  appearance of, **196–7**
  cross flags, *see under main entry*
  early modern flags, 32–6
  heraldic flags, *see under main entry*
  modern national flags, 36–50
  post-historical *or* counter-nationalist
    flags, *see under main entry*
  post-imperial national flags, 53–6
  theoretical aspects, 27–8
  tricolour flags, *see under main entry*
national personification, 11, 131,
  134–**6**, 188, 197
nationalism, theoretical aspects, 1–10,
  17–20, 28, 57, 82–3, 99, 117, 151,
  155, 195–200
Netherlands
  Dutch anthem, **142**
  Dutch flag, *also Prinsevlag*, **35**–6,
    50–**2**, **62**, **88**–9, 187–8, 198
  Queen's Day, *also Koninginnedag*,
    99–101, **135**–40, 192, 198
Nettle, Paul, 143

New Zealand
  Maori community, 179–80
  New Zealand flag, 41, 79, 191
  Waitangi Day, 179–80
Nora, Pierre, 151
Northern Ireland
  Northern Irish flag, 38–**9**, 50, **88**,
    189
  St Patrick's Day, 96–7, 123, **135**
  Remembrance Sunday in, *see under
    main entry*
Norway
  Bokmål *and* Nynorsk, 114
  bunad, 8, 16, 121, 172, 176
  Children's Parade, 119–22, 172–7,
    193
  Citizens' or People's parades, *also
    Borgertog or Folketog*, 115–16
  Constitution Day, *also Gunnlovsdagen*,
    12, 23, **99**–100, 112–22, 131,
    135–40, 150–1, 166–77, 192–4
  Norwegian anthem, **142**, 145
  Norwegian flag, 45–50, **62**–3, 79–81,
    88–9, 169–**70**, 187–9

oneness, *also* sameness, 3, 7, 9, 49, 80,
  88, 94–5, 115, 122, 131, 137,
  151–3, 177, 187, 191
Ortner, Sherry, 58
Ozouf, Mona, 23, 105, 111

parade, *also* procession, 95, 138–41,
  178
  civilian *and* children parades,
    115–22, 172–6, 183–4, 193
  military parades, 21–22, 29, 64,
    106–12, 126–28, 132, 159–60,
    162, 168, 174, 194
participation, public *or* mass-, 4, 7,
  12–14, 95–6, 115, 121, 138–40,
  158–61, 165–7, 174–82,
  193–4
patience, politics of, 3, 173–9
personification, *see under* national
  personification
Place de la Concorde, Paris, *see under*
  ceremonial routes
Pledge of Allegiance, 79–80, 84, 91

230 *Index*

Poland
  National Day, *also* Constitution *and* Army Day *and* Independence Day, 99–100, **135–8**, 160–1, 192, 198
  Polish anthem, **142**
  Polish flag, 33, 53–5, 75, **88–9**, 187, 198
poppy
  as a national symbol, 129–31, 156, 160, 172
  Poppy Appeal, 129–31, 160
  Poppy Day, *see* Remembrance Sunday
  white poppy, 160
Portugal
  Portugal Day, *also* Dia de Camões e das Comunidades Portuguesas *and* Day of the Portuguese Race, 97–8, **135–8**, 140, 198
  Portuguese anthem, **142**
  Portuguese flag, 53–5, **62**, 75, **88–9**, 187, 198
post-historical *or* counter-nationalist flags, 5, 19, 56, 76–9, 86–8, 190–1, 198
Protestant, *also* Protestantism, 87, 195
public holidays, 24, 95–6, 122, 171, 178, 188, 194, 198–9
public spaces and nationalism, 59, 146, 149

Rainbow flag, 92–3, 191
Ranger, Terence, 17, 58, 113, 134
recognition, apology and regret, politics of, 2–4, 20–6, 46, 61–3, 109, 158, 175, 179, 191
reconciliation strategies, 108, 134, 175–9
religion
  and nationalism, 28, 32–5, 81–6, 96–8, 124–9, 134–6, 139–40, 151–7, 178, 186–99
  religious ceremonies, 14, 152, 189
  religious holidays, 4, 96–8, 171, 188, 198
  religious symbolism, *see under* symbols

remembrance ceremonies, 3, 9, 20, 155–60
Remembrance Sunday
  as National Day in Britain, 12–13, 95, **102**, 122–31, 149, 153–60, 175–8, 181–3, 189
  Cenotaph Ceremony, *see under main entry*
  religious services, 123, 126–9, 143, 154–5
  Fields of Remembrance, **130**–1
  Great Silence, 25, 125–30, 154
  in Northern Ireland, 122–3, 156, 172
revolutions, 33, 36–37, 58–61, 89–91, 187–8
Right, political, 168
Rimmer, Mark, 12, 180–1
Roman Empire flags and symbols, 29–30
Romania
  National Day, **102**, **135–8**
  Romanian anthem, **142**
  Romanian flag, 37, **53**, 60–1, **88–9**, 188
Royal British Legion, 128–31, 160
Russia
  Russia Day, *also* Day of Accord and Reconciliation *and* Day of the Great October Socialist Revolution *and* Victory Day *and* Day of the Fatherland *and* National Unity Day *and* Independence Day, 23, **102**, **135–9**, 152, 160–1, 174, 192, 198
  Russian anthem, **142**
  Russian flag, 32, 36, 40, 50–**4**, 59, **62**, **88–9**, 187–8, 198

sacrifice and membership in the nation, 9–11, 16–20, 82–3, 127–8, 132, 149–60, 190
saint days, 96, **135–6**
Salmond, Alex, 123
sameness, *see under* oneness
Sami community
  Sami flag, 49–50, 92–3, 176, 191

Scandinavia, rival nationalisms in, 49–50, 80–1, 169–70
schools, *see under* educational institutions
Scotland
  Scottish anthem, **142**
  St Andrew's Day, **97**, 123, **135–8**, 171, 190
  St Andrew's flag, 32, 38–41, 51–2, 64, 189
Second World War, 21, 37, 99–100, 122, 135, 139, 145, 151, 156–65, 175, 182, 188
Serbia
  Constitution Day, **102**, **135–7**
  Serbian anthem, **142**
  Serbian flag, 53–5, 62, **72–5**, 77–8, **88**, 195
Shore, Cris, 76–7
Simmel, George, 23, 166
Slovakia
  Constitution Day, *also* Victory Day *and* National Slovak Uprising Day, **102**, **138–40**, 160–1
  Slovak anthem, **142**
  Slovak flag, 37, 53–5, 63, 75, **88–9**, 188, 198
Slovenia
  Independence *or* Statehood Day, 101–2, **135–8**
  Slovenian anthem, **142**
  Slovenian flag, 53–5, 74, **88–90**, 187, 197
Smith, Anthony D., 7–8, 14–18, 75, 146, 149, 152–3, 166–7
Smith, Whitney, 28–44, 59, 67–8, 71, 82, 87, 91
Spain
  comunidades autónomas, 70–1
  Día del Pilar, *also Día de la Hispanidad and* Day of the Spanish Race, **97–8**, **135–40**, 190
  Spanish anthem, **142**
  Spanish Civil War flags, 67–8
  Spanish flag, 32–3, 51–3, **62**, **69–70**, **88–9**, 187
  Spanish Republican Tricolour, 67
sponsorship, 95, 170–2, 192–4

sporting events, 2, 81, 86, 106, 180–5
'Stars and Stripes', 36
state
  nation-state, *see under* nation
  state-reconstitution, 89, 99, 187
  theoretical aspects, 7–8, 61–5, 189
Stråth, Bo, 18, 116–17, 167
supra-national symbols, 88, 140, 153, 166, 189
Sweden
  Midsummer Eve, 161
  Sweden National Day, *also* Day of the Swedish Flag, **96–100**, **135–9**, 161, 166–71, 189
  Swedish anthem, **142**, **170**
  Swedish flag, 32–3, 47–9, 51–2, **62**, 79–81, 85–90, **170**, 187
Switzerland
  Confederation Day, *also Die Ur-Kantone*, **96**, **99–100**, **135–8**
  Swiss anthem, **142**, 145
  Swiss flag, 24, 34, 51–2, **62**, **88–9**, 187, 190
symbols, *also* symbolism
  moral *or* religious, 3–7, 14–21, 33–5, 63–65, 81–3, 85–90, 96–8, 124–6, **135–6**, 150–6, 165, **178**, 189–93
  feelings associated with, 3, 14, 25–6, 124, 129, 146, 153, 172, 191
  success or failure of, 3–10, 15, 18–19, 23–4, 91–5, 133–7, 160–8, 177–9, 190–4
  theoretical aspects, 1–10, 14–19, 59, 63, 81–4, 194–9
symbolic regimes, 1, 4–6, 24, 28, 51–3, 86–9, **136–7**, 186–200
  modern (ca. 1789–1914), 99–100, **136**, **196–7**
  post-imperial (ca. 1914–), 100–3, **136**, **196–7**
  pre-modern (pre-1789), 96–98, **136**, **196–7**

television coverage, 111–12, 120, 129, 140–1, 159, 164–5, 172, **178**, 194
Therborn, Göran, 15, 146–9
totem, 13–14, 29, 82–3

traditions, invention of, *see under* invented traditions
Trafalgar Square, London, *see under* ceremonial routes
tricolour flags
 tricolour flag as symbol, *also* tricolourization, 4, 24, 36–7, 44, 51, 86–90, 188–90, 195
 tricolour flag in, *see under country entries*
Turner, Victor, 15–16, 19, 58, 63

Ukraine
 Independence Day, 101–2, **135–8**
 Orange Revolution, 66
 Ukrainian anthem, **142**
 Ukrainian flag, 53–**5**, 60–2, 75, **88**–90, 187, 195
Union Jack, 38–41, 66, 84–86, 187
Union of Soviet Socialist Republics (USSR)
 collapse of, 20–3, 140
 Soviet flags, 20–2, 56, 59–65, 79, 83, 188, 191
United Nations, 61–3, 109
United States of America
 American flag, 36, 66, 76, 79–85
 Martin Luther Day, 179
 Veterans Day, 159

unity, *also* unifying narratives, 3–5, 13–14, 19–25, 71, 80–2, 137, 166–8, 177–9, 185–94, 199
Unknown Soldier, cult of the, 20, 105–6, 124–30, 143, 153–6, 174, 190
Uzelac, Gordana, 25, 124

Valdemar II, King, 34
vexillology, 28–30
Victory March in London on Armistice Day 1919, 124–5
Victory Parade in Moscow, 21–2, 64, 139–41
Vietnam, *also* Vietnam War, 22, 66
Volkstrauertag, 163

warfare, flags in, 4, 33, 58, 88–9, 151, 187
Wales
 St David's Day, **97**, 123, **135–8**
 Welsh anthem, **142**
 Welsh flag, 38–**9**, 41, **55**, 75, **88**, 172, 189, 195
Westendorp Commission, 72–3, 77
whiteness, 83, 181
women in armed conflicts, 21, 158–9, 175
World Value Survey (WVS), 25–6
Workers' Day, *see under* Labour Day

The manufacturer's authorised representative in the EU is Springer Nature Customer Service Centre GmbH, Europaplatz 3, 69115 Heidelberg, Germany. If you have any concerns regarding our products, please contact ProductSafety@springernature.com

Printed and bound by CPI Group (UK) Ltd, Croydon, CR0 4YY

23/03/2026

02076459-0018